DEPTH PSYCHOLOGY:

MEDITATIONS IN THE FIELD

Depth Psychology:

Meditations in the Field

Edited by Dennis Patrick Slattery, Ph.D.
and Lionel Corbet, M.D.

DAIMON

ISBN 3-85630-701-X

Cover photo of Big Sur, California, by Dennis Patrick Slattery

Contents

Foreword

In the mythology of the Dogon of West Africa, the original creation of the world from multiple twin ancestors in the womb of life was marred by the premature birth of a rebellious soul called Yurugu, whom the creator turned into a fox. Forever afterward, Yurugo prowled around the edges of human villages creating disorder and breaking rules, though being out of civilized time and space also gave him access to divination and prophecy. To rectify the situation, four other sets of twins, each male and female, were sent out into the world to help found the arts of ritual, culture, technology, and speech. With these skills, the ancestors, who are reborn again and again in the form of children, could constantly help us to creatively repair, reweave, and renew our human environments, so communities might survive and grow vibrant. Over the course of eons, a philosophical understanding might come to see both order and disorder as fundamental to the equilibrium of the universe.

In these diverse essays by members of the faculty of Pacifica Graduate Institute, there is evidence that Yurugo has been actively prowling through our worlds, causing all sorts of disorder, loss, and longing, much in need of renovation. Writing at the frontiers of depth psychology, the authors seek out spaces of transition, moments of insight, and projects of social repair in dialogue with individuals and communities around them. An energetic engagement with multiple perspectives, antecedents, and goals has created a lively intellectual environment within the container of the Institute that is apparent in this work. We do not all agree about everything; but ongoing, intense, no-holds-barred discussion helps us to clarify, deepen, and impassion our work. Together with the rest of our faculty and students, and many others in the contemporary milieu, we are involved with the work of the ancestors, trying to find equilibrium in a world unbalanced.

This collection is a wonderful example of both the range of thought and the standards of agreement in contemporary depth psychology. While we are in dialogue with diverse thinkers from many disciplines, genres, cultures, and eras, we also all share an appreciation for symbolic language, reflexive exploration, rituals of healing and transformation, metaphors in symptoms and dreams, and mythological thought. Like Yurugo, we each sometimes disorder public discourse in reaching for what is numinous, or prophetic, or not-yet conscious. Containing within our perview the entire range of contradictory potentials for creating both order and disruption, we are continuing to develop our own origin stories and creation myths in ongoing projects of renewal. Here is a depth psychology in process and in community, alive and well as it carries on the work of culture.

Helene Shulman Lorenz
Academic Dean
Pacifica Graduate Institute

Pacifica Graduate Institute: Unfolding a Dream

In the beginning was ... what?

Two small rooms bearing the name "Isla Vista Counseling Center," located on the second floor of a modern California building. One part-time staff member, a work study student (me), paid by the University of California at Santa Barbara, and five volunteers.

From its beginning in 1974, this modest first form has gradually evolved into Pacifica Graduate Institute, an accredited graduate school with degree programs in Clinical Psychology, Depth Psychology, Counseling Psychology, and Mythological Studies, nestled on a 13-acre, estate campus overlooking the Pacific Ocean.

I have tended this institution through its various permutations. To introduce this book, which holds a remarkable array of ideas which live at Pacifica, I will try to weave a story about the evolution of Pacifica, using the threads of our institutional history, the cultural forces which shaped us, and the extended community of people who have dreamed and worked together to make a living tapestry – Pacifica Graduate Institute.

The seeds of Pacifica seem to have been born out of the baby boom generation's experience in the 1960's. In our formative years, we witnessed the Vietnam War, the peace movement, the civil rights struggle, and a radical exploration of a consciousness that penetrated the facade of the American middle class. Our cultural psyche was breaking down.

I was drawn to humanistic education, which emerged out of the human potential movement. There was something alive and active that had to do with redefining our sense of a human life and establishing our personal worth in relation to others, as well as redefining a way of being in the culture that was different than the dominant ethos of the time. Many of us were participating in events at the Esalen Institute in Big Sur, California, studying with Gregory Bateson, Joseph Campbell, Fritz Perls, and others with their challenging and innovative approaches to education, mythology and psychology. Theirs was an attempt to heal the cultural wounds of the psyche.

During this same period, I also had the opportunity to hear James Hillman at the Wright Institute, where he added to the prevailing dialog the notion of *anima mundi* (soul of the world). He explored how that idea was connected to cultural activism. With this crucial addition, humanistic education, imaginal psychology, and a way of being politically active in the world started to coalesce.

I came home to Santa Barbara wondering: What would it be to actually live life through this perspective, to collect people around me in a community that would begin to cultivate this material in order to open up its diverse possibilities? What would it be like to work with other people putting these ideas into relationship within an institution and out to the world? Looking back, I believe that those seminal experiences, 26 years ago, were in fact the beginnings of Pacifica Graduate Institute.

As all of these ideas and dreams asked for expression, several of us were engaging the world in action in our work at a small counseling center in Isla Vista, the student residential community adjoining the campus of the University of California at Santa Barbara, where we were studying Confluent Education. This specialized area of study grew out of the emerging field of humanistic psychology to combine affective and cognitive learning in order to develop curriculum and teaching strategies.

In 1978, we opened a second counseling center in nearby Goleta and began offering counseling skills classes to the public. At the same time, I was also teaching at the local campus of the University of California, at Antioch University, and through Goddard University. I taught courses in introductory psychology, counseling skills, process of psychotherapy, and social psychology. These experiences led to the development of a counseling skills certificate program which was offered under the auspices of our newly-formed Human Relations Center, which also provided a variety of counseling and social services to the community.

The counseling skills certificate program found a receptive audience and proved resonant with the goals of individuals who wished to enhance their skills in a variety of employment and volunteer situations while exploring their own psychological growth. Many of our students also wanted to pursue careers as professional counselors or psychotherapists. From this, we went on to develop a graduate degree program in counseling psychology which honored an imaginal vision of psyche in world. In the early 1980's, as the

Human Relations Center, we received California State approval to grant the degree of Master of Arts in Counseling Psychology. This approval qualified our graduates to sit for state licensing as Marriage, Family and Child Counselors (MFCC's) once they completed state internship and examination requirements.

The Master's program became increasingly oriented around its depth psychological underpinnings. It became clear that the mission and operations of our social service agency and of our graduate degree program required different structures to support their work. At that point it became appropriate to found an independent school of graduate instruction grounded in the convictions of depth psychology coupled with an intention to conduct theoretical, phenomenological, and social action research. At this juncture, a separate institution began to emerge, which was eventually to take the name of "Pacifica Graduate Institute."

In the mid-1980's, the founders and faculty decided to offer the M.A. in Counseling Psychology with an emphasis in Depth Psychology, and to structure the program through three-day weekend sessions held once a month. Since that time, the M.A. Counseling Psychology curriculum has featured interdisciplinary courses in three instructional "tracks" – Humanities and Depth Traditions courses; Theory/Praxis courses; Marriage, Family and Child Counseling courses.

The weekend format enabled the school to invite renowned depth psychologists from other institutions to serve as contributing faculty for the "Humanities and Depth Traditions" courses, and to offer their valuable, specialized knowledge to the Institute's growing student body. The weekend sessions are also crucial in making it possible for mid-career students to study at Pacifica while continuing to fulfill personal and professional commitments in cities all across the United States and Canada.

In 1987, the Institute inaugurated an interdisciplinary Ph.D. program in Clinical Psychology, with an emphasis in Depth Psychology. The program offers courses in the following areas: Research and Professional Courses; Interdisciplinary Courses in Cultural Studies; Clinical Courses in Psychology.

Our two, unique degree programs were enthusiastically received by students and faculty. We were well on our way to teaching and studying in a manner which hosts an individual's personal process while giving back to the profession, the community, and the culture the fruits of our studies. We adopted a motto, which states our mission succinctly: *animae mundi colendae gratia* – for the sake of tending the soul of the world. This motto expresses Pacifica's dedication to cultivating and harvesting the gifts of the human imagination so that these insights may be brought to bear upon the personal, cultural, and planetary concerns of our era. The beneficiaries of our studies, we believe, should not be limited just to those who study here, but to the larger world in need of attention, nurturing and healing.

It is perhaps appropriate at this time to step away from the chronological narrative of Pacifica's history to answer the question which is foundational to the orientation and development of this institution: "What is the vision of Depth Psychology which provides focus for the educational orientation of Pacifica Graduate Institute?"

Depth psychology has its contemporary origins in the work of Sigmund Freud and Carl G. Jung, both of whom called attention to the importance of what lies below the surface of conscious awareness. These deeper and broader dimensions of psychic reality are revealed in dreams, images, symptoms, intuitions, and other non-volitional experiences. Depth psychology also attends to the way unconscious processes express themselves in society and culture. A main tenet of this orientation is that the world itself is ensouled and must therefore be related to responsibly and responsively. Depth psychology draws upon the insights of literature, religion, and mythology to understand the human psyche and to address the contemporary problems of our time.

Returning to the chronology of the Pacifica dream – in the late 1980's the school was flourishing and needed therefore to find a permanent home. In 1988, we located a property just below the foothills in coastal Carpinteria, a community a few miles south of Santa Barbara. After extensive renovations to the property, a 13-acre agricultural estate which had been built in the 1920's by the philanthropist, Max Fleischmann, we began holding class sessions there in late 1989 and formally dedicated it in the spring of 1990.

The founding vision of Pacifica was clear. We felt it was important to ensure that the vision would pervade the educational programs and administrative operations of the school. During the 1990 dedication ceremony for Pacifica's current campus, I spoke of the principles to which the school is dedicated. The following excerpts offer a sense of the school's guiding vision, a sense which still rings true today, a decade later, when the Institute's programs have evolved, adding graduate degrees in mythological studies to our earlier curricula in psychology:

"One level of truth is that Pacifica Graduate Institute is a graduate school in psychology with an emphasis in Depth Psychology. We offer Master of

Arts and Doctor of Philosophy degrees. ... We believe psychologists have an ethical obligation to participate in the psychic life of the world community of human beings, earth, coyote, ocean, rocks, buildings – all being. This school is dedicated to the individual soul being in conscious relationship with the soul of all things.

"We are dedicated, in part, to all the dreamers who have created the imaginal lineage of the imaginal body we call Pacifica. We are dedicated to the alchemists, poets, and philosophers. We are dedicated to the traditions and figures of myth, literature, and religion.

"And we are dedicated to ourselves as dreamers, to our piece – an evolving image in a larger ongoing dreamscape. ...

"Now more than ever we are asked to maintain our insight – our ability to see into the inner dance beneath the external forms.

"That which guides this Institute must remain connected to soul ... to psyche. And not simply the fantasy of the individual psyche, as if the individual can be separated from the web of all being. No. We are asked to remember that we are sourced most deeply in a ground of being that demands a sacred partnership among all forms of life. The soul of the world is making this request."

Renowned archetypal psychologist, James Hillman, who has mentored the development of Pacifica from its early Human Relations Center days, was our keynote speaker at that ceremony, and his words guide us to this day. Here are some excerpts:

"We are here this afternoon for a ceremony of dedication. In dedication of what? To dedicate what? Not merely these physical buildings, this ground of gardens, this blessed site. Not merely to dedicate a school of gifted faculty, imaginative staff, and intelligent students; or only a unique program. More likely we are here in dedication to a vision that formed this site and its buildings and brought to it these unusual persons who comprise the Pacifica Graduate Institute – its particular vision of psyche and an education in psychology dedicated to its vision.

"An education in psychology, a psychological education, requires today indeed a vision. For we are not where we were. A hundred years of solitude behind the walls of the consulting room since Freud in the 80's and 90's of the last century cannot be carried forward unless blindly as a repetition compulsion, into the new century coming. The unconscious does not stand still – that's what the word itself implies. As we gain in awareness in one area, something else falls into shadows. Where, what is the unconscious now and in the coming years? What requires investigative research and therapeutic attention?

"... So the psychological education provided by the Pacifica Graduate Institute can lead the soul out of its century-long and once necessary confinement within the personal, individual, and humanistic walls that have kept it from the world and the world soulless. This vision toward the world can also re-dedicate our dedication to Psyche with a visionary's fantasy-inspired imagination that would aim for nothing else, nothing less than re-souling the world – giving it the gift of each one's specifically peculiar dedication."

One of our challenges was to become accredited with Hillman's insights in mind. Pacifica was working toward formal academic accreditation with the Western Association of Schools and Colleges (WASC), achieving "Eligibility" in 1991, "Candidacy" in 1994, and fully "Accredited" in 1997. Enrollment has grown from 40-60 students in 1984 to the current year 2000 student body of 510 active students attending classes, as well as over 180 individuals in candidacy status working on thesis projects or dissertations.

One of the supporters of the Institute's vision in the early years was the late mythologist, Joseph Campbell. Renowned for his groundbreaking work in comparative world mythologies, his scholarship integrated various fields: literature, anthropology, mythology, world religions, and art history. Campbell offered mentoring and guidance as we went about developing the school; he appeared many times as a guest speaker in the Institute's public conference series. After his death in 1987, his widow, Jean Erdman Campbell, felt that Pacifica would be able to carry her husband's work into the future. She concluded that the Institute would be the most appropriate home for his archives. After careful consideration, she donated his 3,000-book library and archival collection to The Center for the Study of Depth Psychology, an independent non-profit organization housed on the Pacifica campus.

The presence of this unique collection at the Institute and the scholars who were drawn to the continuation of Campbell's work, led Pacifica to develop a new M.A./Ph.D. program in Mythological Studies, which began offering classes in 1994. In keeping with the vision of the school, and that of Joseph Campbell himself, the curriculum of the Mythological Studies program is also framed in the traditions of depth psychology. The Mythological

Studies curriculum includes courses in the following three instructional tracks: Mythology, Literature, and Religious Studies; Myth, Culture, and Depth Psychology; Research and Imaginal Studies.

In 1995, following several years of careful design, Pacifica announced the development of an innovative and unprecedented doctoral program in Depth Psychology, which examines the philosophical, cultural, and experiential foundations of the depth perspective. Program developers, who included many core faculty members, envisioned a revival of the original motivation of depth psychology: to understand and be sensitive to the forgotten, marginalized dimensions of the cultural-historical soul and to provide voice for the archetypal forces that shape the human condition. The Ph.D. program in Depth Psychology began offering classes in 1996. The curriculum is arranged in three tracks: Depth Psychology and the Humanities; Traditions of Depth Psychology; Depth Psychology: Research and Praxis.

Pacifica traces many of its central ideas to the heritage of ancient storytellers, dramatists, and philosophers from all lands who recorded the workings of the imagination. The legacies of these early men and women have evolved in multiple cultural contexts and perspectives.

The depth psychological lineage has been carried forward by many of the contemporary scholars, psychotherapists, mythologists, and philosophers who have also contributed so generously to the growth of Pacifica Graduate Institute. Our "Scholars-in-Residence" program has had the honor of hosting such luminaries as Patricia Berry, Marion Woodman, Andrew Samuels, and Ginette Paris for extended teaching and research residencies at our campus.

Shortly before her death in 1994, archaeologist Marija Gimbutas, preeminent scholar of Neolithic, matrifocal society, who presented her last classroom lectures at Pacifica, decided to place her personal research materials at the Institute. She based her work on archaeological artifacts, linguistics, ethnography, and folklore in order to support her thesis that the European prehistoric culture was female-centered and worshipped a Mother Goddess as giver of all life. Her discoveries have taken on great symbolic importance for feminist theologians who found in her vision of a peaceful, egalitarian, nature-revering society a sense of hope for the future based on this foundation in the distant past. Her papers are now part of The Joseph Campbell and Marija Gimbutas Archives at Pacifica.

James Hillman, the founder of archetypal psychology, has also chosen Pacifica as the repository for his working papers. Other collections at Pacifica include the books and papers of Joseph Wheelwright and Jane Hollister

Wheelwright, who trained with Carl Jung and became leading figures at the Jung Institutes in Zurich and San Francisco.

Marion Woodman, Robert Johnson, Andrew Samuels, and Rudolf Ritsema have honored Pacifica by accepting Doctor of Humane Letters degrees from Pacifica, which were awarded to them for their significant contributions to the field of depth psychology. These individuals, along with Russell Lockhart, Jean Houston, Robert Bly, David Miller, Christine Downing, John Beebe, Charles Boer, are part of Pacifica's informal council of elders, providing guidance and renewal as our school and our understanding of the mission of depth psychology and its potential contributions to the individual and to the soul of the world evolves. Pacifica has also been blessed by the vision and stewardship of our Board of Trustees. We are deeply grateful for their ongoing support and involvement with the dream that is Pacifica.

The Pacifica dream has many dreamers, and they each have contributed (and continue to contribute) to the evolving co-creation of this school, this academic community. Through the years, our faculty, administrative staff, students, alumni, and friends have given so much of themselves, their passions, their skills, their talents, and their vision to Pacifica.

I think that what Pacifica does best, and what we aspire to as an educational community, is something different than what is found in traditional academic settings, where more content, more information, more mastery are the primary aims. At Pacifica, we are aware that students and faculty come to the school with a generative calling of their own, with an innate talent that asks to be tended and cultivated. Facilitating students to meet the material through their own particular originality is the art of education at Pacifica. When we are at our best, the process here really is as much poetic and aesthetic as it is informational.

Pacifica is most interested in the imaginal perspective – seeing through visible content to the invisibles of imagination, the living essentials who frequent persons as well as the creatures and things of the world. As these figures of dream and meditation reveal themselves, they interact with text, behavior, and various community structures ... and something different happens. What we are most curious about is the alchemy of entities in relation to one another – the surprise that happens betwixt and between. We spend hours thinking and talking about how to foster imaginal connectedness. How does one write a dissertation from that perspective? Not only does the topic call the person, but the person goes into her own experience and wonders how she is affected by the topic. When the person and the topic come into relation, the other possibilities emerge. Dreams also contribute –

offering that subtle body experience which lies beyond the personal and beyond the story line.

As Pacifica continues to develop and more people are drawn to our programs, our learning community faces the challenge of keeping a place for soul in the midst of success and growth. In the daily activities on campus, we are coming to appreciate the custodial nature of this work. A thing of beauty calls for a measure of protection. We are stewards of a vision, an ideal which has selected us.

Our purpose is to bring the creative depths of the human psyche into relationship with the citizens, the institutions, and the forces of nature that make up the world. In so doing, we consciously acknowledge the social landscape of which we are a part. We are committed to contributing back into this world an awareness of the unfolding richness of the human psyche. As institutional, academic, and political challenges converge, it is vital to the Pacifica vision that we reflect on and embody a larger sense of the needs of the planet.

Each of us holds a piece of the dream that is Pacifica. Pacifica is not formed out of one philosophy or of one perspective; it is not exclusively rooted in Jung, Hillman, Campbell, Gimbutas, any individual Pacifica faculty member, or myself for that matter.

The essays in this volume are the first gathering of the diverse voices that inform the vision of place, that sustain the energy of the programs and that welcome the voices of the future. They demonstrate ways we can bring the creative depths of the human psyche into relationship with the citizens, the institutions, and the forces of nature that make up the world. These authors consciously acknowledge the social landscape of which we are a part and contribute back into this world an awareness of the unfolding richness of the human psyche. These writings give voice to the desires and to the sufferings of the soul's journey, portals through which we sustain connection with the vitality of the Pacifica dream into the new millennium.

Stephen Aizenstat
Founding President
Pacifica Graduate Institute

A Note from the Editors

Every book has a biography and every collection of essays a collective history. This first harvesting of essays from many of the faculty who teach at Pacifica Graduate Institute is witness to how Depth Psychology has established itself as its own unique field of study with its own ontological awareness of the human person. Developed in the spirit of C.G. Jung, extended by the work of James Hillman, *Depth Psychology: Meditations in the Field*[1], grows directly from the soil of the Romantic Movement of the 19th Century, itself a rebellion against the legacy of Enlightenment fundamentalism, which emphasized the literal reality of the world, and feasted on measurement and the quantification of all knowledge. Perhaps its flagship was Denis Diderot's *Encyclopedia of 1746* which signaled the belief that all knowledge could finally be categorized, alphabetized and objectified.

By contrast, the legacy of Depth Psychology sees human nature quite differently; it extols, for example, the symbolic, metaphorical, spiritual and embodied orders of being. It pays close attention to the poetic, the mystical, the mythical and the emotional condition of the human person. It is diverse in its approach and multi-disciplinary in its attitude. It is to this tradition that the essays herein submit and amplify.

The lenses through which to grasp any cultural and personal phenomena are multi-varied and original in this collection. Stemming from a single tree of belief – indeed having its own mythos – this tree planted in the field of Depth Psychology, with its roots deeply set in the ground of poetry, literature, religion, cultural criticism, the imaginal and oracular realms of being, promotes an abiding belief that there is an achieved form to an individual's

---

[1] The following essays were originally given at Pacifica-sponsored conferences in Santa Barbara, California.

life as it interacts with the larger sphere of being. We hope that you will agree with us that this field of Depth Psychology and the tree that gains nourishment from resting within it, is rich and thick. The faculty perspectives gathered here are only a sampling of the rich diversity of approaches to studying the human being through all of its mysterious prisms.

We acknowledge the debt owed to Dr. Stephen Aizenstat, founder and president of Pacifica, for making both the institution and this volume a reality. We thank Dr. Robert Hinshaw of Daimon Verlag for assisting us with such an important project. We acknowledge with great respect the hundreds of students who have entered the field with us through one of the four graduate programs offered at our institution. We extend much deserved recognition to all of the faculty who have submitted their passions to this volume. We graciously thank Ms. Nina Falls at Pacifica who has been instrumental in several ways in formatting and indexing this volume for publication. Her magic on the computer is without compromise or parallel.

Dennis Patrick Slattery, Ph.D.
Lionel Corbett, M.D.

CHAPTER 1

The Contemplative Self
The Spiritual Journey and Therapeutic Work

Charles Asher

Turning off Highway One is not easy. Gerd Cryns made such a turn toward the end of his life. He turned off Highway One at a simple wooden cross just south of Lucia. He followed a long winding road up the mountain side to the Camaldolese Benedictine Hermitage where he became a monk. There he lived out a monastic life, one form of the contemplative life.

This road itself begets silence, muffling the noise of car engines on the highway below. It is a narrow road, cut through thick, high chaparral with the Los Padres Mountain Range rising in the background. There gnarled oak trees and stately redwoods stand watch. Like silent sentinels observing the winding uphill road below, they mark the comings and goings of guests, and wanderers, and searchers.

The road ends at the monastery, at a walled enclosure, shelved on the edge of mountain heights and ocean depths. The perimeter of the Hermitage is surrounded by individual monastic cells and by an occasional hermit living alone in the woods. Inside the enclosure is a library, chapel, kitchen, eating area and work areas. The deep silence that descends upon the monastery from the surrounding forest is broken by a few well timed bells that order the day into work, prayer, study, meditation, and the divine office. The road Gerd Cryns took up the mountain ends in silence, not unlike some moments of analytical silence. Even the crunching sound of gravel beneath guests' car wheels, or the approaching sounds of footsteps are absorbed by the silence, a pre-condition for solitude. The sound of the screen door closing at the entrance to the bookstore seems strangely out of place. Out of the depths of this soundlessness, depending on the time of day, you may hear the monks slowly reading the Psalms, chanting and singing the divine office: Vigils, Lauds, Vespers and Eucharist as well.

Gerd Cryns went there to live the contemplative life in this Camaldolese branch of the Benedictine Order, founded by Benedict in Italy in the sixth century. The present Camaldolese Hermitage was founded in Big Sur in 1958. Gerd Cryns went there to sing the song about the turn from Highway One even as we, in our analytical work, choose an enclosure to meet those who no longer are able to travel the usual way. We too meet such travelers in our analytical practices, and we host their psyches which, as Jung reminds us, are creating reality each day. (6:78)

I'd like to reflect with you for a few moments about the relevance of the contemplative self, the contemplative moment, to our analytical work. Monastic life is, as I want to state clearly in the beginning, one enactment of the contemplative life. Furthermore, the contemplative life, and monastic life are found in many different religious traditions. I speak of the Western Christian tradition in honor of Gerd Cryns and because of my own novice understanding of this tradition and loyalty to it. I am silent about other traditions simply out of my limited understanding of them.

The experience of contemplation is archetypal. It is the attentive pause at the heart of human life, a gazing upon what is immediately given, even if that be "the end of all things." All human beings enact this archetype in various ways ... some more visible than others, as in monastic life and practice. The contemplative dimension of the monk or the hermit is alien to no person. And you never know when a contemplative may appear, over there on the edge of town, off the main road, in a forest, on a mountain, hiding out, starting creation all over again, fleeing the empire for a vision of what could be.

The word contemplation, with the syllable "temp" in it, has ancient origins. "Temp" suggests something like making a notch in a piece of wood, a simple mark. The word "symbol" has a similar origin. From that mark you had a way to begin to measure and count, noting the distance between your notches, a marked off space. We derive from the word contemplation such words as temperature, temperament, and tempo. Temple comes from this same root, an enclosed space, a templum. Likewise we have the notion of a "template," a basic ordering structure functioning much like the archetype.

At first contemplation referred to a marked off area in the sky. The

Roman augurs and priests gazed with sustained attention on a particular section of the sky to intuit a favorable course of action. Later this measured area of the sky came down to earth, and sacred spaces were marked off for attention, places like consulting rooms, and temples and park benches, and porches on old farm houses, and the hospital bed enclosed by shiny, metal railings.

It became the task of some, perhaps monks and analysts, to attend to these patternings, these marked off places. If it will not offend your linguistic sensibilities too much, I would suggest that the con-templative and the "arche-typlative" have similar resonances. Both involve sustained attention to God, or the Self from moment to moment. We gaze upon such moments to discern favorable courses of living for ourselves and others. It is the Self itself that makes the originating mark in our living, suddenly sequestering us, excavating a hollowed out place from which we view the Self or God unfolding in what Jung called the individuation process.

Under the simple question mark, shaped like a monk's hood, we muse about our existence. These places appear, even as God or the Self appears ... slightly beyond the reach of our conscious capacities. We are marked, questioned, folded into our fetal position, curled up around an elusive center. We find our niche. We need these natural indentations in life, even as Moses did. He, as you recall from Exodus 33, was hidden in the cleft of a rock. He was covered by God's hand, lest he die from the blinding glory of God. He could glimpse only God's back in passing. This glimpse was from a rock cleft left for him. Jungian psychology itself may be such a place cleft for us. How else could we view the numinous in our daily work and survive?

Contemplation, the contemplative moment is the Self or God protecting us from our inability to absorb directly the archetypal, transpersonal power of the Self. So we cover our eyes when we contemplate, lower our eyelids, enter into mystery, and hide wherever we can. A talk like this one is simply a notch, a mark in a piece of wood, a hiding out place, a time and place for us to gaze upon what appears before us, a time and place to contemplate our work. In these contemplative moments we return to a perspective, a God perspective, a Self perspective that alone is radical enough for an approach to the various crises inherent in our times and our profession. How else could we deal with spiritual hunger in the age of the quick fix? What else is radical enough? All else would seem to be an escape, a temporary fix for the soul or psyche which has lost its solitude.

Yet the act of contemplation is not particularly "relevant" ... a charge it has long endured. Rather it is an act in and for itself. The contemplative lives fully into the present as it is given in a series of events. She finds in that moment what has been and will be, what is particular and universal, what is temporal and eternal. The moment is complete in itself although I think, following Whitehead, the Self or God moment participates in creating the next event. The Self or God as one such moment offers what is possible to what is actual. This is an incarnational psychology and theology. There is no intention of dissolving the richness of the analytical process, the complexity of transference and counter-transference issues, the work with images, emotion and behavior, into a romantic notion of contemplation, however much Romanticism historically infuses monastic life and practice. Rather the Self or God is what-calls-us-forward in our concrete actuality by addressing us with what could be. This Self moment is then consequently influenced by and takes into account our choices. The Self then offers us new possibilities. Attention to this process, the presentation to us of discrete events in, for example, the analytical hour, is the work of contemplation. What follows from this sustained attention may be language as word and gesture or further focused attention.

While both contemplation and analytical psychology have traditionally favored being over becoming, the universal over the particular and the eternal over the temporal, I would contend this could be reversed with salutary effects. Embedded in the moment of becoming is also the contemplative moment. In the midst of a raging stream are pools of silence. The historical, concrete, personal, and particular could also be given priority. Such a metaphysical shift would, of course, have implications for the inclusion of other psychological theories within Jungian theory and practice. It would serve as the philosophical basis for healing the split between the archetypal, personal and interpersonal emphases in Jungian theory. It would hedge against the tendency to merge the particular in the universal rather than using the universal or archetypal to vivify the particular, the concrete and the personal.

According to one estimate, a person in the analytical hour has 30,000 discrete experiences, each experience being about a tenth of a second. Add the therapist's experience to this multiplicity, and the interaction between them, and the sum of discrete experiences is staggering. The contemplative and the analyst attend to such moments in themselves, in others, and in the relational interaction. These moments, these passing thoughts, are to be watched as Romuald, the co-founder of the Camaldolese, suggested "... like a good fisherman watching for fish." The contemplative also attends to how the world of nature and culture of soul in the world, impacts those, in William James' phrase, "drops of experience."

It's hard to imagine anything more radical than this contemplative life. The hermit may sit in a hollowed-out tree, and pray, meditate, study, sing, chant and work at hollowing out the tree a little more. There the hermit monk attends to life from moment to moment. This commitment is an astounding way to live one's life. You may well ask what's the usefulness of this attentiveness? It's a question disturbing to many. I don't know. I don't see it solving any of our professional woes. It won't help us compete, fill out insurance forms, or sign up for managed care programs. You can't access the contemplative moment on Internet unless you attend to the moments when the computer is too slow, when you have to wait to down-load. I don't see how it's going to satisfy our hunger for power, money, sex, food, alcohol and drugs. Contemplation is a strange psychoactive medication that would make us more alert to the pain of our human condition. The contemplative moment seems a waste, a waste of time, of human life as we know it. Depth work is similarly accused. Contemplation, like long term analysis, is a lavish waste of time by a few people who took a turn and seem madly in love with the divine. Like analysts they are particularly attentive and fascinated by the workings of the Self, and waste hour after hour attending to its surprising desires for our individual and collective lives.

The contemplative life isn't focused on rewards later, or a brighter future, or a higher position, a better practice. The "Center" for the monk is not higher up. It's not within the monk. It's not between monks. It's not in nature. Yet it may appear in any one of those places. When the divine reveals itself, you will find some monks celebrating. They gather at a particular place, or sit on top of a pillar in the desert, trying to get away from what does not serve God or the Self. From their place of reclusion, a series of concentric circles seem to radiate. The circles order the surrounding area, infusing and permeating it with something like fire.

The celebration of this divine center is based on the rather peculiar assumption by monks like Gerd Cryns that there was a time in which the world began over again, at such a center, and even more remarkably that it began in a Person who was responded to by a community of followers later called the church. They say this creation is still going on, so that such a beginning place is the place to Be. It is the place of Being, of contemplation and hence it is natural to celebrate such a happening. It is an oft-rejected assumption that the world begins again, though as analysts we know the person is recreated many times over through images and personal interactions. We also know about the fire, about the heat and light and energy radiating from the center of a person's fascinations. This energy has the power to infuse the entire person's archetypal, personal and interpersonal living and interconnectedness with the world.

Contemplation is furthermore not a work that is product-oriented; it is more process-oriented – "working" rather than "the work." The work of contemplation is done for itself. It finds little justification from current assumptions of our culture. Its success rate is hardly measurable. Contemplation may or may not be good for your health. There are some rituals, and disciplines, and trainings that go on about contemplation. In the end, just as in analysis, there you are in that moment when the hungry soul is flung toward the Self or the divine presence. And who knows why? Or why it is so enjoyable? Or why some think we are meant to enjoy such moments forever.

Contemplatives of many different traditions hold certain beliefs, but they have a rather disconcerting indifference toward constricting belief systems, even though their way of life may be deeply offensive to the so-called active life. They would hardly ask us to "believe" anything I'm suggesting here. An experience that has to be justified by something external to it, like beliefs, is itself suspect. The contemplative seems to know something, as Jung suggested in the B.B.C. interview, that is deeper than belief. They "know." In a world of fast food information they know something from within the contemplative moment that feeds the hungry.

Romuald gave simple job descriptions to his monks; "Sit in your cell as in paradise." Most of us would not sit in our analytical chairs as in paradise – or would we, some of the time? The contemplative sits, and is. What is for him now is forever. Paradise is now. The cell is already there in paradise. Gerd was here, one of us, living and breathing; now he's there, and the there is now here once again living and breathing. The contemplative moment does something radical to both space and time, just as the dream does in our analytical work. It's an embarrassing moment, especially if you intend to mask progress in your analytical or spiritual work for yourself or others. If you are mirror hungry, ideal-hungry, or alter-ego-hungry in this age of spiritual hunger and the quick fix, I wouldn't suggest eating at the ritual meal of the monastics.

These monastic meals may not feed our hunger in this present age of the quick fix. Monks fast. They get hungry enough to feel their desire for what they need and not only for what they want. Monks tend, with few exceptions, to be emotionally lean and a little empty, carrying the beggar's cup, forever homeless in this world, not quite fitting in. In the long tradition of monasticism they accept anyone as a guest, even as we entertain the personified guests of the unconscious in our analytical hour. But all you can be sure of to eat is a piece of bread and a sip of wine. As a guest you are not refused care, though you may not get what you expect.

What then would an undeveloped self, a depleted self, do with more hunger, more emptiness, even poverty of spirit? You can imagine how a person's ego would easily regress under contemplative conditions, or how a regressed psyche would further splinter. How would silence help that? Contemplation seems hardly useful in developing a more cohesive self or filling in all the gaps left by the founders of depth psychology – unless in the midst of emptiness and gaps there's something about not doing, about just sitting there, attentive, waiting, but not waiting for something to occur. Or perhaps there is something about seeing, gazing, as mother and child gaze at each other. Perhaps this gazing upon a rich flurry of images in the midst of a relationship is what heals. Perhaps there is something in the waiting "with" – with another, with the divine, with the Self. The contemplative says: "Sit in your chair. Sit in your cell. Dream. Enjoy. Like You will forever." How useless! Or do people come to see us, sensing they may find a moment when they are not used for some other purpose than being with us? Contemplatives do another rather useless thing; they sing – a lot. We could sing together as monks in many traditions have done for thousands of years. We imaginally enter our choir stalls. There we face each other. In my talk I will sing some lines to you. You respond silently. Later I will be silent and listen. Some of you will sing out loud to me. Perhaps after we leave each other today we will continue to sing to each other. Maybe some songs go on forever. In the singing itself, in the silence between the notes, in the silence between my words and your thoughts, there is the contemplative moment. What use is that moment? What use is singing? For what reason do you sing? If the contemplative is singing to the divine through singing to his brothers and sisters in choir, then there is something about listening to this antiphonal singing. It gives birth to what I would call the "antiphonal self."

There is something about the song being sung, or chanted between the large S and the small s. Some of us have larger S/S in our practice than others. But the relation between the ego and Self is also going on in our ritual analytical exchanges: the set time, the place, the greetings and farewells, fee payment, cancellations and new appointments. Is it not going on as both analyst and analysand listen to the Self and its complex relationships with the ego? Perhaps people come to us to listen to this antiphonal singing within us, between our own ego and Self, between us and our analysands, between the analytical hour and the hours of our living. A song is in the contemplative's heart and the song needs to be sung. It is the song of the Psalmist, the sound of "the ten-stringed lyre and the lute, the murmuring sound of the harp." It is a song about a new creation. Perhaps we are healed by these sounds, murmurings in the analytical hour. Perhaps people come to us to listen to the "murmuring sound of the harp playing in the background of our analytical meetings. I do not know. It is a great mystery why some people come to meet us. I awakened on All Souls Night to Gerd Cryns murmuring something to me. What? I'm not sure. I'm trying to find out. In life I talked with him twice; they were brief, pleasant conversations. Lately when I've gone to the Hermitage I've spent time at his simple headstone. It is sunken in the earth in an obscure place by the chapel. I clear the grass off his headstone. I wonder about his life, his death, his turn-off-the-road. But what did he want now? And what did that have to do with this call for papers? Like a star falling into the night, there was a contemplative moment when I resolved to sing a song back to him, to this community and the Camaldolese community as well.

After the resolve came the letter from the present Prior, Fr. Robert Hale. He wrote about his discussions with Gerd Cryns who died at the monastery on November 5, 1987. He wrote about how helpful Gerd was to his fellow monks, about his skill at interweaving dream, biblical texts, and liturgical motifs. He also spoke about the conscious, intentional process of his dying, about how he was "… habitually the calm, spiritual wisdom figure." Yet he was not beyond, "… pulling out a squirt gun from under his mattress and popping someone." According to Fr. Hale, Gerd was critical of the Church when it has institutionally wounded others. But he was likewise critical of any dogmatic Jungianism, and was not so much inclined toward "… correcting the Christian faith through Jungian truth, but if anything vice versa." (Personal Correspondence, Dec. 30, 1994, Fr. Robert Hale, OSB, Cam.)

Gerd Cryns took-a-turn, pulled the monk's cowl over his head, found a cleft in a rock of ages and lived the contemplative life informed by his analytical life. What I discovered was that Gerd was murmuring something to me about this. I don't know if it's relevant here. It's something about living into the incarnational reality of our lives as a way of deeply appreciating the particularity of other people's lives in a pluralistic world. It was within his Roman Catholic Camaldolese living and dying that Gerd followed his individuating road. This turn toward the particular, I suspect, is a bit heretical to many of our worldly and perhaps analytical values. We are perhaps more comfortable with our Platonic universalizing approach to our work. His stand may evoke unease, dis-ease, a vague sense of restlessness, or even anger and hostility. There's something disconcerting about a person taking a stand in a particular place, taking Benedict's vow of stability. It is an easy stance to disparage.

Gerd himself struggled with this unease. When he was 34, he wrote to Jung on the occasion of Jung's 85th birthday. He wrote a two page letter. Jung replied with a single spaced two page letter. Thanks to the Hermitage, and particularly to the Prior, Fr. Hale, I can at least paraphrase for you this correspondence. At some time I hope to get the necessary permissions so that you can read for yourself this entire exchange. As far as I know this exchange has never been published or referred to before.

Gerd opens by saying he'd like to see Jung but realizes it's easier to see the Holy Father in Rome than to do that. He says his relationship with Jung's thought has made him a better Catholic in a deep religious sense and a better clinical psychologist. He then goes to the core of his concern. It has to do with individuation. He suggests that among Jung's followers there are differences of opinion about this process. And then comes what seems painful to Gerd, a place where he had been wounded. He says he has the certain impression that some Jungians feel someone, namely himself, who is a sincere, practicing Catholic cannot individuate as easily or reach as high a level of individuation as a person who is not. He asks Jung to respond to this.

Jung's response is quite lengthy, with many interesting elaborations and asides. The heart, and I mean "heart," of his response is on the second page. Jung says, and here I will almost quote his words, that nobody can hope to accomplish complete individuation. It is therefore blatant nonsense to say that one's particular faith is a hindrance or a prohibitive condition in achieving individuation.

It seems that when Gerd Cryns died at the age of 61 at the monastery, he had lived out his questions in his letter and Jung's response as well. It must have been hard for him. How to live his monastic and analytical life? He had to carry expectations of himself and from others that could not have been easy to bear. In fact Fr. Hale mentioned that at one time, while in the process of dying, he cried out angrily, against the monk attending him, "You're expecting too much of me." According to Fr. Hale the monk was astonished and was quite clear that nothing extraordinary was being expected of Gerd in his dying process. His cry seemed to come from another place – perhaps the turn-off-the road, marked by a simple cross. But who among us does not know such pain – so much expected of us – so much we expect of ourselves? Is it not too much to live fully and deeply into our own particular religious traditions and also deeply into our Jungian work? Who, except for a few, such as Jung, are able to bear the unbearable tensions of what comes our way, tensions that those who organize this book sensed for us all? And who can bear it all without a cleft in the rock, a place of contemplation?

The contemplative knows something about there being more in less, something about the hidden life. Perhaps it is foolish to think our analytical profession is going to get better, that we're going to get our fair share of the competitive market, or that we are not entering a period of long decline and hiddenness in our work. Enough may be less, a lot less, and in that there may be more than enough. Can we live in our analytical caves when no one comes? The contemplative does not want to be useful, does not want to accomplish, succeed, prove his worth, get somewhere. Contemplatives sit, waiting, attentive, listening, singing, pausing, gazing, holding something, but what or whom?

These contemplatives just seem sort of mad, sort of madly in love, madly in love with God. As analysts we know something about this madness, about being seized by what is just beyond the horizons of our understanding, and yielding. Monks do this each day. What else could account for their choice to live as they do? And the analysts I've respected the most have always seemed singed with a similar burning desire in relationship to the Self – a madness that spills over into a desire to understand, and into weekly rituals of searching called analytical practice. You can put many a fine point on this passion for the divine, but I have no doubt that Jung was madly and fiercely in love with God, scorched by the divine fire. Because of this he has given us a magnificent vision of how we may experience and approach the divine reality. This is all very strange, isn't it? I'm not particularly rational, but the monastic contemplative way of being is a bit embarrassing to whatever rationality I have. (My wife says I'm going through monk-a-pause!) Perhaps its a pause we all come to or finally allow closer to us. It's all a bit irrational, not that being madly in love has to be rational. But it all goes on in a kind of hidden way, these contemplative moments. It's hard to speak about the unspeakable. The monk "just" is, "just" sits. He, like Gerd Cryns, sings, prays, meditates, gets up when it's dark for Vigils, lives in a cell with a simple wooden stove and cot, eats mostly alone, reads and sings the Psalms and sings the divine office many times a day. In all of this he contemplates the appearance of the divine, in the bakery, doing dishes, changing bed sheets for guests. The contemplative sits in her cell as in paradise, and lives on the edge between the conscious and unconscious, time and eternity, surface and depth. You never know when contemplatives appear, or as history has taught, disappear for awhile. Their presence begins with a rumor, sort of like a possible referral circling our practice. There's someone you ought to see. Over there, in the forest. Up there on a mountain. In there, in a cave, in a hollowed-out tree. In a car while commuting home. In my daughter's long gaze at the incessant rain. In the surfer, curled under a cresting wave. Sometimes you see the contemplative in the look, the long loving at the beauty of life's intricate patternings in the soul of our world. Is the contemplative moment the simple cupping of the hand around the ear so that we can hear the world amplifying itself toward us? Is it found in an educational setting, like Pacifica or in our Jungian training programs, where we draw out what is there to hear more fully? Is the contemplative moment found in the hollowed-out place in my cheek bones, when I am old, have lost weight, have come to die, a comfortable sagging place between my bones, a place I hope someone will compassionately touch, where I will find rest?

This contemplative self, or moment, is a point of view. It is to view with attention. It is concentrated focus. It is to focus on the Self's unfolding, the individuation process. It is a perspective on the world from the Self, or from God's perspective. It does not deny the world. It attends to the world as it is given from moment to moment. It does radically turn from a world that rejects the God or Self perspective, for such a world is not sufficient to sustain human life. It is a perspective that we seek, search for and yet it seems to search us. It is a moment of focus, a place where originally divination took place. So the contemplative self constellates a place from which we, from moment to moment, find our rest. Our contemplative rest, the place where we are arrested, may be in our bodies, in our pathology, in our imaginal life, and in our relational life with others, nature and our complex world.

The contemplative moment is the pause between sounds. It is the silence in the analytical session. It is the sigh of relief. It is the breath taken away by beauty, the moment after love making, the little death, la petite mort. It is the poetic imagination unfurling itself in words that charm us forward. It is the moment of longing which Jung said was at the core of the complex and of which we know so little (8:716). It is the moment of attending to what is most immediately given to us, with little attention to what has been or might be. The contemplative self attends to the new creation of the person and the world and celebrates its appearance. Only a psychology or theology that is able to contemplate such moments is radical enough to act in relationship to the human condition, and to participate in its ongoing creation by responding to its next possibilities.

For Jung, "individuation is the life in God ..." (18:1624). Contemplation and analytical work are likewise the careful attention to the unfolding of this life in God or the Self as it reveals itself from moment to moment. Such moments may evoke action, or silence, or language, or song and dance. But such contemplative moments almost always create awe and an unspeakable desire that our lives and life itself be fulfilled in the divine, that our gnawing hunger will finally cease or at least be partially eased.

Gerd Cryns attended to such moments and what they create. He did this as a contemplative monk and analyst. I think we do this as well in our analytical work. Our work has its own peculiar contemplative experiences. Perhaps analysands seek us out for a few such moments when lives are turning off high-ways, when feelings are aroused, when our imagination takes flight. One such moment for Gerd was a turn-off-a-road to a place not far from here. Who knows how far from here he now is? Unquestionably he still makes visible the contemplative in us and in our work. And so with gratitude we contemplate his life and his death, and the strange fire that is Not-Consumed – even when we are consumed with hunger for more in an age of the quick fix.

CHAPTER 2

Creativity as an Archetypal Calling

Dianne Skafte

Sometimes, quite unexpectedly, we come upon a mythological figure who sets the imagination aflame. It may hail from a time and culture far removed from our own, but we feel an uncanny thrill of recognition. If the relationship is allowed to unfold – if, as James Hillman says, we engage the figure as a fully autonomous "other" with its own nature and intentions – the psyche may find a guide of profound value.

The mythological Muse came into my life during a period of drought. My internal springs of creativity had dried up to such a degree that I despaired of ever again producing anything. I would pour over my own past lectures and publications, trying to remember how I wrote them. But I felt so alienated from the material that I sank farther into gloom. Meanwhile, the region where I lived was suffering from a severe rain shortfall of five years' duration. I watched the landscape gradually pass from straw gold to stunned brown to moribund gray. Inside and outside, life was becoming dust.

Colleagues asked with more frequency what I "was working on" lately. My classroom lectures in the psychology department remained competent enough but lacked the sparkle of true engagement. Kindly students began inquiring if I were "all right." Knowing that I must do something to get back on track again, I turned to the collective wisdom of my own field and undertook a review of the literature on creativity. I found over 6000 professional articles on the topic indexed in *Psychological Abstracts*. Perhaps by osmosis my creative faculties could be re-educated, I reasoned. I now spent all free hours scanning abstracts, retrieving studies that promised insight, and taking notes until my fingers failed.

The task was not unpleasant. I noted how earnestly psychologists have tried to penetrate the mysteries of creativity, approaching it from countless angles and points of view. Numerous psychometric tests to measure creative ability had been developed by the mid-twentieth century, many of them inspired by the success of intelligence test instruments. But questions of how creativity should be defined, what constitutes "measurement," and how cultural factors bias the results virtually doomed this line of testing. Today, few psychologists believe that we will ever be able to define and measure a "creativity quotient." Considerable research was also devoted to correlating creativity with clusters of personality traits. But these efforts produced few significant results. It appeared that no particular type of personality had a monopoly on the creative imagination. Other studies sought clues to creative power in reviewing the developmental life histories of outstanding artists, writers, and scientists. Researchers also emphasized the close connection between artistic imagination and psychopathology, pointing out examples of creative artists with serious emotional problems. While this body of work made for fascinating reading, none of it offered explanatory frameworks that met with widespread acceptance in the field.

Not surprisingly, psychologists from different theoretical orientations have seen creativity through very different lenses. Some psychoanalysts, following Freud's reflections on Leonardo da Vinci, maintained that creative heat is fueled by sexual libido that fails to find expression in personal life. Some followers of this theory went so far as to suggest that all highly creative persons suffer from serious sexual problems – a view that makes one reluctant to begin that next novel or sculpture! Classical Jungians saw dreams, images, and inspired ideas arising spontaneously from the personal unconscious and the collective unconscious shared by all humankind. Creative work flourishes when the ego enters into a participatory relationship with the larger Self, they emphasized. Cognitive-behavioral psychologists have downplayed or dismissed the role of unconscious processes and focused on the patterns of thoughts, attitudes, and actions we habitually bring to creative endeavors. They stress that each person can maximize creative output by identifying and reinforcing behaviors that lead to desired results.

Fostering creativity in the workplace took a lion's share of attention in the 1990's literature. Researchers asked how physical and interpersonal environments could optimally be designed to support a favorable "human ecology of the office." Japanese researchers observed that allowing employees to make phone calls from reclining chairs and work at mobile computers increased quality of ideas. Placing living plants in work areas was found to influence both performance and personal satisfaction. More generative work environments can also be fostered by instituting employee benefits such as four-day weeks, job sharing, and on-site day-care, the literature suggests.

After completing my survey, I possessed much information but felt as barren as ever. The image arose of a person who had sampled food from the tables of a smorgasbord six blocks long but went home empty. My research had stimulated many thoughtful reflections, but nothing I found in the vast and respectable literature truly nourished me. Whether creativity was a personality trait, a developmental artifact, a sexual problem, a pattern of attitudes, a result of good office ecology, or something yet unnamed, I was still failing on all counts.

One day I was hiding out in the lower levels of the university library stacks, thumbing through volumes of ancient history. I have always found comfort wandering around imaginally in centuries of the past – especially when things aren't going very well in the present. By chance, I opened a volume of lyric poetry from the Greco-Roman world and came upon a fragment of verse written by an obscure author. Mesomedes of Crete was a slave who lived in the second century of the common era. He gained his freedom, probably as reward for writing beautiful lyrics, and became a musician at the court of Hadrian. While other poets were praising the glories of war and the feats of heroes, Mesomedes wrote little odes to a mosquito, a sundial, and a sea sponge. Yet the emperor appeared to be fond of his bemused poet.

My eyes fell upon a stanza in which Mesomedes prayed to receive inspiration for his work. I could imagine him walking up a hillside in the glow of late afternoon, looking down upon the sacred groves surrounding the temple. Then he intoned this invocation:

> Sing to me, beloved Muse,
> And I will answer with my song.
> Breathe your breath across your groves,
> And all my soul will tremble.

When I read these lines, a thrill passed through me. I caught a glimpse of the poet's relationship to his source of creative inspiration, a relationship that was hauntingly immediate, intimate, and tender. Whereas I had been groping within the interior of my mind for something original to say,

Mesomedes turned his face outwards towards a larger presence beyond the personal self. If you will open your voice to me, the poet seems to say, my own voice can find itself and give answer. Then the spirit of inspiration seems to merge with Anima Mundi (world-as-soul) itself, caressing each branch of the trees below. The poet's soul, in perfect synchrony, also trembles. When Mesomedes later descended the hill, he surely carried with him a song that would always stir each heart with strange yearning.

I fell into a deep reverie for many weeks after this experience opened to me. All of my life I had heard references to the Muse, but had no personal connection to the image. She was nothing more than a well-worn (perhaps worn out) symbol. But through a poet long dead, I connected with this personification as a living archetypal force. Now I longed to know everything I could learn about her.

The Muse began her mythological existence not as an individual but as a constellation of sentient forces of nature closely associated with springs and bodies of water. Those who drank from certain pools, legend tells, could suddenly be filled with divine vision, hearing, movement, and speech. Water has long been revered as a generative force, and terms like "creative well-springs" still reflect these ancient sentiments.

Eventually the Muses assumed more personal identities. As first they were worshipped as a triad of goddesses who inspired and preserved knowledge in all its forms. The word "Muse" denotes "remembering" or "reminding" (similar to the English "mind"). Before the widespread use of writing, poets and teachers needed to learn thousands upon thousands of passages by heart and recite or sing them to audiences. Knowledge and the arts were bound closely together, and both depended upon the precious gift of memory. English words such as music, museum, bemuse, amuse, and still preserve recollections of these deity's gifts to arts and education.

Various stories provide accounts of how the Muses came into being, but the most common one identifies them as daughters of the goddess Mnemosyne ("Memory") and the great father, Zeus. One daughter was born for each beautiful night they slept together. Zeus's inexhaustible power to generate something new, combined with Mnemosyne's genius for holding, ordering, and preserving, gave the arts their unique character.

By Roman times, the number of Muses was established as nine, each with her own specialized work to do. Thus it came to be that Clio ("Proclaimer") blessed historians; Eurepe ("Giver of Pleasure") inspired music and lyric verse; Erato ("The Lovely") kindled love songs; Calliope "The Great") became patroness of epic poetry; Polyhyma ("She of many Hymns") governed oratory and sacred chant; Melpomene ("Songstress") fashioned tragic drama; Thalia ("Flourishing") gave comic plays their humor; Terpsichore ("Whirler") moved through dancers; and Urania ("Heavenly") assisted all astronomers. Because each artist or scholar engaged in private dialogue with one of these deities, prayers were usually addressed simply to "The Muse." What the supplicant really meant was, "My Muse."

I began to realize that for citizens of the ancient world, these divine sisters were far more than "symbols of the arts." They kindled a special relationship with creativity that heated the mind and warmed the soul. To invoke the Muse was to turn attention away from the personal self-system and direct it towards an incomprehensibly dynamic force whose very nature was to make things happen. Muse-inspiration was therefore oracular in nature. Like an oracle (from the Latin *orare*, to speak,) creative imagination arrived as a visitor from Elsewhere. It ushered the psyche into realms beyond time and space, offering guidance on how to bring each vision or idea into expression.

The link between creativity and oracular knowing is everywhere evident in world mythology. Native Americans of the southwest revered Tse Che Naka, Grandmother Spider Woman. Whatever she thinks about, appears. She spins all creation from her cosmic web, and weaves our fates moment by moment. Among the Ijaw of Nigeria in West Africa, one might pray to the creator-deity, Ogboingba, who inspires intelligence and creativity as well as governing magic, fate, and prophecy. Among the Aztecs of Mexico, Oxomoco is the moon deity who confers divinatory powers. She and Cipatonal, the Sun, created time, fate, and the first human beings. Vak is the primal goddess of ancient India who gave humankind the gift of language. Her name gives rise to English words such as "vocal," "invoke," and "vocation." She was also an oracular goddess who taught us how to see into the future and speak of hidden things. One of her manifestations, Sarasvati ("The Flowing"), created all the arts and sciences. The Greek god, Apollo, (brother of the Muses) served as patron of all artists, and he also was the voice who spoke through priests and priestesses in many oracle sites, including Delphi. The ancient Celts honored their deity Ogma as god of poetry, literature, and eloquence. He gave humankind Ogham writing, whose letters are still used today as a divination tool.

In many indigenous cultures, all art is regarded as a manifestation of divine presence. Creators of masks, poems, music, or other works let themselves be guided by supernal inspiration before picking up a knife or uttering the note of a song. A divination procedure of considerable impact was practiced among the Ostayak Samoyed shamans of the arctic. When wood had to be found for making a drum, they put on a blindfold and stumbled into the forest until they ran headlong into a tree. Then they thanked the tree for guiding them to its side and offering its body. The tree's living essence would thereafter always sing through the drum and assist the shaman's soul journeys.

It seemed clear to me from these and countless other examples that people throughout history have experienced creative generativity not as a personal ability but as a relationship between the individual self and a larger Something. Perhaps creative inspiration and oracular knowing are linked in mythology because they belong to similar domains of psychic life. Both types of experience thrive best when imagination is given a spacious arena and the mind releases its demand for predictability. Both types of experience come to us through an agency that we can only thank, never understand.

I began to pay more attention to reports by creative individuals about their own process. I noted how they often described the original impetus for work as coming through images, dreams, synchronicities, or the body – the same channels through which oracles appear. Prize-winning author Gloria Naylor, whose novels give voice to the diversity of Black female experience, said that she often receives an image in her mind or hears the name of a character years before the rest of the story unfolds. For example, in her imagination she often saw a young man and woman in love, walking past a wooden building by the water. She knew they were in trouble, but nothing else was given. One day, while looking for an apartment in an area of town she had never visited before, Naylor saw an old café by the lake. With a jolt, she knew it was the exact location she had seen in her inner vision many times. Immediately the young couple's names came into her mind: George and Cocoa. Her novel, *Momma's Boy*, grew from these characters. The author knows which images are important, she says, for they hit her powerfully, "almost like psychic revelations" (Epel, 1993, 122-3). Naylor relates that "for me, at least a great deal of what I do is mystical. I feel very blessed that I've been able to do justice to the images and stories that have been entrusted to me." (Epel, 1993, 122-3)

Dream life continually offers new perspectives and helpful guidance. Jungian analyst June Singer recalls that when she was finishing her analytic training, she was required to write a final thesis, a very long work that had to combine extensive scholarship and creative ideas. Singer felt overwhelmed by the task. Fantasies of failure engulfed her, and fragments of ideas kept swirling around in hopeless chaos. One night, shortly before she was required to present her thesis proposal to the faculty committee, Singer went to bed in a state of anxiety and drifted off to sleep. Deep in the night, she became aware of herself drifting in a border region between dreams, feeling very calm. Suddenly she saw an outline of her thesis take form line by line. Each theme presented itself clearly, complete with detailed subheadings. She quickly grabbed the big pad of paper next to her bed and wrote down her vision. The next morning, Singer vaguely remembered a pleasant dream but could not recall its details. She reached for pen and paper in hopes of retrieving a few lingering images. Her astonished eyes met a fully developed thesis outline filling page after page of the notebook. It provided unflawed guidance for writing her fully developed proposal. Singer's faculty committee accepted her submission with enthusiastic praise, and from that point onward, the writing proceeded very smoothly to completion (Singer, 1988).

Spontaneous inspiration may come directly from the body. Dr. Roberto-Juan Gonzalez, who is director of instrumental music at Napa Valley College in California, told me about a memorable experience he had while conducting Stravinsky's *Firebird*. During rehearsals, Gonzalez repeatedly felt frustrated because he could not induce the violin section to play an important passage softly enough. He would motion them to bring the volume down, down, down, but they never managed to handle their bows with sufficient delicacy to achieve the right effect. Performance night opened to a full house. Gonzalez sighed inwardly, knowing that a problem area lay ahead. But when the moment came, his hand suddenly knew what to do. He drew the baton close to him and let it flutter gently against his breast like a small bird. Mesmerized, the orchestra stared at him, hardly paying attention to their instruments. Soon a soft, unearthly sound filled the room. The violinists looked around them and wondered where it was coming from, until they realized that it originated from their own bows. "The music was gossamer," Gonzalez later smiled. "It was incense." People remembered their experience of the music that night as touching upon the uncanny.

Accounts like these gave me heart, not only because they told of remarkable outcomes, but because they affirmed the boundless vigor and playfulness of archetypal creativity. Everyone loses their way during the creative process. Everyone runs out of ideas or solutions, especially when the pressure is on to produce "something good." But the creative imagination seems almost to relish these desperate moments, using them as occasions to rush on stage in a merriment of lights and bells. Or, like Gloria Naylor, we may be asked to live with fragments and figments of ideas for years before they materialize into something recognizable. (Epel, 1993). When they finally reveal their identity to consciousness, we greet them as old friends.

It also seems clear that receiving inspiration from the archetypal realm is only part of the creative equation. Mesomedes promised that if the Muse would sing to him, he would *answer*. We answer the call with our discernment, our labor, our struggle. Only a few rare individuals have produced masterpieces directly from the creative unconscious, unedited by further work. (It is said that Mozart didn't write music, he took dictation.) Most of us must apply our best skill to transforming the original magma into developed works of art or learning. C. G. Jung often emphasized "that the unconscious mind functions satisfactorily only when the conscious mind fulfills its tasks to the limits" (CW 8, paragraph 568). In other words, we cannot substitute dreams and imagination for the active work of life. Author Mary Heaton Vorse perhaps summarized the point best when she quipped that "the art of writing is the art of applying the seat of your pants to the seat of your chair" (Bettmann, 1987, 55). As I was dwelling on these matters, I received an invitation to speak at a symposium on developmental psychology. My topic was to address "old age" as the final stage of the life span. I almost said no, for I could not bear to write another dull academic paper, particularly on a fairly demoralizing topic. Most psychological texts emphasize the declining abilities and narrowing spheres of activity that typify this stage of life. Some books frankly suggest that the best approach we can take as psychological professionals is to help the elderly give up unrealistic expectations and adjust to the inevitability of approaching death.

On that same day, while shopping, I happened to glance at an old woman sitting on a bench outside a grocery story. Her eyes met mine for a long moment. They gazed at me, yet through me, as though contemplating a secret world behind my irises. Contentment, gentle as pale pastels, diffused through me, and I knew that her state of being had somehow touched mine. I smiled, and a soft, dreamy version of its reflection came back to me. The theme of my conference talk shaped itself before I reached my car. I would celebrate a special kind of consciousness that may attend the final stage of life. I would quote from the lived experiences of elderly poets, artists, and depth psychologists who offered us a glimpse of their vision. Perhaps I would accompany my talk with slides of beautiful old faces from all walks of life. No one would leave that presentation with an arid heart, I vowed. As though to affirm what I dared not yet hope, the impossible happened that night. It rained.

When we sincerely respond to creativity as an archetypal calling, our thought and work inevitably shift. The world increasingly reveals itself as a living presence that is always communicating with us. Tidings of inspiration begin to stream in through voices of birds and "visions of the night," through books falling open and words overheard in a crowd. We feel held by something larger than our own personal constructs and endeavors. Creativity may become a less solitary endeavor. We might find that our best work is accomplished when we pool efforts and resources with other people. Inspiration arcs from one mind to another, filling the interpersonal field around us with more creative energy than one individual could ever generate. Modern society's over-emphasis on the "ownership of ideas" might be reconsidered, for if creative promptings come through us from an inscrutable background of collective reality, to whom do they belong? I am not suggesting that we should ever appropriate other people's work and call it our own. But the more freely we give away ideas, the more readily they will return to us, amplified and elaborated by the contributions of others. Proprietary boundaries already are melting away as internet communications instantaneously link individuals with a vast matrix of other minds. We take pleasure in sending stories, tips, warnings, and jokes around the world, unsigned and free.

As a final reflection, I am aware that increased connection with the world psyche increases our connection with the world's suffering. We may feel a stronger and stronger urging to turn our creative energies in the direction of social or ecological needs. The depth psychology program at Pacifica Graduate Institute, for example, encourages students to hear into the unique and specific ways the world calls them to responsible involvement. Students devote two summers of their program to carrying out community or ecological fieldwork projects that bring archetypal activism to life. The work seems to unlock the gates of creativity as students use the media such as film, writing, sculpture, and music to give expression to their experiences. At a conference attended by people from all over the United States, one student brought the audience to its feet in a standing ovation when she described how the inner life of prisoners flourished when given a chance to write creatively.

My encounter with a fragment of ancient poetry showed me that mythological images never lose their power to teach and guide. After two thousand years, the Muse (together with her kindred personifications around the world) still invites us to remember. She offers a connection with realities beyond the self, whispering that we need not struggle alone. Her call to beauty deepens our communion with the world's joy and the world's suffering. Like Mesomedes, each of us may climb up that hillside to sing – and be sung to in return.

Works Consulted

For an informative synopsis of creativity research, critiqued from a cognitive psychology viewpoint, see Weisberg, Robert (1986). *Creativity, Genius, and Other Myths: What You, Mozart, Einstein, and Picasso have in Common.* New York: W.H. Freeman and Co.

For a scholarly review of creativity research, see Sternberg, Robert (1999). *Handbook of Creativity.* Cambridge, MA: Cambridge University Press.

On psychopathology and creativity: Storr, Anthony (1972). *The Dynamics of Creation.* London, Deutsch.

On creativity and sexual problems: Eissler, K.R. (1962). *Leonardo da Vinci: Psychological Notes on the Enigma.* London: Hogarth Press.

On plants in the workplace: Larsen, L., Adams, J., and Deal, B. (1998.) Plants in the workplace: The effects of plant density on productivity, attitude, and perceptions. *Environment and Behavior.* Vol 30(3), 261-282.

On human ecology in the workplace: Powers, M. (1998). New ways to structure the workplace. *Human Ecology Forum*, Vol 26(2). 19-22; Moses, B. (1997). Building a life-friendly culture. *Ivey Business Quarterly*, Vol 62(1), 44-50.

My translation of Mesomedes' invocation is a slightly modified version of those found in the following sources: Anderson, Warren (1994). *Music and Musicians in Ancient Greece.* Ithaca: Cornell University Press. Pages 220-4 contains information about Mesomedes. Web site: Opsopaus, John (1995). *An Ancient Hymn to the Muse.* http://www.cs.utk.edu/~mclennan/BA/HM.html#music

Information on the Muses was drawn from the following sources:

Bell, Robert. (1991). *Women of Classical Mythology: A Biographical Dictionary.* Santa Barbara, CA: ABD-CLIO.

Monaghan, Patricia. (1990). *The Book of Goddesses and Heroines.* St.Paul, MN: Llewellyn Publications.

Murray, Alexander: (1988). *Who's Who in Mythology: Classic Guide to the Ancient World.* New York: Crescent Books.

Web site: Circle of the Muses. http://www.eliki.com/portals/fantasy/circle/define.html

For a psychological discussion of the Muses and their connection with Pegasus and Medusa, see: Jenks, Kathleen (1992). *The Feminine in Zygote and Syzygy: Gender Studies in Violence, Drama, and the Sacred.* Doctoral dissertation. University of California at Santa Barbara.

Creative deities from various cultures may be referenced in:

Jenks, Kathleen (1992). *The Feminine in Zygote and Syzygy: Gender Studies in Violence, Drama, and the Sacred.* Doctoral dissertation. University of California at Santa Barbara.

Imel, Martha Ann and Myers, Dorothy (1993). *Goddesses in World Mythology.* Santa Barbara, CA: ABC-CLIO.

Leach, Marjorie (1992). *Guide to the Gods.* Santa Barbara, CA: ABC-CLIO.

The Shamans of Ostyak Samoyed are referenced in: Eliot, Alexander (1976). *Myths.* New York: McGraw-Hill, p. 128.

References

Bettmann, O. (1987). *The Delights of Reading*. Boston: DR Godine in association with Center for the Book in the Library of Congress.

Epel, N. (1993). *Writers Dreaming*. New York: Carol Southern Books.

Jung, C.G. (1953-1976). *The Collected Works of C.G. Jung, Vol. 8*. (R.F.C. Hull, Trans.). Princeton: Princeton University Press.

Singer, J. (1988). *Modern Woman in Search of a Soul: A Jungian Guide to the Visible and Invisible Worlds*. York Beach, Maine: Nicolas-Hays.

CHAPTER 3

Psyche's Silent Muse: Desert And Wilderness

Dennis Patrick Slattery

"To wage war against despair is our wildness."
Thomas Merton: *Thoughts in Solitude*

Desert and Wilderness are broad archetypal places, ones that I thought I understood, even minimally and which I want to give you a sense of through some of my own experiences during the past year. For approximately three months, I traveled through six states and retreated into 11 monasteries and one Zen center in the western half of the United States. In several of these places I came up against the terror and the comfort of desert solitude and silence. The 14th century theologian Meister Eckhart, one of the mystics who I read during this time out of the familiar world, writes that "the closest thing to God is stillness." And that stillness, from my perspective, is found nowhere more intense and terrifying than in the desert wilderness.

We all know the pain and discomfort of being still, It goes against the mythic grain of our culture not to be active, doing, probing, talking, making something – and being on the move. We also know the crucial place of the desert in the history of the Old and New Testaments. So what follows is part of my reflections on what silence and solitude feel like and what it might mean to one willing to engage them. This solitude that wilderness embodies and at the same time indemnifies, or compensates for, is at the heart of Carl Jung's observation that "only when all props and crutches are broken, and no cover from the rear offers even the slightest hope of security, does it become possible for us to experience an archetype that up till then had lain hidden.

... This is the archetype of meaning ..." (CW, 9.1, 32). I would say that the physical desert is literally powerful as place and spiritually potent as disposition, for the desert is a disposition, and what it disposes is everything that one is. It is a place where solitude is intensified through its barrenness. It is a sparse, empty, monotonous, scarce, yet beautiful landscape – when in it, in solitude – for to be in the desert with others changes the terrain radically – is to confront or feel in oneself those same qualities – not to be filled up with noise, activity or desires, but to be emptied of the superfluous so that what is truly important to one's existence has a chance to spread out.

I have grown to love the desert and to fear it, for it calls up something of my own solitary nature – which we all have if we can hear it and give it a chance to speak. Desert solitude is the deepest form of solitude, I believe. It asks only one question when you enter it for even a short time: What are you willing to give up? Moving in the desert landscape, living in it for days or weeks, allows one to ponder relinquishment, or as William Faulkner will call it in relation to wilderness in that part of his novel, *Go Down, Moses* that he entitled "The Bear," an abrogation of all supports, giving up and over what sustains us everyday. I sensed during my time hiking, sitting, meditating in the high desert retreats of Utah, Oregon, Colorado and New Mexico, that each of us possesses a wilderness within that is not often visited – but within it is something very essential and vital about who we are that needs to be recognized and given a voice.

Part of this experience is that in solitude it is not so much being alone, as it is being in relation to a presence that offers nothing – nothing comes from silence – silence, in its fullness, breeds nothing, encourages emptiness. It is, as Father William McNamara, co-founder with Mother Tessa of Nada Hermitage in Crestone, Colorado, and Nova Nada in Nova Scotia, calls a place of stillness. But what is stillness really? And what is it in the desert, the wilderness that brings one to stillness? It does not, for one thing, mean stasis. I believe the Israelites, for their 40 years of wandering in the desert, were a still people for most of that journeying. No, stillness is not stasis, it is something more.

And I have felt that such a stillness in the archepoetic space of desert and wilderness gives something back to us; it is a place of paradox, for it simultaneously engages relinquishment and retrieval – a gain and a loss. It is a place, according to William McNamara, that is "uncrowded, naturally beautiful, uncluttered, unhurried, solitary and still. One is free to be one's self here" ("The Desert Experience" 84). This sense of freedom in austerity, in sparseness is what most interests me. For just a moment I want to return to Carl Jung's sense of archetypes in that same essay, "The Archetypes of the Collective Unconscious." After discussing the more familiar archetypes of the shadow, the anima and the wise old man, and almost at the end of the chapter of perhaps his most famous volume, he adds:

> the course of this process [of the archetypes' manifestations] appear as active personalities in dreams and fantasies. But the process itself involves another class of archetypes which one could call the *archetypes of transformation*. They are not personalities, but are *typical situations, places, ways and means*, (my italics) that symbolize the kind of transformation in question. ... These are true and genuine symbols that cannot be exhaustively interpreted, either as signs or as allegories. They are genuine symbols precisely because they are ambiguous, full of half-glimpsed meanings, and in the last resort inexhaustible. (38)

He ends by observing that they "are in principle paradoxical, just as for the alchemists the spirit was conceived as 'senex et iuvenis simul' – an old man and a youth at once.

The desert wilderness as a place of half-glimpsed realities, symbolic and paradoxical and inexhaustible – such is the uncanny power of place. As Ahab suffers the wilderness of the ocean's vastness, in Herman Melville's *Moby-Dick*, he meditates on the head of the Sperm Whale and even commands it to give up its secrets, so deep into the ocean's wilderness has it plunged. Such a reverie prompts in him this insight which ends the chapter: "'O Nature, and O soul of man! how far beyond all utterance are your linked analogies! not the smallest atom stirs or lives in matter, but has its cunning duplicate in mind" (264). Such a profound metaphysic carries my image of the desert as something both within and without with all of the attendant qualities mentioned. The desert has its mimetic reality in psyche as psyche has a natural impulse to express those qualities of the desert. Its power of place is archetypal in energy and condition and pulls us radically out of the ordinary.

On a day-to-day basis, and perhaps in a shallow reflection, we all worry about this or that, about having enough means, of wondering what is next, feeling anticipation of what can't yet be seen or fathomed. But in the desert silence daily cares seem irrelevant, not worth the energy it takes to keep them alive. The silence of the desert swallows them up, dissolves them, gives them a smaller place in the scheme of one's life.

But the other side is true as well: what surfaces out of the silence is a deep and clear intuition of what is important – -family, the work that sustains me, my writing, my studies, my students, the imagination and its relation to the real. In fact, the desert teaches me that there is an imagination of silence – even a silent imagination – something of an ordering principle awakens in the silence of the desert; the scarcity, silence and indifference of the desert promotes in me a way of ordering what matters.

I want to risk here that it is just at this juncture of desert, silence and my own interior solitude that myth is born, myth as an ordering principle, a way of seeing, a perspective on reality, itself a liquid quality that won't be pinned down. The desert is a place, I believe, which matters because it shows me what matters. Myths give back to an individual or even an entire people a felt sense, through images, of what matters and of what is at stake if what matters is lost, trivialized and muted. My experience of desert wilderness revealed to me on a mythic level of knowing what seems a paradoxical action.

Desert solitude, with its attendant scarcity, monotony and indifference – all of which force one to look more closely, to take more time to observe – brings one closer to oneself, to God, to a sense of what is not me, but at the same time increases by deepening the mystery of these qualities, these presences. Intimacy in the desert breeds a strangeness – intimacy is more a mystery than a clarifying. And whether the sense of the sacred is in nature herself or in a God who manifests itself through nature, one can begin to hear this divinity as solitude deepens. This deepening pulls me, or any of us who relinquish control on entering the wilderness, off the horizontal relation with other life and into the vertical dimension; scarcity allows for the vertical descent, unencumbered, free, and open to a sense of grace in all things.

Hiking the Piedras Lisas Trail in the Sandia Range of the Cibola Mountains northeast of Albuquerque, I come across two rangers. One of them shows me the piñones seeds dropping all around the base of the Piñones tree. I take a handful and put them in my pocket for later as I hike up to 8400.' There I sit on a rock and just try to notice what is around me in the wind and the solitude as the scruffy life forms around me shudder in the wind. I see the subtle purple burn of color along the top ridge of the prickly pear cactus, the hard pods of the piñones conifer that drops its seeds for the animals to feed off of and the earth to absorb to begin another tree. I taste 4-5 seeds in the hard shell as my teeth sink quickly into the soft meat inside. It has a subtle taste, careful and exquisite, a bit woody, like chicory, or even mesquite.

I see as well by my stone seat the many prickly pears with their prudent needles extending not too far, subtle in length, modest in its range, and all around their base rests the ground, porous and spongy to absorb every drop of rain water so as not to be beaten hard by the sun all summer. The silent soil and the gentle sound of the wind passing through conifer and cactus evoke in me the feeling that I am inhabiting a subtle atmospherics of grace itself.

This voice cannot or is not often heard amidst the noise of the city or in our own homes. It needs the wilderness, the desert, a deep solitude to be heard. What we might hear in solitude's small utterance is minimalist, a little voice, a whisper. If one listens attentively, one hears the little voice – not the boisterous boom of hollow speech but the stiller, fuller voice that invites a meditation. One hears the small voice by opening up wider to its resonance – the desert experience emerges in that small voice. Smallness, a miniature mind set, a getting by with little, with a scarcity that is at the same time more than enough, almost an abundance in its smallness.

The miraculous paradox of the loaves and the fishes occurs within a desert disposition. The desert is an archimedean point, a reference, in its particulars and its expansiveness, its sameness wrapped round in its subtle differences, and in its quiet, whispering economy. This experience of still-ness allows one a center point to rest in – to be still in. The desert is of its nature quiet and still; moving within it day after day, one feels a certain contemplative place open within; something opens in stillness – a slow steady movement that begins, in silence, to show how deeply one is con-nected to the natural world and, through it, to others. I want to say that in our individual solitude is our true communal solidarity. Solitude and soli-darity. That is desert realism. Max Picard tells us that "the silence of nature is permanent; it is the air in which nature breathes" (*Silence* 137). Solidarity in silence, our more natural state than speech perhaps is more permanent, more originary. When we speak, our words are dying before they pass our lips and teeth. We speak into the teeth of death all the time; but silence links us permanently with everything else – there is a power in silence that speech lacks.

Perhaps this is why instructions on silence follow obedience, those on obedience precede instructions on humility in St. Benedict's *Rule for Monas-teries*. There he writes, quoting The Prophet: "I will guard my ways that I may not sin with my tongue, even in saying good things." Something in the nature of speech itself voids the silence, even as all words eventually fall back into the darkness of silence and are absorbed by it. But in this information age – and some irony exists in that phrase – silence is banned to the edges, if even allowed to breathe at all. And with the banishing of silence, solitude is impossible. Distraction, diversion, chattering all blunt the blade of silence and solitude and with them, any deepening of self's disclosure and the reckoning of divine imminence.

The silence I am speaking about, moreover, is not the silence I enjoy each morning when I rise and am reading, or writing in my journal by 5 am, and more often it seems, at 4:30. There I enjoy the darkness outside, pushed back by the light of my lamp as I hear only the faint ticking of the clock in the living room. Notes I take I write in longhand because I want to move slowly, closer to the speed of silence, not sound. I do not want to hear the efficient hum of the computer or stare at the blue screen with white letters popping up on it like popcorn from another galaxy. Yet with all its soothing properties, this silence and solitude does not touch the deeper – may I call it older and more natural? – silence of the desert, which is in its physical placeness, both foreign and familiar to my deeper solitary self.

The silence that holds the desert in place – with its tan, tawny stillness, its delicate bushes and sharp spears of cactus plants, is different and more profound – it is, for lack of a better term, an ancient silence, even a wilderness silence, a wild silence, refusing all efforts to be domesticated. By this I mean that desert silence is more enveloping, powerful and deeper – it is like an envelope of non-sound. And part of its majestic power resides in the deep darkness that accompanies it. Silence and darkness together – almost a lethal combination for the uninitiated because it acts as both strange attractor and terrifying obstacle. Together they create an atmosphere in oneself – and that condition or atmosphere is a solitude that wishes to be felt. It touches something inside me. Together they challenge me to become as still inside as it is on the outside. Stillness within everyday activity. It settles the rages, worries, anxieties, confusions.

The darkness of such a world is so profound that, waking up at 2am at Nada Hermitage at 8500' in Crestone, Colorado, I blink my eyes and can detect no difference between the darkness in me and the darkness of my hermitage. All is porous, open, almost undifferentiated. Now the head wants to hold on, to adhere to the familiar, to grasp at the ordinary for safety. It waits impatiently to think its way convincingly out of this darkness – to shine the flashlight of reason on it, even as I would use my flashlight to break the solitude's darkness. But the body goes with and into the darkness with little resistance; the flesh finds its way into darkness and silence and actually feels at home there.

If, after a few days in this world, and altitude sickness I learn, is not fatal, I begin to carry this atmosphere into my ordinary movements during the day; I begin, for example, to move more slowly, more carefully, and even more quietly. Banging a pot against the sink as I prepare breakfast is a minor assault on the silence. I begin to eat in silence and in a prayerful solitude. I find myself giving thanks for the simplest joys: watching the light gather in silence in the morning and the darkness descend from the ground up in the evening as I perch on my window covey that looks out on to the steep slopes of the Sangre de Cristo Mountains, which climb to 14,000 feet. Even they, however, are swallowed by the darkness each nightfall, so powerful is its presence.

As the days went by I found myself moving *in the silence*. A quiet begins to take over. I move with more economy. I actually began to feel and see through the silence to the world I had left behind. Solitude and stillness are the apertures through which one moves to silence. To see the world, one's own past, where one is destined in life – the destiny that has found you – through the eloquence of deep silence, is remarkable. Actually, it is miraculous. There in the silence is a clarity, uncluttered and manifest – a wildness and tameness at once. Or is it a wild nothing? A tame emptiness? I cannot agree totally with the Cistercian monk, Thomas Merton when he writes, surely in a dejected moment, that today there are no deserts, only dude ranches. The dude ranch is the secular, the pathologized desert place stripped of its simplicity and its austerity. No abrogation exists at the dude ranch, and no terror of the silent unknown. No mystery then either, for the two go together in some ineffable coupling. And yet in his other writings, especially in *Bread in the Wilderness*, he shows a profound understanding of nature's elements:

> Light and darkness, sun and moon, stars and planets, trees, beasts, whales ..., all these things in the world around us and the whole natural economy in which they have their place have impressed themselves upon the spirit of man in such a way that they naturally tend to mean to him much more than they mean in themselves. That is why ... they enter so mysteriously into the substance of our poetry, of our visions and of our dreams. (59)

Solitude and silence I believe are the apertures through which these natural living beings gain in symbolic significance. I felt this most strongly in Psalter chanted at each monastery and in the prayers of the Zen Center.

Each monastery or zen center allows and creates a particular form of silence. It invites the listening self in without suggesting any promise of a vision or of an insight that transcends the everyday. I discovered nonetheless that solitude itself promotes a way of listening more closely, listening into what another is saying, what one is reading, perceiving, imagining, even remembering. To imagine *through solitude* allows more of what is at hand to be taken in.

Here is another paradox that the desert silence taught me: There exists a connection between wilderness, desert, solitude and silence that almost naturally brings one to empty one's own will to the will of the desert, to its indifference. To wander in the desert is humbling because it is to grasp, after the mind has ceased its incessant whirring, a fullness in its emptiness. Silence truly felt contains a fullness in its absence of sound. Silence empties sound; it promotes a serenity that is hard to engage in any other way that I know. Meister Eckhart is instructive when he observes that one must learn to cultivate an inward solitude brought forth, perhaps, through the outer solitude of the desert.

Later, in the 19th century, in one of the great classics of world literature, Henry David Thoreau observes in one of the most beautiful chapters in *Walden* entitled "Solitude," that the solitude he experienced at the pond yoked in him *sympathy* and *serenity*. In the solitude he began to observe nature clearly and closely: "every little pine needle expanded and swelled with sympathy and befriended me. I was distinctly made aware of the presence of something kindred to me. ... Some of the pleasantest hours were day long rain storms in spring or fall which confined me to the house for an afternoon or a whole day." (109) His days of solitude created one of the profoundest nature writings of all time, in part because in his deep kinship with nature he observed what Melville was to give fuller expression to in *Moby Dick*: "We live in an ocean of subtle intelligences" (243). Exploring this sea of intelligences made Thoreau aware that "I never found the companion that was so companionable as solitude." (112)

Wilderness Animals and Solitude

As I hiked in the Cibolo Mountains northeast of Albuquerque where I was staying at a Dominican priory, I found myself in snow at 8500' in early November. The tracks of animals, their hooves and claws and padded feet were a criss-crossed maze in the snow. Alone on a well-marked trail, I had reached the summit pointed out to me by two rangers. I had only an orange and some water to revive me, so I ate the orange, skin and all, drank some water and turned to the descent. Tired and worn thin by the lack of oxygen, I started down, taking my time so as not to slip over a sharp incline and become fodder for the local life that had left all those footprints in the snow around and below me.

Moving slowly and quietly, I reached a point in the trail where the stillness was suddenly broken by some life vigorously crashing through brush to my left. Even with many of the trees stripped of their leaves and foliage, I still could not see but a few feet into the thickness. Suddenly across my path about 15' ahead of me glided a magnificent buck with a large and involved rack of antlers. His deep black eye, almost oily in its slickness, and opened wide, spied me at a perpendicular angle as he crashed into the thicket to my right. I will never forget the sound of his antlers clacking like wooden swords with the bare tree branches as he moved with speed and tremendous dignity into the woods, head held majestically high and followed almost immediately by a doe and then a young fawn slipping and sliding behind her. Only an instant later, two large dogs, in hot pursuit, were thankfully so taken by the chase that they did not see me, or did not care. They charged barking across my path and into the woods in a howl of sound, breaking the silence as they enjoyed the hunt. All of this happened within the space of 15-20 seconds.

The magnificent image of the three deer has been with me for months and will be one of those images that somehow changes something inside. I realized that I had been a witness to something that my nature needed. I was grateful that my silence and slow movement put me in that place at that instant to witness such majesty in nature. Such is the blessing of solitude – the revelation, the illumination, the confrontation, with what one can never really prepare for. Such an image, an experience, erupts unbidden, most often unearned, from out of the stillness; for an instant, something sacred, natural and pulsing with life in its wildness makes its appearance in a kind of spontaneous theophany, and then, speechless, voiceless, without utterance, but instead enveloped in the deep wild silence out of which it has emerged, becomes visible and auditory for an instant, breaking the natural silence with natural sounds, and then is swallowed just as quickly by the wilderness that opened for its appearance just an instant before.

Silence and solitude may afford the best opportunities for the surprise in life. Not desiring, not seeking, but being simply present to what is directly in front of you, even off to the sides, if we can tame our aggressive spirit not to grasp, to reach out, to have it, to possess it. Then something is offered to us in solitude and in the wilderness that would not come our way through any other means of being present. This is what I mean when I say that solitude and silence are places in which other elements that we need but perhaps don't know it, can come forward. Something of divinity was present in that magnificent body and dark black glistening eye of the buck – a deep darkness that solitude and silence eventually take us to.

How beautifully William Faulkner gives us solitude in the poetic space of his story, "The Bear," just one section from the longer, more epic work of the south, *Go Down, Moses*. The part of the story I am interested in finishing this essay exploring is its beginning, which describes the annual pilgrimage of a group of men from Jefferson, Mississippi into the big woods, there to engage for one week a ritual hunt of "Old Ben," a large bear "with one trap-ruined foot" that forever eludes them, and which they are content to being cheated of in a pageant of "the old bear's furious immortality" (186). But all of these men are worried, because with the advent of the locomotive, and with its penetration into the wilderness and its passengers of loggers and developers, they see the "wilderness, the big woods, bigger and older than any recorded document" (183), being constantly eaten away by progress:

> that doomed wilderness whose edges were being constantly
> and punily gnawed at by men with plows and axes who
> feared it because it was wilderness, men myriad and name-
> less, even to one another in the land where the old bear had
> earned a name. ... (185)

As a young boy being initiated into the hunt, the ways of nature and the annual ritual with the men into the wilderness, Isaac McCaslin falls under the tutelage of old Sam Fathers, part negro slave and Chickasaw chief, who knows all the ways of nature and every tree and shrub within a 50 mile radius. To him Isaac apprentices himself until one day, in early summer in June, during an outing to celebrate some of the men's birthdays, when Ike is only ten, he decides he knows enough to enter the woods in solitude to see the bear. But in so doing, Sam Fathers tells him, "choose." Either the gun or the vision of the bear – you cannot have both. Relinquish the rifle as you enter the immemorial woods or do not set your heart on the bear's presence being revealed.

And so Ike rises one morning before dawn while the rest of the men are sleeping and enters the wilderness: "the wilderness closed behind him as it had opened to accept him – opening before his advancement as it closed behind his progress" (187). Equipped only with a biscuit-thick silver watch that had belonged to his father, a compass, and a stick for snakes, Ike enters the woods and heads back to where they had the day before found "in the thick great gloom of ancient woods" the rotted log scored and gutted with claw-marks and beside it in the wet earth "the print of the enormous warped two-toed foot" (192). Now, without his rifle, he is no longer in the hunt but on another journey of his novitiate; he gives up, abrogates, "all the ancient rules and balances of hunter and hunted" (198).

As he journeys deeper into the wilderness, he crosses a threshold separating what is familiar terrain into territory never before traversed – it is alien territory for which compass and watch still give him direction and timing. They alone give him direction and place as noon crosses him overhead. Now he is in a markless region but still feels alien to it and finds himself suddenly without direction: "He stood for a moment – a child, alien and lost in the green and soaring gloom of the markless wilderness" (199) and standing there in the deep silence he realizes that he is still "tainted" by the instruments marking his space and time. "He removed the linked chain of the one and the looped thong of the other from his overalls and hung them on a bush and leaned the stick beside them and entered it." (199)

Almost immediately he becomes lost and begins to cross his back track, as Sam Fathers had taught him. Without his tangible guides, he now begins to move more slowly, more deliberately as he prescribes a circle. When he does not end up back where he left the watch and the compass, he begins a second circle, counterclockwise to intersect at some point with the first one. Trackless and unmarked, the land in front of him offers up no traces of animal or mortal having traversed it.

After a time, Ike comes upon a fallen tree that he had never seen before; as he sits on it to rest he sees by it "the crooked print, the warped indentation in the wet ground which while he looked at it continued to fill with water until it was level full and the water began to overflow and the sides of the print began to dissolve away" (200). As he looks he sees another and yet another moving beyond him; he rises and begins to follow the slowly-filling paw prints, without haste or panic or fear; they "appeared before him as though they were being shaped out of thin air just one constant pace short of where he would lose them forever and be lost forever himself … panting a little above the strong rapid little hammer of his heart, emerging suddenly into a little glade and the wilderness coalesced." (200) At this very spot he suddenly sees glinting in the sun the compass and the watch; he has been led back to them by the prints filling with water.

And then he saw the bear – not appearing, but "just there, immobile, fixed in the green and windless noon's hot dappling, not as big as he had dreamed it but as big as he had expected. …" (200)

> Then it moved. It crossed the glade without haste, walking for an instant into the sun's full glare and out of it, and stopped again and looked back at him across one shoulder. "Then it was gone. It didn't walk into the woods. It faded, sank back into the wilderness without motion as he had watched a fish, a huge old bass, sink back into the dark depths of its pool and vanish without even any movement of its fins. (200-201)

I wonder as I read this passage if this young boy will ever be as free as he is at this moment in time, which is simultaneously out of time? And what do we notice has happened in this solitary journey into the wilderness, where relinquishing what gives us direction and familiarity, even a certain control, is surrendered, where one yields oneself to another dimension of being? We watch Ike enter the wilderness and give up direction. He turns himself over to another guide – an animal in nature and to the voice of Sam Fathers – the two coalesce. He is in fear, but he trusts, even in the fear. Lost, he begins to circle, not move in a straight line, and doubles back on himself, remembering to locate an intersection, a marked crossing point; and he follows instructions given to him in the crooked print in the mud filling with water and marking the memory of the bear – the print filling with water is the fading memory of what has just passed across the earth's surface – the subtle motion of water covering the markings in the earth appears just behind the bear's luminous and lumbering presence in which Ike senses another reality or dimension of a familiar reality.

Entering a true wilderness is a timeless excursion, a mythic motion; true wildness is to go into alien and unfamiliar territory by traversing first what is known and familiar, until in that alien space there is a blending together of psyche-world through animal image. It is a moment of experience that is poetic in its contours, wherein a deep correspondence of emotions set up here. And Isaac is given this vision, which is like the one he has dreamed for years, by abrogating, relinquishing, minimalizing, giving up the familiar.

As I read these few pages of a much larger action, what do I enter? I ask myself, as I read this meeting in the alien ground of wilderness. Something of my own wilderness? Where have I been without watch or compass? Where the path was vague or nonexistent, *the selva oscura* of Dante, and here *the selva antica* of Isaac.

Certainly, as Jung reminded us, "when the props and crutches are broken and no cover from the rear offers even the slightest hope of security," there/ then can the world open, like a wound in the wilderness, to let emerge what has remained hidden and to offer us something far richer than any of the instruments we have been courageous enough to let go of – and to feel in that poverty a richness of soul that could not be had in the grasping.

Stillness in Motion

Things move gracefully in stillness
Even in the tomb is there movement
A sacred friend of stillness

In death stillness has an inner
motion –
A slight turn, the flame up of
Breakdown –

A stillness comes over me in the
desert's subtle body.

In the Sonoran desert Poison Milkweed
grows into stillness
No one can really see its white bloom
breach from out the green waxy plant.

If I can be still as death
then a bit of commotion emerges from under
a broken bottle, or beside an abandoned
truck tire
its rubber smelling of Albuquerque and
San Antonio, Houston and New Orleans.

Death's stillness settles over words squiggling
to life on a blank white page,

The words, wounds that dry to scars, immobile and
in motion on the back of a desert landscape,
futile attempts to scratch past death.

But the silent scrub oak and Beavertail cactus
send words home into the dark silence where
even Death's roilings are muted for a time.

References

Faulkner, W. (1952). *Go Down, Moses*. New York: Vintage.

Jung, C.G. (1971). The archetypes and the collective unconscious. In *The Collected Works of C.G. Jung, Vol. 9.1* (H. Read, Ed., R.F.C. Hull, Trans.). Princeton: Princeton University Press.

McNamara, W. (October, 1998). *The Desert Experience*. Xeroxed material at the Spiritual Life Institute, Nada Hermitage, Crestone, Colorado.

Melville, H. (1967). *Moby Dick* (pp. 1-470). H. Hayford and H. Parker (Eds.). New York: Norton.

Merton, T. (1953). Poetry, symbolism and typology. In *Bread in the Wilderness* (pp. 52-67). New York: New Directions.

Merton, T. (1993). *Thoughts in Solitude*. New York: Noonday.

Picard, M. (1988). *The World of Silence*. Trans. Stanley Godman. Washington, DC: Gateway.

St. Benedict. (1948). *St. Benedict's Rules for Monasteries*. Trans. Leonard J. Doyle. Colledgeville, MN: The Liturgical Press, St. John's Abbey.

Thoreau, H.D. (1993). *Walden and Other Writings* (pp. 1-276). New York: Barnes and Noble.

CHAPTER 4

Sigmund Freud's Mythology of Soul
The Body As Dwelling Place of Soul

Christine Downing

Sigmund Freud's *Interpretation of Dreams*, though it bore the date 1900, was actually published in 1899. Freud deliberately misdated the book because he had the chutzpah to assume his was a book that belonged to the new century. A chutzpah that in retrospect seems well justified. For as Paul Robinson wrote in a review of the recent Freud exhibit at the Library of Congress, "We may safely pronounce him the dominant intellectual presence of our century." (Robinson, 1998, 12)

The exhibit gave voice to Freud's detractors as well as his admirers; it made clear that there are many Freuds, many ways of understanding Freud. Freud has been read as both jailer and liberator, as scientist and artist, realist and romantic. There's an enlightenment Freud and a post-modern Freud. Many seem tempted to identify Freud with but one of these positions, whereas I see Freud's texts as "over-determined" and am persuaded they cannot be reduced to one level of significance, one interpretation. After all, to look for latent meanings in the manifest surface of Freud's texts, to discover the under-texts, is to participate in a mode of reading which he himself taught us in his interpretations of dreams, parapraxes, symptoms, and literature. To honor the tensions, the contradictions in Freud's thought – that, I believe, is where the juice lies.

My reading of Freud thus seeks to allow him to say as much as he can, to teach me as much as he can, aims at allowing him to enrich, challenge, deepen my thinking. I've been reading and rereading Freud (and much of the secondary literature) for almost 40 years now. I keep rereading Freud because I have found in him language for what matters most to me (although, of course, I realize another language may do so more fully for others).

My reading of Freud is undoubtedly in large measure shaped by my having come to Freud from Jung. So that my reading of Freud is in some significant ways a Jungian one; not one that reduplicates Jung's reading of Freud (which I regard as distorted) but simply that of someone who knew Jung's work first and reads Freud in a way that emphasizes the poetic, metaphorical, mythic dimension of his psychology. I see myself as someone whose thinking has been deeply influenced by both. Together they have parented my vision of my self, my vision of the human soul.

I knew Jung's work first – as we know the mother long before we know the father – and still experience him as mother of my soul. In my early twenties he gave me myself, a vital, nourishing relationship to my inner life, my dreams and imaginal capabilities. I continue to recognize this gift as an unequivocal blessing. But there was a sense in which Jung for me was too much like a soft pillow; some spark necessary to my own creative activity was missing. And that I found when a few years later I turned to Freud – whom I have learned from by contending with and rebelling against, as one does with a father. In the intervening years I have learned that my vision still needs to be both mothered and fathered, that I remain unwilling to respond to the imperative: You must choose between them, between the divorced parents.

To speak of "my" Freud is to speak of his sense of the inextricable intertwining of body and soul. Because Freud viewed the body as the dwelling place of soul, he found that to speak of the soul, of its deepest longings and most profound terror, is to speak of the body, of sexuality and death. And that to speak of the body as the soul knows it, is to speak metaphorically, imaginatively, mythically – to speak of Oedipus and Narcissus, of Eros and Death. I want to look at the role these three myths play in the development of Freud's understanding of the soul – how he finds that behind the myth of Oedipus lurks the myth of Narcissus and behind that the myth of the eternal struggle between Death and Love.

But first I need to make clear that Freud does speak of the soul. It seems to me signally important to recognize the degree to which his lifelong love of classical culture shaped Freud's way of understanding the psyche. He spoke often of his schoolboy delight in Greek poetry and philosophy. And of how as an adolescent he dreamt of becoming an archaeologist. He was reading Schliemann's account of the excavations at Troy and Mycenae while writing *Interpretation of Dreams* and by then understood himself as engaged in an archaeology of the soul. As an adult he was an avid collector of ancient near eastern antiquities and in a letter to Fliess spoke of the figurines gracing his writing desk as his "gods." This enduring immersion in the ancient world led him to be attuned to the etymological overtones of psychological terms in a way most of us Americans aren't. So that we are likely to hear as professional jargon what he heard as having mythological resonance.

Rightly to apprehend Freud's logos of the psyche it seems to me essential to know that he consistently used the word *Seele* where the English translation gives us "mind," "mental structure" or "mental organization." *Seele* is the German word for soul and Freud meant by *Seele* the psyche of Greek mythology and philosophy. In his invaluable book, *Freud and Man's Soul*, Bruno Bettelheim says that, for Freud, Seele *refers* to the fragile insubstantial essence of the self which needs to be approached gently and with love (Bettelheim, 1983, 15). Freud's *Seele* is the Psyche of the Hellenistic fairy tale about Psyche and Eros which describes how the soul's journey to self is motivated by love of an other for whom one does what one couldn't quite do on one's own and which relates how Psyche had to journey to the underworld to become psyche, become herself.

Freud's *Seele* is the soul of psychology, not of religion. Freud was not religious in any conventional sense, not a theist and most emphatically not a monotheist. His *Seele* is *psyche*, not *pneuma*, not the transcending spirit but the embodied soul. It is the soul of Hebrew scripture, of Genesis, not of Christian theology. Not that aspect of us which is literally immortal, but what enlivens us while we are alive. The soul is the breath of life. It enters at birth, leaves at death. It connects us to world, each time we breathe in or out, and enables us to be speaking beings. Soul is in a sense a metaphor, a myth. It has no physical correlate, though we can't help but imagine it spatially. It dwells in the body but can't be located anatomically. Freud's understanding seems to me close to that of the ancient Greeks who located psyche in the diaphragm, in one of the hollows, the empty spaces, of the body.

Freud was not religious in any conventional sense, and just as his book on lay analysis shows how important it was to him to distinguish psychoanalysis from medicine, so *Future of an Illusion* shows how equally important it was to him to distinguish it from religion. He was not a theist and most emphatically not a monotheist. He identified the God of Judaism and Christianity with dogmatism and repression, with an ego-consciousness dominated by the super-ego, and believed that the fatal flaw of this god lay in his claim to be the only god. Yet religion was a central subject in the writing of his later years. He saw it as a response to our deepest, most urgent longings, longings which are never outgrown, and wondered whether most of us could really do without religion's consolation, without religion's promise that these longings – for cosmic order, for the rewarding of ethical behavior, for immortality – will ultimately be fulfilled.

Although *Seele* is Freud's word for the whole of the psyche, it is not the equivalent of Jung's "Self;" it does not refer to a harmonious totality nor to a single center. In Freud's view each element within the psyche – ego, id, and super-ego – claims to be and strives to be dominant. To see this more clearly it may help to note that it is only in English that Freud writes of the "ego." In German he simply uses the everyday word for "I", *Ich* – a word with deep emotional association, rather than the distancing, objectifying, technical term, ego. And for Freud *Ich* always implicitly has a double referent. It means both "Me" in its fullest sense, the whole of the psyche, *and* one of the aspects of psyche, the reasonable conscious aspect, the me that's trying to comprehend the whole (an appreciative interpretation) and the me that's trying to dominate the whole, that claims to be the whole (a more critical interpretation) – the me that has to learn it's not really master in its own house.

Whereas in ego psychology the assumption is that the ego is appropriately the agency of the total person, for Freud the relationship is seen as metaphorical: the ego is seen as a displacement of the totality and ego psychology is seen as buying into the ego's own illusions. Thus when Freud says "Where the id was, let the ego be" – or rather, to translate *Wo es war, soll ich werden* more accurately, "Where the it was, let the self become" – he is not aiming at a reduction of psyche to ego in the narrow rationalistic and utilitarian sense, but is rather calling for an expanded self which includes a conscious relation to what he called the *It* in us, the *that* in us. For Freud himself spoke not of an *Id* but of *das Es*, a word which (as Bettelheim noted) for native German speakers like myself evokes immediate association with our childhood selves, with those earliest years when we were spoken of as *das Kind*, and thus with those situations where we are drawn to describe our experience in the passive voice, situations where Greeks would have said that the gods are at work in us.

It is the ego that looks upon the rest of the soul as the UNconscious. But in Chapter 7 of *Interpretation of Dreams* Freud suggests that it might be more appropriate to recognize that the animistic, subjective, mode of apprehending and organizing experience which brings together thought and feeling and works by way of symbols and association is the original mode of psychic functioning, the psyche's *primary process*. This more poetical, mythic, way of functioning is not a distortion of normal psychic process but rather the form of the psyche's uninhibited activity; it represents the core of our being. This primary process way of responding to experience is actually going on – unconsciously – throughout our day, organizing our experience on a different basis from that of rational consciousness, of the ego, on the basis of memory and feeling and similarity. We tend, however, to be so involved in our practical concerns and activities that we don't attend to this and only become aware of it at night through the testimony of our dreams

Freud's psychology is thus a psychology that focuses on soul, not ego, and for Freud to speak of the soul, of its deepest longings and most profound terror, is to speak of the body. He sought a language for the self that takes seriously that we are embodied souls, ensouled bodies. He sought to give voice to the speech of the soul (psyche-logos) rather than to speak objectifyingly about it, and discovered (in his work with women suffering from hysteria) that the soul speaks through the body, that the psyche uses the language of the body to express itself. He learned to hear somatic symptoms as language, not as gibberish but as expressions of an otherwise silenced soul; he learned to read symptoms as symbols. "Symptoms are like mythological figures," he writes, "all powerful guests from an alien world, immortal beings intruding into the turmoil of mortal life" (Freud, 1953/1974, 278).

I believe Freud was able to enter so deeply into the hysterical imagination because he in a sense participates in it, He, too, has a predilection for body metaphors, for speaking of the soul through the language of the body. His favorite figure of speech is synecdoche. The taking of a part for whole. Thus oral and anal become ways of talking about fundamental life-orientations, not just food or feces; castration anxiety and penis envy become ways of talking about some of the most fundamental concerns associated with our gendered existence. We wholly misunderstand Freud if we fail to hear these terms as metaphor.

Yet it is essential that we recognize that Freud doesn't take the body literally, as his rejection of medical training as appropriate preparation for becoming an analyst ought to make evident. "The theory of the drives is our mythology," he writes to Einstein, and *drive – Trieb* not "Instinct" – is indeed the irreducible, ultimately self-explicable term, the "god-term," of Freud's psychology. This choice of language is intended to emphasize the ultimate unity of soma and psyche, body and soul. Drive is need become wish, energy become meaning, physiological instinct transformed into mental activity.

Freud's poetics of the psyche focuses on the drives and their vicissitudes, their transformations, whereas Jung, I believe, severs body and soul more radically. For Jung our bodies are more animal, our instincts less malleable. For Freud "drive" is the meeting-place of body and soul. For Jung "instinct" means body in lieu of soul, refers to those processes which are uniform, regular, automatic, unalterable, blind, and compulsive. "Archetype" is his word for instinct become meaning. Jung's teleological emphasis leads him to see Freud's perspective as reductive. Thus Jung refuses to see the child's affection for its mother as "sexual," and Freud insists that we do. Jung understands his focus on archetypal rather than sexual interpretations as healing, as transformative, as teaching us to appreciate the symbolic, the imaginal, the spiritual. Whereas for Freud to speak of sexuality *is* to speak of the soul.

For Freud, as we have already noted, to speak of the soul is to speak of the body, and thus necessarily of sexuality and death. His insistence on the inextricable enmeshment of body and soul leads to a logos of the psyche which takes seriously our sexuality, our mortality, and our inescapable involvements with other desiring, acting embodied beings, with family and with society. Long before he begins to speak of Eros and Death, Freud responded to sexuality and death as numinous, as sacred. Though he claimed a deafness to the mystical, it is evident that he felt the transcendent here.

Our sexuality is not only the meeting place of body and soul but also the meeting place of self and other. Freud speaks of the importance of the human move to face-to-face intercourse, of a lovemaking which involves not only the connection of body to body, but of eye to eye, soul to soul. He sees our sexuality as taking us out of ourselves, beyond an intra-psychic psychology. We are directed toward world and particularly to human others – *and* we are narcissistic, would often wish to deny, to escape, this inter-dependence.

Freud's understanding of sexuality was always transliteral, always meant more than genitality, more than normal, adult, heterosexual, reproduction-directed sex. He saw human sexuality as connected to our capacity for metaphorical thinking, for symbolization, for myth making. His awe of the sexual is also awe of our imaginative capacities. There's a two way vector of interpretation: culture means sexual energy but human sexuality also means the possibility of culture.

He reminds us of the unique features of human sexuality, especially of its malleability. The nonperiodic aspect of our sexuality, our continuous openness to arousal, means we have to learn to choose, to delay, to substitute. He views this ability to substitute as lying at the heart of sublimation, of symbolization. Arousal can be diverted to what we'd still call sexual: not now, later; not here, there; not her, him – or to what might be more difficult to recognize as such, to a poem, for example, which may not even be about my longing for her but about waves crashing on the shore.

We learn from Freud that we are more sexual than we had hitherto suspected - and more symbolic. He encourages us to celebrate our capacity for sublimation (which he likens to alchemical magic), to take conscious delight in writing the poem instead of fucking the stranger, in being able to love again when the first love is irretrievably lost – at the same time that we mourn what once was or could never be. He encourages us to honor our exuberant inventiveness, the resilience of our imagination.

But Freud's mythology of sexuality is never a salvific myth; he never suggests that sexuality could save us, fulfill us. From his perspective we have both defined sexuality too narrowly – and asked too much of it. He sees our sexuality as an expression of our deepest human longings – our longings for full expression and full acceptance, for physical closeness and emotional intimacy – and sees how our sexuality is always a wounded sexuality. He aims to help us recognize the perversity of normality, of adult socially-approved sexuality – the cost of being cut off from our rebellious, regressive, unconscious sexuality, from our bisexuality, from a full-body sensuality. He seeks to remind us how in the beginning, in childhood, sensuality and affection are closely intertwined, and to help us recognize how easily, how frequently, they become separated. He sees how our sexuality seems always to carry with it an impossible longing for complete satisfaction. He speaks of the sadness that seems always to follow upon coitus and believes that in love-making we are always really looking for the first love, the mother, and even further back to our enclosure in her womb, to that time when there was no separation between self and other.

For Freud to speak of the soul or of the body is always to speak of being wounded, of suffering. Ernest Jones wrote that Freud "taught us that the secrets of the human soul were to be apprehended only in connection with suffering; through being able to suffer oneself and thus entering into contact with the suffering of others." For Freud the starting point of any depth psychology was pathology – *pathos-logos* – the speech in us of that in us which seems to happen to us, our passivity, our feeling, our suffering; that which hurts and is vulnerable, what is anxious & destructive. He believed this pathological aspect has its own voice and wishes, longs to be heard and understood; he believed that we all suffer, are all conflicted.

To speak adequately of this suffering, he learned, is to speak mythically. I see Freud's discovery of the living reality of myth as marking the real beginning of psychoanalysis. As it was this in turn that first drew Jung to Freud. The first pages of *Symbols of Transformation* communicate the powerful impact of Jung's first reading of *Interpretation of Dreams*, especially of the pages on the Oedipus myth. Suddenly, he says, "the gulf that separates our age from antiquity is bridged over, and we realize with astonishment that Oedipus is still alive for us."

Freud's discovery of the erasure of this gulf grew out of his own experience, his self-analysis. I am my most difficult patient, he told Fliess, and the one from whom I've learned the most. Freud (like Jung) had the chutzpah to assume the archetypal, the universal, the mythic significance of his own experience. He believed he had discovered through the exploration of his own psyche clues to what is true of the deepest experience of all of us.

His self-analysis was provoked by the death of his father, a loss which issued in a sustained period of depression, introversion, and of being flooded by dreams and new insights. His father's death seems to have functioned like a "shamanic wound." Until then for Freud the unconscious was something that others had, an important force in the life of his hysterical patients but not really in the psyches of normal persons like himself. His grief, his suffering, his discovery of the ambivalent feelings he had toward a father he had thought he loved unreservedly, brought Freud into touch with his own unconscious.

The starting point was suffering. His father died in October, 1896; almost exactly a year later Freud had the dream from which he awoke knowing: "I am Oedipus." (Not: "I have an Oedipus complex.") For Freud "Oedipus" was not an illustration or clever designation for an insight which might have been articulated otherwise but the *medium of discovery*. Indeed, his understanding of the Oedipal continued to unfold for decades. He came to mean by "Oedipus" everything associated with the hero of Sophocles' *Oedipus The King* – and later also with the Oedipus of *Oedipus at Colonus*.

He especially wanted to suggest that he had discovered as still alive in himself – and he believed in all of us – a profound inextinguishable longing for the unconditional love we knew at the breast, in the womb. Pointing to the persistence in us of incestuous wish and parricidal longing was his way of calling our attention to that voice still alive in us which cries: I want her; I want all of her, all to myself. And to our deep murderous resentment of anyone who intrudes between me and her, between me and the fullness of love I imagine I once had and still long for.

Self and other – self and lack – appear together. To be a person is to be wanting, in need, wish-driven, lacking. We become aware of being persons, of being a self through the discovery of our insufficiency, of our helplessness. Freud sees the Oedipus myth as making visible the primacy of desire – and the inevitability of its frustration, the inescapable connection between sexuality and the unattainable, the pain of being human. The loss of that imagined blissful first love issues in unavowable grief and rage, in unappeased longing, and in unmitigated terror. Having lost our first love, we always feel threatened by loss. Indeed, the knowledge of the loss somehow precedes the knowledge of the love. (We know Eden as Eden only after the gates have closed behind us.)

Incest and parricide are thus not to be understood literally, and yet they are connected to actual experience, bodily experience, childhood experience. Thus we misread Freud – make him into a Jungian – if we understand incest and parricide as "only metaphor."

Freud also meant by "Oedipus" the commitment to self-knowledge (even when painful) exemplified by Oedipus's persistence in his search to discover the true identity of the one whose murderous dead had brought death to his city. (It is actually this aspect that is emphasized in *Interpretation of Dreams*.) The Oedipus myth also shows how the story never begins with us; psychologically we enter into a world already there, a world of others, become ourselves in response to their desires, their fears. As Oedipus's life was shaped by his parents' fears, by the curse laid on his father – and in turn his dying curse fatefully impacts his children's lives.

In his later years of suffering from the unremitting pain of his cancer, Freud identified with the blind exiled Oedipus utterly dependent on being led by his daughter Antigone – as Freud had become dependent on his daughter Anna to insert each morning and then remove each night the prosthesis that separated his oral and nasal cavities, and to deliver his speeches when he, Sigmund, Siegmund, the victorious mouth, no longer could. "My Anna, my Antigone," he called her. In those years he identified with the Oedipus who had come to terms with his finitude, the Oedipus who was ready to die.

I am Oedipus, he said. Fully to know myself is to acknowledge this identification. And in saying this he was rediscovering what myth-oriented cultures have always affirmed: we find our identity through discovering a mythic model. Freud learned that to be a self is to be others, we become ourselves through a series of identifications. Though there is no question that the myth of Oedipus has particular power for him, almost as important to Freud were his identifications with several biblical figures – Jacob, Joseph, and Moses – and with other classical mythic figures – Psyche and Eros, as we've already noted, and Narcissus.

It was Havelock Ellis, not Freud who first introduced the term "narcissism" into psychology, but in Freud's use the term becomes much more than simply a fancy word for auto-eroticism or masturbation. He brings some of the full richness of Ovid's telling of the myth back into psychology, particularly the close association of narcissism and death. Ovid's Narcissus is a beautiful youth who rejects the love of the nymph Echo and of many male admirers, one of whom implores the gods, "May he too fall in love with another and be unable to gain his loved one." So at the edge of a barely moving stream Narcissus falls in love with his own reflected image, unaware that it is his own. Only when he discovers this does he fall into immobilizing despair – and not knowing whether to woo or be wooed, slowly wastes away and dies.

Narcissus in the myth is someone who takes his own reflection for another, who can't distinguish between self and other. As, so Freud believes, none of us can at the beginning, when enmeshed in what he calls primary narcissism, that early pre-psychical, pre-verbal stage in which there is no self and no other, a stage which exists only in memory, in fantasy, only for the imagination – only afterwards. Consciousness, as we noted earlier, begins with the experience of separation and loss. Self and other are co-created – and thus arise the twin possibilities of self-love and other-love. The Oedipus myth expresses the soul meaning of one, Narcissus of the other.

Some of the originally undifferentiated libido is directed to the self, some to others. Consciousness entails a departure from primary narcissism, a transfer of some of the love that might be directed toward ourselves to another. Often we may try in some way to have it both ways, to love someone who reminds us of ourselves, or of our earlier selves, or of our ideal selves. We are also likely to over-estimate the beloved to make up for the forfeited self-love – and to need to be loved back to recover the forfeited self-love. And when we aren't loved, there is always an enormous temptation to entirely withdraw libido from the outer world and thus fall into what Freud calls "secondary narcissism."

Narcissism thus represents an earlier, more primary stage than Oedipal love; it arises in response to the separation between what is not yet an ego and not yet an object, out of longing to deny the loss, the dependency, the neediness, to claim a self-sufficiency. Our initial turn to an other expresses our impossible longing for an other to give us back that lost wholeness. It is really an expression of fusion longing, and expresses a desire to *be*, not to *have*.

Only after the full acknowledgment of the loss, only after what Freud calls the work of mourning, does there really arise the possibility of turning to other as other, as a genuinely separate object with its own desires which are not just for me. Only, we might say, when we acknowledge the existence of a rival, admit that the mother does not exist only in relation to us, only as we enter the Oedipal world, does the possibility of real loving, of Eros, emerge.

Narcissism is an illusion; we are in a world with others; we are not self-sufficient, we are not the world. And thus narcissism is death. Freud often quotes Heine: "We must learn to love in order not to fall ill." But it is also true that the narcissistic longings never die. For we all long to return to that earlier fantasized world where self and other were one, all long to believe that separation is not the ultimate truth. As Julia Kristeva puts it, "The lover is a narcissist with an object" (Kristeva, 1997, 147). Eros is the long way round back to narcissism, to death; Eros is an *Aufhebung* of narcissism, its overcoming *and* its continuation by other means.

From the time of that dream from which he awoke knowing "I am Oedipus," Freud knew that to speak adequately of the psyche requires recourse to mythological and metaphorical language. In the writings of his last years the figures of the twin Titans, Eros and Death, come to loom as large as had the figure of Oedipus earlier on. In her *Tribute to Freud* the poet H.D., who was a patient of Freud's in the early 1930s wrote: "Eros and Death, these two were the chief subjects, indeed the only subjects of the Professor's eternal preoccupation." And as he told her, "My psychology lays the basis for a very grave philosophy."

During the last two decades of his life, Freud's emphasis shifts from the psychological to the metapsychological and to the period in our lives where the mother is the most important figure for both boys and girls, a period Freud sees as equivalent to the Minoan-Mycenaean period in Greek history when goddesses were more important than gods. During this time death also became an ever more important theme in Freud's writing. Among contributing factors we might name the painful breaks with Adler and Jung, the outbreak of the First World War which he saw as making evident the costs of the repression of aggression and death wish, the deaths of one of his daughters and of a beloved grandson soon after the war's end, and his own cancer which served as a constant reminder of his own oncoming death.

As Death becomes an ever more important theme, Freud comes to speak of Eros, the cosmic life principle, rather than of sexuality. It is important, however, that we recognize that this does not represent a move from body to spirit, but rather an even deeper contemplation of the meaning of our embodiment and finitude. Freud has become deeply aware of how precarious our love of life is, how there is something inside us which works against that in us which wants, against that in us which is turned to the future, to others, to the new, against what he now calls Eros.

He looks upon Eros and Death as two primal powers, as cosmological not just psychological energies, forces that are at work in us, through us, and in the whole outer world. He speaks of them as twin brothers, engaged in a dramatic struggle with one another and sometimes in so close an embrace that we cannot distinguish between them. To speak of them as mythological figures is to engage in an age-old human way of figuring the most powerful forces at work in the universe. Freud does not call upon us to worship these Titans but simply to acknowledge their power – and to remember that they do not constitute a moral dichotomy. We should not fall into the trap of regarding Eros as good or Death as bad.

Freud's Eros is, of course, not the childish Cupid of popular imagination. He is the Eros of Apuleius and of Plato, and of Hesiod and the Orphics, the creative principle which is the source of all being, all life. Freud clearly distinguishes Eros from what he calls "oceanic feeling," from fusion longing, which Freud viewed as regressive, narcissistic, directed by death longing. His Eros is clearly an active "masculine" figure, an energy directed outward, toward real, particular others. Not to all, that would be fusion longing once again, but to an ever widening, more inclusive circle of others. His Eros is one of the parents of civilization; he is, as Auden puts it, the "builder of cities" (Auden, 1976, 218). Freud sees civilization, communal existence, as dependent on libidinal attachments, not just on the containment of aggression. Society is based on love *and* on our fear and hatred of others. We want and resent society; it fulfills and frustrates us; we accept it and rebel against it; part of us adapts to the restrictions it demands, part doesn't.

The twin brother of Eros is Death. Freud never calls this figure Thanatos, the name of the minor the Greek god who carries us to the underworld, nor Persephone or Hades, but simply: *Death*. Early on Freud had focused on the importance of overcoming the repression and literalization of sexuality; in this later period he comes to emphasize the importance of overcoming the repression and literalization of death.

Death, as Freud speaks of it, is of course psychical and not simply biological reality. He suggests that narcissism may be the most intimate and archaic expression of the death drive. The goal of all life is death, he tells us, with ever more complicated detours. Death is something we both long for and fear. He associates death fear with our fears of: the unknown, the uncanny, the unconscious; with our fears of vulnerability and passivity; our fears of not being loved, of being abandoned, of not loving. Death wish is associated with all in us that is pulled toward repetition, inertia, regression; all that longs for a tension-free existence, for Nirvana resolution, completion; the voices in us that cry "leave me alone, let me have my way, don't make me change; let me stay a child, let me return to the womb." Death wish shows itself in our longing to be immortal, to be remembered, in our longing not to die. This is a paradox that Nietzsche also articulated: the wish not to die is itself a death wish, as is all resistance to change, to movement, that is, to life.

When denied, death-fear and death-wish both become destructive, become aggression. Again Freud reminds us of our resentful hatred of anything that intrudes between me and that longed for peace, that reminds me of my incompleteness, my wanting, my separation from the all. But remember: death is not the enemy. The death drive is not bad; it represents a given direction of the soul. Freud hopes to help us recognize the importance of accepting this as part of who we are, of learning to bear the conflicts within us, of curing our demand for cure, for resolution, of coming to view conflict as enduring and enlivening. But, then, that's Eros's view. Death itself might say: we need to honor also that in us which continues to want happiness, resolution, fulfillment.

In the early 1930s, as Nazism was becoming more and more powerful, Freud saw a world more and more dominated by Death - and saw how our fear of Death leads to its gaining more and more power over us. Yet he ends *Civilization and Its Discontents*, what Adam Phillips calls "his great elegy for happiness," (Phillips, 1998, 72) not with words of despair, and of course not with words of easy cheap consolation, but with what comes as close to a prayer as we are ever likely to find in Freud: "But now it is to be hoped that the other of the two heavenly powers, eternal Eros, will make an effort to assert himself in the struggle with his equally immortal adversary." (Freud, 1953/1974, 145)

This evocation of hope, of Eros in the light of, not denial of, Death, brings to my mind the last stanzas of the poem, "In Memory of Freud," that W.H. Auden wrote a few month after Freud's death in 1939:

> But he would have us remember most of all
> to be enthusiastic over the night,
> not only for the sense of wonder
> it alone has to offer, but also
> because it needs our love.
> Our rational voice is dumb. Over his grave
> the household of Impulse mourns one dearly loved:
> sad is Eros, builder of cities,
> and weeping, anarchic Aphrodite. (Auden, 1976, 218)

References

Auden, W.H. (1976). In Memory of Sigmund Freud. In *Collected Poems*. New York: Random House.

Bettelheim, B. (1983). *Freud and Man's Soul*. New York: Alfred A. Knopf.

Freud, S. (1953/1974). Introductory lectures. In J. Strachey (Ed. and Trans*.*), *The Standard Edition of the Complete Psychological Works of Sigmund Freud* (Vol. 16). London: Hogarth Press.

Freud, S. (1953/1974). Civilization and Its Discontents. In J. Strachey (Ed. and Trans.), *The Standard Edition of the Complete Psychological Works of Sigmund Freud* (Vol. 21). London: Hogarth Press.

Kristeva, J. (1997). Freud and Love. In K. Oliver (Ed.), *The Portable Kristeva*. New York: Columbia University Press.

Phillips, A. (1998). *The Beast in the Nursery*. New York: Pantheon Books.

RobinsonP. (1998, November 12). Symbols at an Exhibition. *New York Times Book Review*, p. 12.

CHAPTER 5

A Depth Psychological Approach to the Sacred

Lionel Corbett

Given the huge variety of spiritual practices found in contemporary culture, it may seem excessive to make yet another suggestion for our spiritual smörgåsbord. But the spiritual life of a culture periodically demands renewal; the same (albeit ancient) truths benefit from being restated in a modern idiom. It is as if each emerging culture has to rediscover and reword its connection to the sacred – and what could be more in tune with the spirit of our times than depth psychology, one of our culture's newest disciplines?

When depth psychology turns its attention to spirituality, we hear familiar spiritual themes – but we hear them spoken about in a new voice. Crucially, we also hear profound spiritual importance attributed to material that the larger culture deems to be secular and nothing to do with spirituality. This happens because depth psychology has its own way of thinking about sacred experience and has its own vocabulary for speaking of it. In particular, we do not restrict our understanding of the sacred to any particular theological system. Our approach is simply stated: rather than dictate the way in which the sacred *should* appear, rather than appealing to tradition, to biblical authority and to dogmatic assertions, we simply try to discover the ways in which the sacred *actually* appears in a person's life. Then we try to clarify the significance of this experience for the subject, using the experience itself as its own self-authenticating statement. We do not try to make the experience mean something in terms of a particular theological system, nor do we judge it in such a light. Instead, we try to relate sacred experience to the psychological make-up of the subject, to his or her background, emotional state, and to the direction that the experience seems to indicate for the future course of the personality.

Accordingly, the depth psychological approach to spirituality is useful in two situations. Some people find that the image or concept of the divine that they were taught in childhood no longer has much personal meaning because it does not correspond to what is really sacred to them. Other people are committed to a particular tradition, perhaps a branch of Judaism or Christianity, but they need to re-mythologize their tradition – that is, they need to give new and personal meaning to its images and sacred stories. In this essay, I will focus mainly on the first group.

When the religious tradition of their childhood no longer resonates with us, our true spirituality has to develop in private, like a secret inner life that we may share with few people, if anyone. This happens especially when the way the sacred actually affects us bears little resemblance to what we were told was sacred in childhood. In such a case, our childhood religion often seems irrelevant; it does not work to comfort us when we suffer, or it does not have an adequate explanation for the evils that we see around us. Perhaps it simply leaves us cold because its image of God is too male, too cruel or arbitrary, too concerned with sin and guilt, or just too remote from the realities of relationships and everyday life. Instead, we may hold some values and experiences very dearly, but it may never occur to us to describe them as "sacred" because our culture does not allow them to be thought of in such terms.

Those of us in this situation may still attend Church or Synagogue at holidays such as Easter, Christmas, Passover or the Jewish new year, per-haps because of an echo of our childhood importance to us, or out of nostalgia, guilt or just plain sentimentality. At these times we may feel pangs of sadness when we think of how important were these religious services to our parents and grandparents, whereas the service leaves us cold because we do not experience the divine in such places. As Jung put it, once the gods have left a temple, they never return. Surely it is important to look at why this has happened, why are we left cold by contemporary religious institu-tions. Does depth psychology really have anything to offer in this spiritual vacuum?

In such a situation, there is often a deep sense of loss, a painful awareness that not only has the institution failed us, but there also seems to be no other way to contact the sacred, which leads to a constant sense that something is missing from our lives. It is then as if we cannot connect with someone we love. Until we reconnect, everyday life may lack fullness or depth of meaning. We would prefer that everyday life would provide constant contact with the sacred, without which those of us with this need are always a little lost, as if we were searching for the way home. Worse, if we stay in the Church when the divine is no longer there for us, we are really worshipping an idol. Therefore, when the traditional ideas and images no longer light the way, it becomes urgent for us to find a way to discover what is *personally* sacred. Depth psychology suggests a way in which we may live an authentic spiritual life without adherence to any established religious institution, without relying on a set of pre-established ideas about the way the sacred is supposed to appear. A man dreamed that a voice said to him: "God dooms us to live a life apart from him." He was distressed by this, until we recalled Meister Eckhart's comment "God save me from God." In both cases, the point is that preconceived ideas about the divine might interfere with the direct experience if this reality does not happen to coincide with our expectation.

The experiential approach concentrates on the particular emotional *quality* of an experience to decide whether it is authentic. The actual content of the experience does not have to conform to any doctrinal notion of the sacred, although of course it may do so – the psychological approach does not *discount* the traditional manifestations of the sacred, it simply expands the number of its possible manifestations. To describe sacred experience, Jung borrowed the term "numinous" from Rudolph Otto, who had coined the word to describe the quality that he thought was at the core of all religious experience. A numinous experience in its most obvious form is mysterious, uncanny and awesome; it obviously comes from beyond the ordinary realm, filling us with astonishment and wonder. It is also alluring and fascinating, often leaving us feeling blessed or humbled, entranced and transported. Biblical examples are those such as Moses at the burning bush that was not consumed by the fire, or Saul on the road to Damascus, suddenly struck by a blinding light and hearing a voice saying "why do you persecute me?" But these kinds of experiences are not confined to the Bible, or to the saints and mystics of the traditions. They may erupt at any time in the lives of ordinary people, or they may be deliberately induced by careful preparation.

The psyche-centered approach suggests that numinous experience is the result of contact with transpersonal levels of the psyche. This idea distinguishes Jung's model of the psyche from those models of the mind that only describe the unconscious in personal terms. For Jung, the psyche is like the air we breathe; we each have a lung full of air, but we are all enclosed in a larger field in which all air is continuous. Analogously, the personal level of the psyche is seamlessly continuous with its transpersonal level. Just as the crest of each wave in an ocean seems to be separate from the tip of other waves, but deeper down is continuous with the larger body of water, so the psyche has personal levels and a transpersonal level in which we all participate.

Within the transpersonal psyche, Jung describes deep structures that he calls archetypes. Archetypes are pattern-formers in the psyche, where they correspond to the laws of physics that determine how the material world operates. Just as matter behaves in orderly and predictable ways, so the behavior of the psyche is ordered archetypally and is not random. Consequently a baby is not born as a blank slate, but rather with the full potential for being human. A baby expects to meet a mother; the Mother archetype is the spiritual potential to experience a mother, whereupon a human being humanizes or fills in this transpersonal potential. In religion and mythology, the Mother archetype is depicted as the Goddess, or the Great Mother, or the feminine aspects of the divine. This archetypal potential is expressed differently in different cultures, where she is given different names and dresses, and different attributes are ascribed to her. She is every Goddess from the Blessed Virgin Mary to Demeter to Durga – these are simply local or folkloric versions of a deep, transpersonal structure of the psyche. Similarly, the baby meets a father, who humanizes the archetypal Father of mythology, who is usually represented by sky gods like Zeus or the biblical Yahweh.

Obviously, beside Her significance for religion and mythology, the archetype of the Mother has major personal importance for the development of the child. This means that the personality has spiritual as well as human determinants, or we could say that the transpersonal and the human levels are continuous with each other within a personality. For example, a woman physician dreamed:

> I enter the room of a woman patient and find her lying on the floor next to her bed in a fetal position. She is weak, emaciated, and two thirds of her body is covered with bruises where she has been beaten. I realize that she has spent all of her life in jail and has been severely abused. She also has a reputation for being dangerous, combative and out of her head. I lift her frail body into my arms and turn her on her back so that I may listen to her heart. I lay her down gently. I can see the terror on her face and I have the sense that she is like a vicious animal and may attack me at any time. I ask her permission to listen to her heart, then gently lift her gown,

revealing no more than is necessary to place the stethoscope so that she will not feel invaded or feel that I do not respect her privacy. Her face and entire body soften with relief and she allows the examination. I come away with the awareness that she is very ill and that she will be my first psychiatric patient – someone I must see through to the end. Her name is Mary, and I realize that she is, in fact, the Blessed Virgin Mary.

Now this is not a traditional manifestation of the Virgin Mary. But for the depth psychologist, the dream depicts the way in which the Goddess is configured in this particular woman's psyche. She has been abused and beaten, which has made her dangerously violent. At the same time, the dream tells us about the way in which the dreamer's femininity was treated in her childhood: it is an image of a complex, or an emotionally charged, painful structure within her psyche. The dream tells us that the divine feminine can be redeemed by the dreamer's care and love, and it also depicts the way in which the Goddess has been treated by the culture, so that the dreamer carries a larger burden than her own difficulties. Her work on her own problem will help the redemption of a larger cultural problem.

This dream is typical of how individual experiences of the sacred are connected to our own emotional and psychological life. Obviously, a person with a different psychological background would experience this archetype in her own, quite different, manner. When dealing with numinous material like this dream, there is no meaningful distinction between psychology and spirituality. Descriptively, there is no difference between what the traditional religions call the experience of spirit and what the depth psychologist calls numinous experience. This is why Jung is able to call the archetypes the "organs of God" in the psyche.

This dream illustrates another of the main differences between the depth psychological approach and traditional approaches to spirituality. The numinous image in the dream has a distinctly frightening tone to it, as if it could be dangerous to the dreamer. The archetype is considered to be potentially both negative as well as positive. It may be that at a transcendent level of reality the divine is all good, but at the level of our experience the Self, or our image of the divine, seems to have a dark side to it. One manifestation of this darkness is our painful psychopathology; at the collective level, the dark side of the Self is manifest in events like the Holocaust and Hiroshima.

The depth psychological approach has no comment about levels of the sacred that are transcendent, or which are beyond experience, and does not speculate about the nature of the divine. We do not make pronouncements about whether the divine is one, or three, removed from the world or totally immanent, or especially strongly felt in Jerusalem. We do not think of the numinosum as a personality in its own right, as a kind of Superior Person. Instead we concentrate on its manifestations within our consciousness. We have no way to tell whether a numinous experience originates within the psyche itself, or whether there is a transcendent level of the divine that is merely mediated by the psyche. What is clear is that without the psyche, experience would be impossible. Consequently, depth psychology does not really encroach on theology. We are only interested in the experience of immanent levels of the sacred, in the ways in which the sacred becomes manifest in our lives, and in the psychological effects this has on us. (See Corbett, 1996 for a fuller discussion.)

For the psyche-centered approach, the numinosum can seem to appear from outside ourselves, as an experience that is infused into us, or it can affect us from within the personality. Thus we see it in dreams, in visions, in relationships, in the body, in the natural world – and most importantly, as this dream example shows, it appears within our psychopathology and our suffering. In such a case, we are gripped from within by a force of which we can try to become conscious. We can then try to relate to this force, which, until then, is relatively autonomous. However it appears, numinous experience is always psychologically relevant to the experiencer, and at the same time it tells us something about his or her true spirituality, which may or may not correspond to traditional ideas. For example, in his *Cosmic Consciousness*, Richard Bucke (1961, p. 214) tells the story of a woman who is gathering flowers when suddenly:

> I looked at the large bunches we had gathered with growing amazement at their brightness ... A wonderful light shone out from every little petal and flower, and the whole was a blaze of splendor. I trembled with rapture – it was a "burning bush." It cannot be described. The flowers looked like gems or stars ... so clear and transparent, so still and intense, a subtle living glow ... what a moment that was! I thrill at the thought of it.

Someone who experiences the numinosum in this way, by means of the natural world, is given a strong clue about her authentic spirituality. This woman was never really satisfied in the Church, and could never reconcile the behavior of the biblical God, removed from his creation, with her profound feeling for nature, so that as a child she felt herself to be something of a wicked skeptic, all the time with a deep vein of sadness that she had to keep out of sight (p. 268). She describes how she would look at the stars with "unspeakable longing" for an answer to her dilemma. She knew there was something missing in her life, a connection to the depths of her own nature that she could not reach. For a long time she tolerated this situation as her lot in life, until her soul demanded an awakening, which for her was triggered by a serious illness. She recovered, and in the process developed great empathy for the suffering of others. But she yearned for a larger life, for a deeper love, and constantly felt that she was like a creature that had outgrown its shell, yet could not escape from it. It seemed that only death would offer some release.

At last, exhausted by her search, she was able to let go and surrender completely. Only then did the numinosum erupt, and she had the sense of a serene and holy Presence pervading nature, with periods of rapture at its beauty. On one occasion she reports that while smelling flowers

> The pleasure I felt deepened into rapture; I was thrilled through and through, and was just beginning to wonder at it when deep within me a veil, or curtain, suddenly parted, and I became aware that the flowers were alive and conscious ... The feeling that came to me with the vision was indescribable. (p. 272)

This experience filled her with "unspeakable awe." Typically for someone whose spirituality is not satisfied by the traditional God-images in which she was raised, these experiences gave her a sense of a real spiritual ground, and an "unfaltering trust" that: "Deep in the soul, below pain, below all the distractions of life, is a silence vast and grand – an infinite ocean of calm, which nothing can disturb; Nature's own exceeding peace ..." She finally felt truly anchored, and during this time she realized spontaneously that her life is a spiritual evolution, a "passing phase in the soul's progression." This is hardly a new idea in the history of spirituality – but it is one thing to be told about it and quite another for such an idea to burst into one's consciousness with such "overwhelming grandeur." As well, it is clear that her experiences of nature are sacramental – they act as a channel of grace, or a means of connecting with the sacred. From this follows two other notions found within the experiential approach. No institution has exclusive hegemony over sacramental experience, which can take many forms. Similarly, redemption can occur in many ways other than that prescribed by traditional institutions.

No matter whether the numinosum grips us by means of the inner or the outer world, the psyche-centered approach suggests that it provides a personal revelation from archetypal levels of the psyche. But the archetypes are configured differently in different people, and in any personality some archetypal forces are more prominent than others, so that we find different things numinous. If we were rather crudely to use the names of gods and goddesses to personify archetypal forces, in some people we would find more Zeus energy, in some more Aphrodite, in others more Hera or Hestia. In other words, some people are more oriented towards power and authority, some towards relationship at all cost, while others find hearth and home most numinous. Because of these differences in our mental make-up, a spiritual idea that is of the utmost importance to one person might leave another cold. Consequently, there can be no normative spirituality that applies to everyone. If a person is drawn to the story of Jesus, and finds that the events of Jesus' life and his teachings are profoundly important to him because they resonate with his own psychology, then that person is an authentic follower of Jesus. But, if we feel that the idea of Jesus' vicarious sacrifice and suffering on our behalf is uncomfortable, or if we are actually repelled by the image of Jesus crucified, then we are not able to participate in this mythology as a mode of connection to the sacred.

Much of this difference in response to the story of Jesus illustrates the fact that the religious mythology to which we are drawn often reflects our personality structure and early developmental factors. Some people grow up in families that require that children sacrifice themselves to their parents' needs, or in families in which parents sacrifice themselves for their children. Some families demand that a child tolerate cruel behavior if he or she is to remain connected to a parent. Sometimes the children of abusive parents excuse their parents by blaming themselves, as in "if I were not so bad, he wouldn't treat me this way," or the child projects her own anger onto abusive parents, as in "he must be angry with me to treat me this way, and it's happening because I am bad." There are many other similar psychodynamic configurations that would draw one to a mythology that describes child sacrifice or brutal pain as a ransom for being saved from sin, or as the price of connection to a Father God. We might then find these aspects of the gospel story numinous. But, if these kinds of parent-child dynamics were not particularly strong in one's early life, the story of Jesus might have less appeal, or at least one might be more attracted to Jesus' stress on love and social justice rather than on sin and the need for redemption.

When the stories and teachings of a tradition reflect our personal psychology, we are drawn to them – otherwise they are uninteresting or repellent. For example, a woman was brought up in a very repressive religious atmosphere in which she was constantly told that the body and sexuality were bad and dangerous. This led to considerable conflict about sexuality and her femininity. In a dream, she is kneeling in Church to take the sacrament and realizes that the wafer she is given is full of raisins, and that these are part of the sacrament. She associated raisins to Dionysus, the Greek god of wine, who was a god of ecstasy, rapture and love. He was close to nature and to women – often he was surrounded by enraptured lovers, the frenzied Maenads or Bacchae who were possessed by him. In Greek mythology, Dionysus is the only god who actually rescues and restores women, instead of raping and dominating them; he tries to free women from the constraints of the patriarchy. Communion with this god means reveling in nature, entering the realm of the irrational and emotional, with frenzied music and dancing to the point of ecstasy. As well as being a god himself, Dionysus is also a priest to the great Goddess Cybele. His deadly enemy was Hera, the Goddess of marriage, which is not surprising considering how opposite are the values of these archetypal forces – Hera insists on the social obligations of marriage, while Dionysus' passion disrupts them and calls on women to not be bound by the usual rules. At Eleusis, the Dionysian sacraments were the body and blood of the god in the form of bread and wine. The dream suggests that this archetypal quality is sacramental for this woman. For her, sensuality is spiritually important, and an intense sexuality could be an ecstatic experience of merger with the sacred. Instead, this important aspect of her soul has been denied and vilified – a clear example of how an important archetypal predisposition is in conflict with a traditional religious attitude. No wonder she is conflicted and unhappy as she sits in Church trying hard to worship a God-image that is not her God.

In its better moments, the Judeo-Christian tradition has recognized the body as a sacred container of spirit; in the tradition's worst moments, the body has been vilified or demonized, but certainly regarded as less important than spirit. However, for some people the body is an important medium of numinous experience. During a meditation retreat, a woman experienced repeated episodes of excruciating pain in her back, at the level of the heart. This was much worse pain than she was accustomed to during such retreats. Suddenly, as she was lying down to try to alleviate the pain:

I experienced sensations of extraordinary energy, light and movement in my body, and heard a voice say that this was an experience of, and an opportunity to observe, Eros and its energy. It was like observing Eros in its pure and intense form – like watching or studying electrical or nuclear energy, but seeing it as an energy of the heart. It entered from above my body from a point mid-way between the pubic area and the navel as a column of white light, with radiating yellow/golden light at its base. The sensations of this energy were simultaneously exciting, sensual, sexual, powerful, hot, vibrant, radiating, expansive, enlivening and frightening.

As the experience subsided, she experienced "an extraordinary sense of both being and being enveloped by a completely open heart that was all-expansive and all-encompassing. It left me with an amazing sense of joy and peace and a feeling of being wholly a part of the cosmos." As a result of severe childhood deprivation, this woman has long struggled with feeling alone, unloved, and unable to love deeply. Relationship is crucial to her psychological make-up, but it has been extremely difficult for her to attain. Here she experiences an opening of the heart, a sense of relatedness with all things and a feeling of unity and belonging. This is why Jung was able to say that contact with the numinous is healing; the experience is directly related to an area of emotional difficulty and brings the help that is needed. Now, behaving with an open heart, with compassion and love, has become an integral part of her spiritual practice – not simply because she has been told of its importance, but because this is authentically who she is.

The problem of the resonance between our personality and our true spirituality is crucial. We cannot be forced into a spiritual tradition that is not in harmony with our nature. I distinctly remember being very perturbed as a child by God's forbidding Adam and Eve to eat of the Tree of Knowledge in the Garden of Eden. This prohibition made no sense to me, especially since the creation was all good. Why would knowledge lead to death (Gen. 2: 16-17)? Surely such a command was only likely to make Adam and Eve yearn to eat from the tree – and how could knowledge be harmful? In any case, Adam did not die immediately, but lived to be 930. At the same time, at school I was told that knowledge and reason were highly valued, and that we should try to discover as much as we can about the world. There are sophisticated responses to this paradox, but this was one of many seeds of doubt that were sown in childhood. I now realize that I was horrified at the time because to me learning is a numinous activity. In the Hindu tradition, *Jñana yoga*, an approach to the sacred by means of knowledge and questioning, is recognized as an important spiritual path for some people. To be told that knowledge is forbidden was completely opposed to this important dimension of my personality. These kinds of conflicts between the teachings and stories of a tradition and one's personal psychology cause us to abandon our childhood religions because they do not work – they do not correspond to who we are, and they do not answer our deepest needs.

Another important manifestation of numinous experience occurs by means of creative work, such as writing, dancing, painting, or music. Sometimes we feel taken over by a force that is actually doing the work, while we simply act as a conduit. When the artist Marc Chagall was asked whether he prayed, he replied that of course he did – he made art. William Blake said that he wrote some of his poetry "even against my will." The sense is that something takes over during these times, producing a result that does not seem to have come out of the ego. During the creative work, we lose track of time, and we lose the sense of being a separate self – there is simply work going on, but not a separate individual doing it. Because the ego is possessed by non-ego forces, we have passed into sacred time and space, which is different from ordinary time and space. I believe that what happens in such situations is that the creative work becomes a form of spontaneous personal ritual, a form of contact with the sacred using the body and non-verbal language. The artist *needs* to do her art, which expresses more than what can be said. The process has a life of its own within her; she has been mobilized and focused by the energy of the sacred, which is an archetypal Other that moves her to create. The archetype is then allowed an image, language, or an action in the body, depending on the art form involved. Thus, the work is an incarnation; it is consecrated, and it makes the sacred dimension accessible.

The psyche-centered approach to spirituality claims that religious systems address archetypal pressures within the personality that are common to all people, and these can be satisfied using the techniques of depth psychology. Our religious yearning can be met without the necessity of thinking of the divine as a kind of personality who took part in Bible stories. Instead, our felt sense is that we are addressed by transpersonal levels of consciousness.

Different methods and ways of speaking about the sacred lead to different results. As a way of contrasting the psychological and the traditional approaches, consider the archetypal notions of salvation and redemption, which are found in some form in all religious systems. Each tradition offers its own brand of salvation by promising us some special good if we behave and believe in the correct manner. Either we will go to heaven, or we will be especially close to God, or we will attain eternal life in the hereafter, and so on. For the psychologist, the need for salvation arises from the sense that there is something wrong with us as we are at the moment. This sense of incompleteness develops when we grow up feeling that something about us is missing, or something needs fixing. Because we do not grow up in perfect childhood environments, the development of our sense of self is incomplete, and a part of the personality either remains unformed or painfully distorted. We feel that we need something in order to become whole. We may search for this something in many ways – a perfect mate, a perfect job, money, substances, or other distractions.

But we really need healing, and it is not an accident that there is a connection between our need for wholeness and the religious idea of "salvation." The word comes from the Latin "salvus," which means saved, but it also means "to be in good health." As Jung pointed out, religions are psychotherapeutic systems – they contain and help us with these kind of important feelings about ourselves. But instead of offering salvation by means of promises of some future benefit in another realm, depth psychology tries to deal directly with what is missing or painful in our sense of self. The necessary element, or the glue that will put us back together, may be provided by a relationship, or it may be given to us in an act of grace as the kind of numinous experience I have described earlier. The healing or saving factor is always numinous in its own right, even if it does not take one of the official forms.

Related to the urge towards salvation is the archetypal pressure for redemption. Some people have a powerful need to be extricated from some sin or evil that they feel about themselves, or they fear danger that they sense from others or from an angry God. Consequently, the idea of a Messiah or redeemer is very important. To meet this need, religious systems offer formulas for how redemption occurs – e.g., Christ's self-sacrifice pays a price on behalf of humanity that allows us to be reconciled with God in spite of our sinful nature. But the depth psychologist recognizes that this formula of vicarious sacrifice may not work for everyone. It does not always seem necessary to invoke the need for a painful, bloody sacrifice in order to relate to the divine. For the depth psychologist, the idea that God is judgmental and punitive and treats us as if we were in a law court is simply a fantasy that arises from experiences with an angry parent who must be pacified or he will be dangerous. Such projections of parent-child psychology onto our image of God are not necessary – they keep us stuck within an infantile way of thinking about the divine. The Judeo-Christian tradition has told us that *God* accuses us of being sinful, but the depth psychological suggestion is that our sense of badness is an *internal, psychological,* difficulty that we project onto our God-image.

We no longer need to project our own violence onto our God-image. If we can become conscious of our own darkness, and heal the frustrations and hurts that make us violent, angry, and guilty, we will be redeemed and saved by that new consciousness. We are redeemed when we peel off the projections of our parents and culture onto our God-image and develop our authentic connection to the Self. As Job discovered, a questioning of our preconceived ideas, and a healthy skepticism about the collective images of God, may lead to the vision of a new and personal God-image that is not just based on hearsay. We may invoke and receive the help of the divine to help us with this process, but this can happen in many ways besides the traditional theological formulas. There is no need to assume that any particular theological plan for our redemption is anything other than a human fantasy. Using the methods of depth psychology, we can stop projecting our need for a redeemer onto someone else, and be responsible for the demands of the Self, our personal image of the divine, as it manifests itself to us directly.

If we appeal to an outside authority or doctrine for redemption and salvation, we are like an addict who needs a constant supply of something in order to feel normal. Unless it is based on direct experience of the sacred, an ecclesiastical fix may only last a short time, and it must be renewed with exhortations to faith, belief, worship services, scripture readings, accusations of sinfulness, and sermons about how to behave. In contrast, the depth psychological approach prefers to deal with our sense of guilt or insufficiency on its own terms, at its own level, as our psychological situation, without projecting this sense onto a punitive God-image who demands belief in order for us to be saved according to a particular formula. In the end, to insist that only the approach of an institutional religion is a way to the divine is no more than a political device.

Finally, there is little point in arguing that the teachings of the Judeo-Christian tradition have not been given a fair trial. We have had several thousand years of such trial. The failure of purportedly Judeo-Christian cultures to seriously implement the compassionate and loving teachings of the tradition is evidence that these teachings do not always resonate with the deepest level of the individual soul. We only deeply engage in our lives with what is inwardly important. When religious ideas do not correspond to who we really are, we pay lip service to the religion but underneath we value something else entirely – witness the fact that Nazi Germany was ostensibly a Christian country, but this was obviously only true at a superficial level. What was really numinous to the Nazis was an entirely different god. The few authentic Christians of that nation, such as Dietrich Bonhoeffer, were ruthlessly eliminated. When the Christian story actually corresponds to the archetypal dynamics of a personality, we know it from his or her feelings and behavior – such a person is not found committing mass murder, and does not need to be told that this is evil.

Profoundly important spiritual teachings are useless if they cannot be applied because of the dynamics of a personality. If someone is full of hatred because of childhood abuse and mistreatment, it is a waste of time to tell him to turn the other cheek. If someone needs to accumulate money and position to bolster a fragile sense of self and low self-esteem, it will be impossible for him to follow Jesus' advice not to lay up earthly goods but to develop spiritually instead. If someone is full of rage and vengeance, he cannot be simply told to develop forgiveness and love for those who hurt him. Such problems are simultaneously spiritually and psychologically important – they are one of the places from which the numinosum grips us. They can only be helped by a gradual process that integrates split off aspects of the self, heals or soothes childhood wounds, develops unused potentials of the personality, learns about real relationships, and forms a connection to the Self. The individual's spirituality has to emerge organically out of such work, aided if we are so blessed by experiences of the numinosum. For the depth psychologist, this process of engagement with our deepest subjectivity and our connection to others is itself a spiritual practice. This practice, as Jung put it, leads us to the paradox that our suffering and our healing come from the same place.

References

Bucke, R.M. (1989). *Cosmic Consciousness*. Secaucus, NJ: Citadel Press.
Corbett, L. (1996). *The Religious Function of the Psyche*. London and New York: Routledge.

CHAPTER 6

Religious Pluralism in the Service of the Psyche

Patrick J. Mahaffey

> Our solidarity precedes our particularity,
> and is part of our self-transcendence.
> The truth of all of us is part of the truth of each of us.
> – *Wilfred Cantwell Smith*

Awareness of the plurality of religious traditions and their diverse perspectives on the nature of human existence and its destiny is a new horizon for religious thought, and presents us with new possibilities for spiritual experience. It also poses a challenge to the authority and self-understanding of particular religions. Adherents of a particular tradition must address or reflect upon questions that religious persons of the past – secure in more self-contained or homogeneous communities and societies – rarely had to face: Why are there so many religions? Why do I belong to one religion rather than another? Can more than one religion be true? And, if so, are they equally true? How should my religion relate to the others? Religious plurality is equally challenging to a person who does not align with any particular tradition but nevertheless feels religious longings, and who seeks spiritual experience and meaning in the context of postmodern, secular culture.

This essay will explore some of the ways in which religious persons have responded to this challenge. My examples will be Christian and Hindu interpretations and responses to other religions. The focus will be on influential philosophical or theological arguments which have been expressed in the history of these traditions.[1] I will also consider what Jung's psychology has to offer with respect to understanding – and embracing – the multiple and diverse forms of religious symbolism.

The term "religious plurality" refers to the variety of distinct or diverse religious traditions in human culture. It is important to acknowledge that each large-scale, transcultural tradition contains its own plurality or diversity. There are three main attitudes one may take toward religions other than one's own. An exclusivist attitude denies that other religions are alternative ways to salvation or liberation. The only valid tradition is one's own. Consequently, one may attempt to convert the "other." The intention to convert, I suggest, is to negate the other *as* other. An inclusivist attitude attempts to incorporate other religions into its own scheme of salvation. Typically, other religions are seen as *partially valid* or as *unconscious versions* of one's own religion. The "other" tends to be seen as a version of one's own religion. One projects one's self-understanding onto the other. A pluralist attitude affirms that one's own religion is one of many valid ways to salvation or liberation. The other is different from oneself but can be genuinely encountered and understood in a way that enriches or deepens one's self-understanding. One may also think of this attitude as "polytheistic" in the sense that James Hillman uses the word – a recognition that the human psyche is populated or visited by a variety of "gods" and "goddesses" or archetypal and transpersonal forces. While my intention is to emphasize pluralistic approaches to understanding the varieties of religious experience, it is important to see them against the backdrop of exclusivist and inclusivist perspectives since they reflect the predominant attitudes toward cultural diversity and religious plurality.

Exclusivism

The primary attitude of the church throughout Christian history has been to deny that other religions are valid paths to salvation. The roots of this attitude may be traced to the New Testament. Two paradigmatic examples convey the attitude in unequivocal terms. The first is the words of Peter in

---

[1] See Paul Knitter's *No Other Name? A Critical Survey of Christian Attitudes Toward the World Religions* for more examples from the Christian tradition. For background on Hindu attitudes, see *Modern Indian Responses to Religious Pluralism*, edited by Harold Coward. Examples of attitudes exhibited by other religions may be found in Coward's *Pluralism: Challenge to the World Religions*.

the Book of Acts: "And there is salvation in no one else, for there is no other name under heaven given among men by which we must be saved" (4.12). The second are words attributed to Jesus in the Gospel of John: "I am the way, and the truth, and the life; no one comes to the Father, but by me" (14.6). These New Testament texts recapitulate the First Commandment of the Hebrew Bible (or Christian Old Testament) from Exodus: "Thou shalt have no other gods before me" (20.3). Yahweh's demand for supremacy in this commandment eventually became a theological conviction that there were indeed no other real gods. A polytheistic pantheon, with one god asserting supremacy, was turned into a monotheistic conviction. As a consequence, the "other gods" disappeared altogether, except as threatening temptations or tempters, and the biblical view or myth held that Yahweh rules all: He is the creator, the sustainer, and the redeemer for the whole world.

Exclusivism in Christian theology is also rooted in the Christological doctrines formulated at Nicea and Chalcedon in the fourth century. For example: "Jesus Christ is unique in the precise sense that while being fully man, it is also true of him and him alone, that he is also fully God, the second person of the co-equal trinity" (Chalcedon). The corresponding ecclesiological doctrine is that the church alone is the way of salvation for all humankind. This traditional Roman Catholic teaching was institutionalized and enshrined in the axiom, "Outside the Church no salvation," which has, until recently, played a decisive role in the Roman Catholic Church's relations with other religions.

Exclusivism has not been confined to the pronouncements of the Roman Catholic Church. The Protestant equivalent of the axiom has been the firm assumption that outside Christianity there is no salvation. This view prevailed into the twentieth century and has formed the predominant attitude of the World Council of Churches until 1970 when a willingness to engage in inter-religious dialogue was initiated by this international and multi-denomination organization. One highly influential example of Protestant exclusivism in the present century is the position of Karl Barth and other neo-orthodox or evangelical theologians. Barth distinguished Christian revelation from religion. Religions, in his view, are human constructions and unable to provide human salvation. Christian revelation, by contrast, is entirely God's initiative. Christianity alone has been created and elected by God to be the one and only true religion. It alone has the authority and responsibility to be a missionary religion. From this perspective, knowledge of other religions is of limited value and dialogue with persons with different religious faiths is useful only insofar as it provides a more effective basis from which to preach the Gospel.

Hindu exclusivism is rooted in traditional attitudes regarding the *Vedas*. Hindus consider these texts to be eternal (uncreated) and the most perfect revelation of the divine truth. From the *Vedas* comes all knowledge of the *dharma* and without the *Vedas* liberation (*moksha*) is not possible. This raises the question of how Hindus view the scriptures of other religions. One response is evident with regard to Jainism and Buddhism. Since both the Jains and Buddhists reject the concept of scriptural revelation and treat the teachings of Mahavira and Buddha (the respective founders of these two traditions) as teachings to be tested out and proven for oneself, it is easy for Hindu exclusivists to simply reject such teachings in relation to the revealed *Vedas*. Another response which developed in relation to the plurality within Hinduism itself has been to give different texts such as the *Mahabharata*, *Ramayana* and the *Puranas* the status of secondary revelation. While this position grants some validity to other scriptures, it still preserves the exclusive authority of the *Vedas*. This approach is applied to the scriptures of other revealed religions such as Christianity and Islam: they are, at best, secondary revelations, carrying less authority and validity. Modern examples of Hindu exclusivism include the approach of Dayananda Saraswati, founder of the Arya Samaj, and the Vaishnava approach of Bhaktivedanta Prabhupada, founder of the International Society for Krishna Consciousness. Both approaches exhibit a fundamentalist interpretation of Hindu scriptures, and an emphasis on converting the adherents of other religions.

Inclusivism

Inclusivist attitudes toward non-Christian religions represent a strand in Christian history opposed to the historically dominant influence of exclusivism. To be inclusivist is to believe that all non-Christian religious truth belongs ultimately to Christ. Christianity is seen as the *summit* and *completion* of all other religions; it is the *fulfillment* of what is best and true in the others. The strategy of inclusivist theologians is to discern ways by which the non-Christian religions may be integrated into the Christian way of salvation.

Although Christian inclusivism appears to be a recent theological development, it dates back to the early roots of the Christian tradition. A paradigmatic source of inclusivism in the New Testament is Paul's speech on the

Areopagus described in the New Testament Book of Acts (17.22-31). In this passage, Paul acknowledges the authenticity of the worship of the Athenians at their altar "to an unknown God" by conferring a name on the God whom they already worshipped but did not truly recognize. By being so included, their religion was brought to completion and perfected.

In the twentieth century, inclusivism was more typical of Catholic theology than Protestant thought. Documents formulated during the second Vatican Council in the 1960s moved away from the exclusivist doctrine of "no salvation outside the Church" toward a more inclusivist appreciation of other faiths. They set the stage for new theological efforts such as the approach taken by Karl Rahner, perhaps the most influential Catholic theologian of the twentieth century. Rahner's concept of "salvation history" attempts to account for the fact that the Christian Gospel has not reached all people – for example, persons who lived before New Testament times, and persons who lived after New Testament times but never, through no fault of their own, encountered the Gospel. This concept maintains that God offers grace to those who have never properly encountered the Gospel, and asserts that it is mediated through the non-Christian's religion. The difference between Christianity and other religions is that Christians claim to name the reality which is *anonymously* present in other faiths, and operative in their rites and practices for achieving salvation. Persons in other religions are accordingly said to be "anonymous Christians." From this perspective, the mission of the Church is to proclaim, to the world religions, the mystery of Christ who works, hidden and unperceived, within their rituals and institutions. The Church, then, is the conscious embodiment of the salvific power of Christ which has always been active in the world even before the Incarnation.

Although most Catholic theologians accept the basic elements of Rahner's theology of religions, they continue to assert that Christ is unique from other religious teachers, prophets or saviors and that he is normative for all the others. To be normative means that Christianity is the necessary *catalyst* for all other faiths. Without Christ's revelation, other religions cannot really understand and appropriate the salvation at work within them. Many Protestant versions of inclusivism follow this same basic pattern of argument.

The paradigmatic source of Hindu inclusivism is the famous passage from the *Rig Veda*: "The real is one, the learned call it by various names" (1.164.46). Sayings conveying the same idea can be found scattered throughout Hindu religious literature including the frequently quoted verse from the *Bhagavad Gita* that suggests that all religions are included and accepted by the revelation of Krishna: "As men worship me so do I accept them; men on all sides follow my path" (4.1). In short, these texts are used by many modern Hindus to express the inclusivist attitude summarized in the slogan "one truth, many expressions" and the corollary affirmation of "one spiritual goal, many paths."

Hindu inclusivism may be described as perspectivism. The various religions are regarded to be different and sometimes conflicting perspectives on the one divine reality. This understanding of ultimate reality is rather like looking at a piece of sculpture from different perspectives. Although each view is different from the others and although some aspects of what is seen and described from different angles may seem incompatible, contradictory reports can yield a reliable overall description of the sculpture, which could not be obtained from only one viewpoint. There is a classic parable in the tradition which makes the same point. A number of blind persons encounter an elephant. Each describes his experience on the basis of touching various parts of the elephant – the ears, trunk, feet, and so on. Each description is based on an actual encounter with the elephant but they vary considerably because of the part of the elephant each describes. In each case, the part is mistakenly taken to be an accurate account of the totality of the elephant.

According to this logic, Hinduism should be *tolerant* and *open* to other religions because the more aspects of the divine we can perceive, the more complete our understanding will be. Within the tradition, tolerance is also required to include all sects (worshippers of the avatars of Vishnu, Shiva, Kali, and so on) and all points of view (the six orthodox systems of Indian philosophy or *darshanas*).

In the Hindu tradition, religious seekers start with whatever path matches their sensibilities and is within their reach (*ishtadevata* or "chosen deity"). It does not seem to matter which path is selected. However, most Hindus qualify their affirmation of other religious paths. The qualification is this: each of the religions moves one toward the goal of release from *karma-samsara* and union with the divine, but only with the aid of the revelation of the Vedas can one go the entire way to complete release. The implication is that other religions are valid as far as they go but that ultimately they require completion or fulfillment through the *sanatama dharma* entrusted to Hindus.

Modern Hindu inclusivism is expressed by a variety of thinkers, religious leaders, and the movements they inspired. These expressions range from the positions of the Brahmo Samaj; Swami Vivekananda and other swamis of the Ramakrishna Mission and Vedanta Society; and the philosophy of Sarvepalli Radhakrishnan. The essence of these viewpoints is summed up in the slogan "many paths, one goal." However, when one examines the teachings of many swamis and gurus, it becomes evident that all paths are *not* equal. The various paths and forms of worship correspond to a person's *stage* of knowledge. This implies that as one progresses, certain forms of worship or spiritual discipline drop off or are renounced because one has arrived at something more efficacious. Thus there is a hierarchy of paths or disciplines. Eventually some forms must be superseded if a spiritual aspirant is to reach the goal. The "path of knowledge" (*Jñana yoga*) is higher than that of devotion (*bhakti yoga*) or service (*karma yoga*). The goal of the path of knowledge is the realization that the inmost self (*atman*) is identical with ultimate reality or the divine (*Brahman*). This is the philosophy known as Advaita Vedanta. The hierarchical perspective applies both within Hinduism and to other religions.

From this perspective, all religious paths are understood as true or good because they point to the ultimate truth of Advaita Vedanta and thus contain, at least implicitly, the truth of this perception of reality. This, in effect, makes adherents of other traditions into "anonymous Advaitins." Thus, the "tolerance" eloquently advocated by many influential Hindus during the twentieth century clearly has its limits. In the final analysis, it is an attempt to reinterpret all other viewpoints so as to include them in a larger synthesis.

Pluralism

Pluralism in the Christian theology of religions is largely the product of the rise of modern historical consciousness in the nineteenth century and the tradition of theological liberalism that developed in response to it. Christian pluralists reject the idea that Christ is the fulfillment of other religions and affirm that these traditions are valid paths to salvation.

I will provide two examples of this kind of thinking – one Catholic and one Protestant. John Hick is a Protestant theologian and philosopher of religion. His theocentric position is based upon a critical reappraisal of traditional Christology and an affirmation of the universal salvific will of God. "Theocentric" means that his theology does not focus on Christ or Christology. He contends that the traditional Chalcedonian "two-natures" Christology (God as fully human and fully divine) represents an unwarranted deification of Jesus, and that a literal understanding of the incarnation has led to attitudes of exclusivity and triumphalism toward non-Christians.

If Jesus was literally God incarnate, and if it is by his death alone that human beings can be saved, and by their response to him alone that they can appropriate that salvation, then the only doorway to eternal life is Christian faith. It would follow from this that the large majority of the human race so far have not been saved. But is it credible that the loving God and Father of all human beings has decreed that only those born within one particular thread of human history shall be saved? Is not such an idea excessively parochial, presenting God in effect as the tribal deity of the predominantly Christian West? ("Jesus" 180)

The traditional Christian attitude, we may say, represents an egocentric and ethnocentric perspective regarding the superiority of Christianity.

Incarnational language, in Hick's perspective, is mythic and metaphorical. He argues that the Christian tradition turned the poetic image "Son of God" into prose, so that the *metaphorical* son of God became a *metaphysical* God the Son, the Second Person of a divine Trinity. The problem is that while the symbols of Jesus as Son of God, God the Son, God incarnate, and Logos made flesh served their purpose well for centuries of Christian history, the doctrine (or abstract concept) of the incarnation has poisoned the relationships between Christians and Jews and between Christians and Muslims, and served as a basis for Christian imperialism. So, Hick urges Christians to become conscious of both the optional and mythological character of traditional Christian language.

This perspective resonates with Joseph Campbell's reflections on religion as an expression of metaphor and myth:

From the point of view of orthodoxy, myth might be defined simply as "other people's religion," to which an equivalent definition of religion would be "misunderstood mythology," the misunderstanding consisting in the interpretation of mythic metaphors as references to hard fact: the Virgin Birth, for example, is taken to be a biological anomaly; or the Promised Land as a portion of the Near East to be claimed and settled by a people chosen by God; or the term "God" is understood as denoting an actual, though invisible, masculine personality, who created the universe and is now resident in an invisible, though actual, heaven to which the "justified" will go when they die, there to be joined at the end of time by their resurrected bodies. (55)

How, Campbell bluntly asks, is a modern mind to make sense of such nonsense? His suggestion is that we understand that myths are productions of the human imagination. Like dreams they contain narratives and images which are psychologically symbolic. They must be read, not literally, but as metaphors (55). Hick's theology moves in this direction by understanding the Incarnation to be a powerful metaphor for the divinity inherent in human beings.

Hick describes his alternative to traditional Christology as a Copernican revolution in theology. Analogous to the shift from Ptolemaic earth-centered cosmology to the sun-centered cosmology of Copernicus, Hick argues that the old Ptolemaic theology (represented by Barth and other exclusivists) and its recent epicycles (represented by Rahner and other inclusivists), props up an increasingly implausible system with either the Church, Christ or Christianity at the center of the universe of faiths. His model, by contrast, puts "God" – or, in more neutral terms, the Real – at the center, with all religions (including Christianity) revolving around this center (*God and the Universe of Faiths*, 131).

Hick distinguishes between a *noumenal* or transcendent reality and the variety of *phenomenal* apprehensions of this reality which arise in the various religions, variously designated as God, Brahman, the Tao, the Dharma, Shunyata, and so on. These phenomenal experiences and conceptions are "images" of the transcendent. The plurality of such images reflects the various ways in which the divine reality has impinged upon human consciousness in its different historical and cultural circumstances. And they may all reflect encounters with the one infinite reality though with partially different and overlapping aspects of that reality – as in the parable of the blind persons and the elephant. Therefore, all religions may be true and complement each other but none can claim to be the Truth in an absolute or exclusive sense (*God Has Many Names 83-84*; 90-94).

Raimundo Panikkar, a Catholic theologian and historian of religions, has been a passionate advocate of dialogue between religions which insists on the need to understand other religions on their own terms. Dialogue, in his view, is both "inter-religious" – between persons from different traditions – and "intra-religious." The latter term means that a genuine encounter with non-Christian religions entails entering into the subjectivity of these traditions. He describes this as a kind of conversion process and insists that it must take place at a level which is much deeper than that of comparing doctrines. Put another way – in hermeneutical terms – this process achieves a "fusion of horizons" – one's perspective or horizon of understanding co-mingles with the perspective or horizon of the other. Panikkar argues, in effect, that a Christian will never fully understand another religion such as

Hinduism if she or he is not, "converted" to Hinduism. Conversely, a Hindu does not fully grasp Christianity unless she or he becomes a Christian. As Panikkar puts it:

> Religions meet in the heart rather than the mind. ... The meeting of two differing realities produces the shock of the encounter, but the place where the encounter happens is one. This place is the heart of the person. It is within the heart that I can embrace both religions in a personal synthesis. And it is also within the heart that I may absorb one of the two religions into the other. In actuality religions cannot sincerely coexist or even continue as living religions if they do not "co-insist" – that is, penetrate into the heart of the other. (*Unknown Christ*, 43)

This is not merely a matter of *assimilating* or *incorporating* other religions into the Christian path of salvation. It is an encounter that mutually transforms each religion and affirms each one's evolving particularity.

Panikkar's pluralism strongly affirms the particularity of each religious or spiritual path. "It is not simply that there are different ways leading to the peak, but that the summit itself would collapse if all the paths disappeared. The peak is in a certain sense the result of the slopes leading to it" (*Unknown Christ*, 24). Similarly, religious symbols are understood to be singular and irreducible. Thus, Panikkar rejects the concept of the one God (or ultimate) who exists over and above the names of the various religions: "It is not that this reality *has* many names as if there were a reality outside the name. This reality *is* many names and each name is a new aspect, a new manifestation and revelation of it. Yet each name teaches or expresses, as it were, the undivided Mystery" (29). This plurality may be celebrated as refractions of light which shade into each other through creative contact and interaction.

> The different religious traditions ... are like the almost infinite number of colors that appear once the divine or simply white light of reality falls on the prism of human experience: it refracts into innumerable traditions, doctrines, and religions. Green is not yellow, Hinduism is not Buddhism, and yet at the fringes one cannot know, except by postulating it artificially, where yellow ends and green begins. Even more, through any particular color – through any particular religion – one can reach the source of the white light. ... If two colors mix, they may sire another. Similarly with religious traditions, the meeting of two may give birth to a new one. In point of fact, most of the known religions today are results of such mutual fecundations. (*Intrareligious Dialogue*, xix-xx)

Sri Ramakrishna, a great nineteenth century saint and mystic who intentionally sought out a wide variety of spiritual experiences during the course of his life, provides a striking example of Hindu pluralism. His earliest mystical experiences were of the Divine Mother in the form of Kali. He subsequently experienced God as Rama and Sita; undertook tantric practices and experienced other forms of the Divine Mother; experienced the formless perception of *Brahman* through the meditative state of *nirvikalpa samadhi*; and later engaged in spiritual practices which allowed him to experience God or ultimate reality within the contexts of Christian and Muslim worship and Buddhist meditation. In the end, he retained his devotional preference for Kali and refused to rank the experience of the formless *Brahman* as higher than his devotional experience of God as the Divine Mother. Thus, he affirmed a variety of ways of experiencing the divine without ranking these alternative modes of spiritual experience.

Mahatma Gandhi presents a second example of Hindu pluralism. Gandhi embraced two Jain doctrines which he considered to be part of the Hindu tradition. The first of these doctrines is that of "the many-ness of reality" (*anekantavada*) – the view that reality is so complex that the many acceptable propositions about it may be very different, and even contradictory depending on the point of view of the observer. The second closely related idea is that all propositions present only partial views. Thus, all views should be qualified or prefaced by the phrase "from one point of view" (*syadvada*). This doctrine allows for the possibility of different or divergent statements being equally true since they depend on the point of view that serves as a context for the statement (Jordens, 5).

Gandhi believed Hinduism to be the most "tolerant" of all religions but came to see that to make this claim was to claim superiority for the Hindu religion. This realization led him to alter his teaching. He substituted the slogan "equality of religions" for the attitude and practice of "tolerance," a phrase which went beyond mere "respect" for religions, and which is grounded in the concept of non-violence (*ahimsa*). Gandhi expressed his new attitude via a metaphor: "Even as a tree has a single trunk, but many branches and leaves, religion becomes many as it passes through the human medium" (quoted in Jordens, 11). Religions are equal because at the root, or trunk, they are really one. This is a metaphor of depth, emphasizing the source of religious experience in human experience rather than a transcendent principle or destiny.

Gandhi's acceptance of the equality of religions was also based upon the conviction that all their scriptures, teachings, and counsels are fallible; none of them articulates ultimate answers. Whatever ultimacy they do contain can only be detected by the application of the acid tests of truth and non-violence. These criteria are not the propositions of scripture and doctrine; they are criteria for deciding right action. Thus, Gandhi's pluralism is essentially *pragmatic* and *ethical*: it is concerned with "experiments with truth" (a phrase he was fond of using) that make a practical difference in our life worlds.

My final example of Hindu pluralism is the thought of K.C. Bhatta-charyya, regarded by many to be the most original proponent of neo-Vedanta philosophy. Religion, from this perspective, involves the recognition that something is wrong with our actual condition, belief in a possible condition that would be better, and a method for actualizing this more desirable mode of existence. There are different religions because different teachers have emphasized different imperfections in our actual condition, envisioned different better possibilities, and taught different techniques for attaining these goals. Thus the problem with our actual condition has been variously identified as ignorance, suffering, and sin. George Burch summarizes Bhatta-charyya's view:

> To attain absolute objectivity or absolute truth is the goal of Advaita Vedanta. Moksha is pure truth purged of all subjectivism and error. To attain absolute subjectivity or absolute freedom is the goal of Buddhism. Nirvana is pure freedom purged of all constraint. To attain absolute togetherness, with God and fellow human beings, or absolute Love, is the goal of Christianity. Beatitude is pure love purged of all separation and the sense of sin. (27)

Unlike Hindu inclusivists, this viewpoint does not hold that religions are different paths to the same goal. They are paths leading up to different mountain peaks. A person cannot get from one peak to another except by making a fresh start at the bottom. He acknowledges that there is no need to follow one religious path rather than another but insists that only one can be followed. "They proceed divergently not convergently, disjunctively not conjunctively, alternatively not jointly" (24). This theory maintains that the forms of the Absolute to which these paths lead are equally absolute and that they cannot be evaluated by each other or by anything higher.

This pluralist perspective advocates commitment and coexistence. *This or that* is the formula of commitment. A choice is offered but commitment is required. Commitment involves the opposition of alternatives. Yet it also allows one to acknowledge the validity of other paths that one does not choose to follow. Therefore commitment promotes the coexistence of different religions. This pluralistic attitude differs from the attitudes entailed by orthodoxy and liberalism. "Psychologically, orthodoxy reflects pride in the exclusive superiority of one's own way. Liberalism reflects excessive humility prepared to eliminate from one's own way anything incompatible with others. Commitment reflects a true and robust humility which, while maintaining its own way without compromise or qualification, still recognizes the equal validity of other ways not as errors to be tolerated but as alternatives that are freely chosen." (Burch 25)

This model presents a radical irreducible diversity of ways to seek religious fulfillment. It affirms each of these ways as equally valid. However, interreligious dialogue – or intrareligious dialogue – has little point from this perspective; accordingly, it offers little possibility for the creative transformation of traditions through their encounter with one another. Though I do not myself resonate with this vision of the irreducible diversity or particularly of religious or spiritual paths, it is important to take this perspective seriously if we really want to grasp what it means to be a pluralist.

I prefer an alternative model of religious truth suggested by Paul Knitter, a Catholic theologian. The traditional model for truth in the West is grounded in the Aristotelian principle of noncontradiction. According to this principle, two divergent propositions cannot be affirmed. One must be true and the other false. Truth, therefore, is defined through exclusion. This is what the word "de-finition" means: to determine the limits, to set off one thing from another. Defining religious truth in this way gives it an absolute quality. For something to be true, it has to be, in its category, the only or absolute truth. One can know it is true by showing how it excludes all other alternatives – or, how it absorbs and includes all other alternatives (217). An alternative model of truth is relational. Truth is defined not by exclusion but by relation. In this view: "What is true will reveal itself mainly by its ability to be *related* to other expressions of truth and to *grow* through these relationships" (219). This model recognizes that no truth can stand alone, that no truth can be totally unchangeable.

Jung's Perspective on Religious Plurality

According to Murray Stein, Jung proposed that all mythologies have a common source in the collective unconscious, and that all human beings are therefore heir to all religions. No god or goddess is utterly alien to anyone; all deities have a place in the psyche's pantheon. This idea is completely counter to the "no other gods" injunction of the biblical myth expressed in Exodus; it embraces *all* the gods. As Stein puts it, "There are no 'other' gods. Each image of God – whether male or female, animal or human or superhuman, concrete or abstract – sheds some additional light on the Wholeness of the God image embedded in the human psyche" (viii). This understanding of the psyche is the antidote to exclusivism, and accords well with the pluralist attitudes we have encountered in the work of Christians and Hindus reviewed in this essay.

Jung's writings affirm the religious function of the psyche, an impulse which arises in each person in all times and places. As he expressed it, "The collective unconscious contains the whole spiritual heritage of mankind's evolution, born anew in the brain structure of every individual" (CW 8: 158). Elsewhere, he observed: "One could almost say that if all the world's traditions were cut off at a single blow, the whole of mythology and the whole history of religion would start all over again with the next generation" (CW 5: 25). The archetypes are common to all religions, but the symbols and myths differ among traditions, depending on their cultural and historical contexts. Figures such as the divine mother, the wise old man, the dying god, the hero-savior, and the divine child, among others, may be found in a wide variety of cultures though the particular images, symbols and stories vary.

Jung discovered that he could not really distinguish, psychologically, the realization of the self from the *imago Dei*, the image of God. The self, the deepest treasure of the unconscious, bears all the characteristics that religious persons and theologians have given to the reality they call God. Paul Knitter points out several parallels: The self, hidden and beckoning within us, is ineffable, beyond all our reasoning powers and concepts. Yet, it is quite real in the effects it has upon us. It is also a reality both transcendent and immanent – truly with us and part of us, yet ever more than what we now know ourselves to be. And, in Rudolph Otto's well-known description of God, it is a *mysterium tremendum et fascinosum* – a mysterious power that both frightens us in its darkness and fascinates us in its promise (58-59).

From his discoveries of the unconscious and the presence of the God-image within it, Jung drew conclusions concerning the nature of the established religions. His psychological interpretation of the notion of revelation provides a common foundation with which all religions can appreciate and speak to each other. All revelation has its origin, or at least part of its origin, in the individual and collective unconscious. In Jung's words: "Revelation is an unveiling of the depths of the human soul first and foremost, a 'laying bare,' hence it is an essentially psychological event, though this does not of course tell us what else it could be" (CW 11: 74). It is the experience of God speaking from within. This "within" is essentially the same for all human beings. The differing dogmas and doctrines are attempts to give symbolic expression to this essentially ineffable experience. They do differ, and yet they are rooted in the same archetypes. Knitter effectively sums up this psychological way of understanding religious symbols:

> Religions play a valuable and a necessary role in mediating between the "divine content" of the unconscious and a person's conscious awareness. In this sense, one could call the world religions the great psychotherapeutic symbol systems of the world; they provide the symbols by which the archetypes can be touched and called forth. They tune us to the mystery within so that we can feel its call and not be frightened by its unknown demands. They assure us that this mystery is real and at work within us. (60)

Another implication of Jung's perspective is that no religion or symbol can claim to be absolute, the one and only. As Jung wrote, "It is altogether inconceivable that there could be any definite figure capable of expressing archetypal indefiniteness" (CW 12: 18). In other words, the God-image is utter mystery, ever beyond our realization; it cannot be captured in any one form. Although these statements clearly show that Jung was a pluralist, he gave special emphasis to Christ and certain Christian theological concepts. For example, Jung said: "The Christ symbol is of the greatest importance for psychology insofar as it is perhaps the most highly developed and differentiated symbol of the self, apart from the figure of the Buddha" (19). Christ represents the completion of the process of individuation, the realization of the self. Jung also regarded the theological concept of the incarnation to be a model for individuation, and understood the passion of Christ to be a further symbol of the pain and trust involved in this transformative process – the experience of surrendering the ego in order to integrate it into the mystery of the self (CW 11: 157).

Nevertheless, while Jesus is for Jung one of the best symbols of the Christ, he is not the only one. Jung has a psychological explanation for the traditional claim for the exclusiveness of Jesus. From the early history of the church, Christians have held that Jesus is "one and only" precisely because he is such an effective symbol. Having been grasped and transformed by this symbol, they naturally attribute to it "a universally binding truth, not of course by an act of judgment, but by the irrational fact of possession, which is far more effective" (CW 12: 36). In other words, "one and only" means "the symbol really works; take it seriously." Jung acknowledged the efficacy of other symbols by saying, "In the West the archetype [of the self] is filled out with the dogmatic figure of Christ; in the East, with Purusha, the Atman, Hiranyagarbha, the Buddha, and so on." (17)

Finally, Jung was an advocate for dialogue among religions. In particular, he felt that there was much to be learned in the encounter of Christianity with Eastern religions. The East, in Jung's estimation, had long been aware of the reality of the unconscious and the necessity of penetrating its depths.

> As we know, this question has occupied the most venturesome minds of the East for more than 2,000 years, and that in this respect methods and philosophical doctrines have been developed which simply put all Western attempts in the same line into the shade. (CW 11: 554)

Jung recognized that just as the West had lost touch with the inner life and the God within, the East tended to ignore the reality of the material world. So he felt there is much to be learned on both sides. He observed that "the East is at the bottom of the spiritual change we are passing through today" but added that "East is not a Tibetan monastery full of Mahatmas, but essentially within us." ("Spiritual Problem" 476)

We see clearly from this that Jung's encounter with Eastern religions underscored the importance of coming to grips with one's own cultural tradition. By doing so, he helps us move towards the realization of more inclusive and vital forms of religious self-understanding in our postmodern world. He offers us a way to appreciate our common humanity through an appreciation of the diverse symbols that issue forth from the plural psyche. In this way, we may welcome our encounters with persons and traditions that differ from our own. At the same time, we may enter into a dialogue with the teachings and traditions that touch and inform us most deeply. Jung's psychology, we may say, provides a psychological basis for a unitive pluralism. It allows us to affirm our interconnectedness with others, and promotes a worldcentric perspective regarding the myths, symbols and images which give meaning to our lives.

References

Burch, G. (1972). *Alternative Goals in Religion: Love, Freedom, Truth*. Montreal: McGill-Queen's Press.

Campbell, J. (1986). *The Inner Reaches of Outer Space: Metaphor as Myth and as Religion*. New York: Harper & Row.

Coward, H. (Ed.). (1987). *Modern Indian Responses to Religious Pluralism*. Albany: State University of New York Press.

Coward, H. (1985). *Pluralism: Challenge to World Religions*. Maryknoll: Orbis.

Hick, J. (1977). *God and the Universe of Faiths*. Glascow: Collins.

Hick, J. (1982). *God has Many Names*. Philadelphia: Westminster.

Jordens, J.F.T. (1987). Gandhi and Religious Pluralism. In H. Coward (Ed.), *Modern Indian Responses to Religious Pluralism* (pp. 3-17). State University of New York Press.

Jung, C.G. (1953-1976). *The Collected Works of C.G. Jung* (R.F.C. Hull, Trans.). Princeton: Princeton University Press.

Jung, C.G. (1971). The Spiritual Problem of Modern Man. In J. Campbell (Ed.), *The Portable Jung* (pp. 456-479). New York: Viking Press.

Knitter, P. (1985). *No Other Name? A Critical Survey of Christian Attitudes toward the World's Religions*. Maryknoll, NY: Orbis Books.

Panikkar, R. (1978). *The Intrareligious Dialogue*. New York: Paulist Press.

Panikkar, R. (1981). *The Unknown Christ of Hinduism: Towards an Ecumenical Christophany* (Rev. ed.). London: Darton, Longman & Todd.

Smith, W.C. (1981). *Towards a World Theology: Faith and the Comparative History of Religions*. Philadelphia: Westminster Press.

Stein, M. (1992). Foreword. In *No Other Gods: An Interpretation of the Biblical Myth for a Transbiblical Age* (pp. vi-ix). Wilmette, IL: Chiron Publications.

CHAPTER 7

The Challenge to Stay Open: Buber and Bion

Avedis Panajian

The concept of the "between" has been explored across many disciplines, including theology, psychology, philosophy, and physics, as a way of describing an experience that bridges the subject-object dichotomy. Theorists must use the different languages that are particular to their own fields of study; however, there are a remarkable number of similarities in meaning when cross-disciplinary notions of the "between" are compared.

An interesting comparison can be made "between" the works of the theologian, Martin Buber, and the psychoanalyst, Wilfred Bion. Both speak about spiritual unification from the perspective of a differentiated state of I-Thou relationship rather than from the perspective of solitude. Both express concern about the human person's tendency to become anybody else rather than him or herself. They emphasize the importance of being present to everyday living and the importance of realizing oneself. Both Buber and Bion value humankind's social nature. Each believes that the human person has an inborn need to be confirmed by another person for what he or she is and for what he or she can become, and that the human person has a need to be approached with faith. Confirmation of the other is only possible through the experience of a whole person being directly present. Interestingly, both theorists speculate that the unborn child has knowledge of the mother and is already involved in containing the mother; and both imagine the unconscious as the guardian of our wholeness that evolves between us and around us.

Both Buber and Bion are open to faith and welcome revelation. Both start from motivated ignorance. They manage to walk a "narrow ridge" without resting on theories; however, neither loses respect for the scientific method. Both value evidence, clarity, precision, and decisiveness.

Buber and Bion are interested in origins. They value the unity of psyche and soma, and each opens up with his heart and integrates the feminine side of his being. Both men enjoy the ability to pause with anticipation as well as restful moments of emptying the mind. Lastly, both Buber and Bion teach us how to listen to ourselves while listening to others at the same time.

Martin Buber

Martin Buber was a leading Jewish thinker who influenced many Christian theologians and religious philosophers. Buber felt that his work was "atypical" in that it did not fit into any one particular academic discipline; it was located between disciplines. His work, *I and Thou* (1958), is often called a philosophy of dialogue. *I and Thou* begins from experience that focuses on what is "human" in man. It begins with the declaration, "To man the world is twofold, in accordance with his twofold attitude" (1958, p. 3). By the term "attitude" Buber means a fundamental position, a way of posturing oneself toward the world either as I-Thou or as I-It. These postures are not rigid categories into which various types of people fit; for example, it would be wrong to insist that the scientist would prefer the I-It posture and that the artist would prefer the I-Thou posture. Rather, these attitudes are modes of experience that alternate in all people, "not two kinds of man, but two poles of humanity" (1958, p. 65).

Within these poles, the two I's are not the same. In the I-It attitude, the I holds back and understands, measures, uses, and even controls the It. This I-It realm originates in our sensations, perceptions thoughts, emotions, and desires. The I-It relationship is based on a perception of the other, but it does not encounter the whole being of the other. Rather, we select those characteristics of the person that are relevant to our inquiry and ignore the others. We synthesize what we learn about the other and use concepts and signs to communicate with the other. This attitude is essential for survival – it allows us to share an objective world. In this way, knowledge is generated and the environment is predicted. We generate a sense of continuity and provide some certainty to our lives. This is the realm of feelings and of using others; it is the subject-object relationship of epistemology and much of psychoanalysis. Here the subject who knows is distinguished from the object that is known. Buber states: "without *It* man cannot live. But he who lives with *It* alone is not a man" (1958, p. 34). The world of It is set in the context of space and time; however, the I-It attitude does not know the present, only the past. It exists only through being bounded by others.

In contrast, the I-Thou relationship can only be spoken with the whole being, and being spoken brings about its existence. The I-Thou relation has no bounds. It is an incomprehensible threat to the I-It order that holds a human person. It is discontinuous and disruptive. What is important to Buber is not thinking about the other but directly confronting and addressing him as Thou, which involves immediate contact. What evolves between the two is ineffable. To speak directly to the other makes the subject realize his own otherness. In fact, it challenges both to break out of the prison of the external object. The I affirms itself only in the presence of the Thou. For Buber, the I is the term for a relation that cannot be expressed by a thought, because a thought dissolves the relationship. The I, in relationship, rediscovers "its original community with the totality of being" (Levinas, 1967, p. 138). For Buber there is a spiritual significance to making social communion, and the I-Thou relationship, primary. The I-Thou relationship cannot be identified as subjective in that the I-Thou meeting does not take place in the realm of subjectivity but in the realm of being. The space between the I and Thou is the space in which the human person is realized. The between cannot be conceived of as a space existing independently of the meeting of I-Thou. The space is inseparable from the adventure in which each human person participates.

For Buber the human person is both open and hidden. A problem occurs when openness and hiddenness are out of balance with one another. When Buber states that one's whole being must encounter the Thou, he never means this to be some kind of mystical fusion. He believes that the Thou teaches you to meet others and to hold your ground when you meet them. In the midst of the encounter, once the I becomes conscious of experience and conscious of listening, the Thou disappears and the I finds itself in the domain of It. The intense momentary encounter cannot last. Buber describes how our "exalted melancholy, (is) that every *Thou* in our world must become an *It*" (Buber, 1958, p. 16). The I-Thou is a relationship of true knowledge because it preserves the integrity of the otherness of the Thou. Commitment is what allows access to otherness. The key to otherness is knowledge through commitment.

Buber states that "[i]n every sphere in its own way, through each process of becoming that is present to us we look out toward the fringe of the eternal *Thou*; in each *Thou* we address the eternal *Thou*" (1958, p. 6). God, the eternal Thou, is both the supreme partner of the dialogue and the power underlying all the other I-Thou encounters. We cannot know God in himself. We can only know Him as a person because that is the way He encounters us in relation. For Buber, God is both self-revealing and self-concealing. Buber is against any systematic theology that takes away the mystery of God. In a way, he is here referring to the mystery of the I-Thou relation to God or to the mystery of the nearness and remoteness of an I-Thou relation with the divine. Buber rejected theology that teaches this or that about God; his religious thought gives primacy to the I-Thou relationship with the incomprehensible.

Buber starts from the human experience of faith, which makes him think of revelation in these terms: "{t}hat which reveals is that which reveals. That which is *is*, and nothing more. The eternal source of strength streams, the eternal contact persists, the eternal voice sounds forth ..." (1958, p. 112). From a reception of revelation, one receives a presence as power. Revelation is an incomprehensible event. He who is receptive to revelation knows that the I-Thou is real in the present.

For Buber, the ability to access the unique wholeness of the other in a relationship is founded on the two innate givens of distancing and relating, which provide the basis of our involvement with the world. Distancing is a prerequisite for relating. Distancing sets the other apart from us, making it possible for us to experience his unified wholeness. When we use distance to hold the other apart from ourselves as a separate being, there is the possibility of an I-Thou relationship.

For Buber, every man has the wish to be "confirmed as what he is, even as what he can become, by men," (1965, p. 182) and we have an innate capacity to confirm our fellow men in this way. In fact, our humanity only exists when this capacity unfolds. Here lies an important bridge between Buber's work and the practice of psychotherapy, since confirmation of one's patient is the most essential attitude of the psychotherapist. It is through such affirmation that the psychotherapist attempts to make the other present. To make present means to imagine the other concretely, to imagine what another person is wishing, feeling, perceiving or thinking. For Buber, the essential element of genuine dialogue is to experience the other side. This means to imagine the real, which demands "the most intensive stirring of one's being into the life of the other" (1965, p. 81). The act of inclusion of the other allows one to make contact with another and still be in contact with oneself.

The dialogical attitude means that the psychotherapist must "walk a narrow ridge." He or she does not "rest on the broad upland of a system that includes a series of sure statements about the absolute, but on a narrow, rocky ridge between the gulfs where there is no sureness of expressible knowledge but the certainty of meeting what remains undisclosed" (1965, p. 184). The psychotherapist who ventures along this narrow ridge holds his own perspective, but only in the context of what the patient brings, with all the surprises of the moment. The "narrow ridge" culminates in the I-Thou, which challenges the person to face surprises and seek deviations in the service of coexistence. The psychotherapist does not take security for granted, nor does he or she use theory to substitute for the encounter. The challenge to the psychotherapist is to be fully present in the "nothing else than process without getting lost in the abyss" (1957, p. 94), since theory can be used as a defense against facing the unknown. The therapist must face the certainty that the unknown will always be there. Like the therapist, Buber's concern was with losing sight of the whole person.

Even when, because of insecurity, an individual refuses to enter relationship with a Thou, the longing for confirmation remains. In the grip of this difficulty, a person who clings to an I-It relationship may speak of Thou but really mean It. Here Buber points out the duality of being and seeming – we may seem to be something other than what we are. A person may seem to be a unified I, and may say Thou, without actually entering into a relationship with the Thou. Buber believes that we all give in to the temptation to possess confirmation of our being while avoiding the risk of a real I-Thou relationship. However, it is essential to differentiate people in whom "being" or "seeming" predominate. For Buber, when "seeming" enters into a child's life, so does evil, because then the essence of Creation is imprisoned in the I-It world. For Buber, evil is both human and cosmic.

Wilfred Bion

In many ways, the clinical work of the outstanding British psychoanalyst Wilfred Bion mirrors Buber's philosophical emphasis on the crucial importance of an I-Thou stance in human relationships. For both Buber and Bion, listening imaginatively to the speech that precedes language, speech that lives in the wider reality of spirit, is essential to understanding whether speech is used truthfully or abusively. This is especially important when we try to address the psychotic person's hopeless longing for a Thou. Bion's work with psychotics reveals such patients' serious problems living in the world of It. But Bion realizes that the realm of I-Thou is dependent on I-It for its meaning. Without the ability for attention, notation, memory, differentiation, knowledge and judgment, every attempt on the part of the psychotic towards a Thou is bound to fail and end in an It. Eventually, this problem leads the psychotic into a fragmented world of It, where a return to Thou is very difficult.

In Bion's early papers on schizophrenia, his main concern had been on intrapsychic links, or the connections between the different aspects of mental life. A major shift towards the importance of the I-Thou is found in Bion's rich paper, "Attacks on Linking" (Bion, 1967), which discusses the links that occur between mother and infant or analyst and patient. He notes that he uses the term "link" "because I wish to discuss the patient's relationship with a function rather than with the object that subserves the function; my concern is not only with the breast, or penis, or verbal thought, but with their function of providing the link between two objects" (p. 102). For Bion, emotional experiences are the links between two people. The concept of linking is an attempt to understand what goes on between people, how creative relationships develop between individuals, and how these relationships can be attacked.

For example, Bion extends the notion of linking to include the therapeutic importance of "containment," or a mother's ability to take in and transform her child's otherwise unbearable mental pain, and the therapist's similar function, which allows an experience of meaning rather than inchoate terror. Containment allows one mind to know and include another mind, which is apparently an inborn need. Containment also implies that one's heart opens up spiritually to the wholeness of the other. In his work on linking, Bion also introduces the idea of normal projective identification as a form of communication that is both important for development and also a form of link between analyst and patient. Bion describes a patient with whom he felt that he was witnessing an early mother-child scenario in which a mother had dutifully responded to her child emotionally; but she was impatient and did not understand that the baby wanted more than only her presence – she did not take in the child's terror that he was dying. This was an unbearable feeling that the baby could not contain, a terror that the baby was trying to cope with by projecting it into his mother, who in her turn could not tolerate this dread and reacted by either denying it or by becoming anxious herself. Bion said that this man "resorted to projective identification with a persistence suggesting it was a mechanism of which he had never been able sufficiently to avail himself; the analysis afforded him an opportunity for the exercise of a mechanism of which he had been cheated" (p. 103). It seemed that the patient wanted to "repose" these terrifying parts of his personality in Bion, apparently because he felt that if these parts were allowed to do so for long enough they would be modified by Bion's psyche and could then be safely taken back into the patient. But if Bion evacuated these feelings too quickly, they were not modified but rather became even more painful for the patient – it was then as if Bion was refusing to accept parts of the patient's personality, so that the patient tried to force them into Bion "with increasing desperation and violence" (p. 104).

Bion movingly describes his inability to be present with this patient with his whole being. He was able to have a competent I-It relationship with the patient, and with himself, which enabled him to realize that he could not confirm the patient's total personality. This was a crucial realization because only opening up with one's whole being allows the analyst the capacity to confirm the patient as he is, and as what he can become. Here Bion acknowledges how frightening it is for both analyst and patient to be fully real and present. Limited awareness of this fear limits our presence.

In his later *Theory of Thinking*, Bion attempts to integrate the feminine in himself, as if he has been thinking too much. Here we see a major transformation as he realizes that thinking has functioned for him as a defense against opening up, as though the masculine side of his personality has limited him to the I-It realm, because opening up to the I-Thou is frightening. When Bion is able to repose himself, he is able to move to another kind of attention that comes from his femininity; this kind of attention allows him to be open to being penetrated by the patient, who is then able to put parts of his personality into Bion. For this to happen, Bion must be able to put aside his thoughts and insights, allow himself to wait and listen, and move from knowledge to wisdom. This is the wisdom of being present and staying in the moment with his patient, and the wisdom of enlarging his heart to enable him to watch over and let emerge whatever needs to emerge. This form of caring waits and protects what is in need of development – it is free to use intuition and imagination. A mother's capacity for reverie about her baby allows her to accept the baby's experience of itself. By extending the idea of repose to include maternal reverie, Bion suggests that in her reverie a mother is able to integrate life and death. He must have been aware that in reverie the soul and the mind are united, which unites conscious and unconscious.

If there is no authentic I-Thou meeting, a mis-meeting occurs; such a mother, however dutiful, does not satisfy the infant's longing for a Thou. She is unable to repose in her femininity without ambitions and projects, so that she is unable to receive the whole infant; rather, divorced from Thou, she is not a whole being, since she lives a life that is classified and determined by rules. Such a mother confuses the infant who needs her as a Thou, since she treats him as an It, whereupon the Thou is lost.

Buber says something very similar to Bion's belief of what happens when we are cheated of the necessary projective identification. Buber notes that when the Thou is lost, an internal contradiction develops. Because our inborn need for an I-Thou relationship is such a priority, it "strikes inward" if there is nowhere for it to develop, leading to problems such as autistic states (Schoen, 1994). Or, the patient takes himself as an It, and lives a life of self-idealization.

Both mother and analyst need to have the freedom – and be aware of such freedom – to go beyond set rules. A mother needs to have the freedom to dream about her infant as well as dream her own origins. The mother and the analyst must have the confidence to enter the realm of the ineffable. Here Bion intuits the limits of psychoanalysis and anticipates new ways of thinking about the unconscious. He moves to poetry and to meditative states in order to spiritually liberate and aid psychoanalysis, and he tries to go deeper into the origin of our being. Bion asks the mother and the analyst to take themselves outside of time and open up to faith, to encounter whatever one encounters. He requires us to have the freedom and the maturity to venture between memory and imagination. Whatever we encounter in reverie is supported with a background of rest and calm. He stresses feminine gentleness, slowness, and peace of mind. He tells us that the images that we receive from the feminine side of our nature are different, and are put to different use, than those that we receive from the masculine side of the personality.

Buber and Bion

Both Bion and Buber believe that the infant has a spiritual origin and that a mother has to confirm her infant in order to awaken his spiritual dimension, while not forgetting that the infant also confirms his mother. But a mother can only confirm and awaken the spirit in her infant if she is able to respect her natural separation from the baby. It is important to note here that Bion does not say that the mother or the analyst has to be in a state of fusion with the infant or patient. If a mother is able to maintain a distance, she might be able to fulfill her infant's longing for an I- Thou relationship through reverie. The infant's longing for union is then satisfied by his mother's capacity to engage in a differentiated spiritual and psychological union with her baby. If the infant is able to reciprocate, then she is able to respond to the mother's independence and is able to be a Thou for the mother and share in giving her a differentiated sense of spiritual and psychological union. Buber says that by becoming mother's Thou, the infant "fills the heavens" for her. But if the mother and infant are unable to accept one another's distance, the I-Thou relationship is impossible. The outcome is a defective and incompetent I-It relationship. Bion's clinical writing provides many examples in which either the mother, the infant, or both are unable to respect each other's distance. In these cases, the longing for an I-Thou relationship goes unmet.

In other words, both Bion and Buber provide us with models for early experiences between the infant and mother. They both imagined the mother's experience of her infant, and the infant's experience of his mother, from a position of mutual reciprocity, a relationship that engages the depths of each of them. Importantly, by the word "relationship" both writers mean something different than the way in which traditional psychoanalysis under-stands this term. For Buber and Bion, relationship means an open, direct, wholly present, forthright, full-hearted, unbounded, discontinuous and unpredictable experience.

Buber and Bion are both concerned with human will. Bion stresses the importance of early freedom of movement that is essential to enhance the freedom of the infant's will. Both mother and infant have to tolerate this freedom; mother's willfulness may crush the infant's freedom of will, just as her envy may destroy the infant's will to live. Instead of having a will to live that has been reinforced by mother, patients who have lost their freedom of will in infancy, because mother could not provide the necessary freedom, tend to choose self-will, or a will to power, as a substitute. Instead of a will to live based on freedom of choice, this strategy provides a pseudo-sense of security in which I-It and I-Thou relationships are confused. In a similar vein, Buber believes that "[h]e who consumes life destroys it. He who hallows life, lives and teaches" (Schoen, 1994, p. 94). For Buber, to hallow life, and for Bion to respect life and patients, is a kind of action that brings forth one's will. This will, which comes from respecting life and people, is "without arbitrary self-will." It is willing without willfulness, and this kind of free will leads to the freedom to discover meaning. Bion notes that "disturbed self-love is accompanied by intolerance of meaning or its lack" (1965, p. 73). Further, "The first requisite for the discovery of the meaning of any conjunction depends on the ability to admit that the phenomena may have no meaning," (p. 81) and an inability to admit this stifles the possibility of curiosity at the outset.

A mother who lacks the ability for reverie will have difficulty respecting the infant's freedom to explore personal meaning or meaninglessness. Infants with strong destructive feelings towards their mothers, or those who have severe separation anxiety, can hold onto their mother as meaning itself, rather than as the source of meaning. Meaning is held onto as a thing because the possibility of meaninglessness is not tolerated. In such situations, I-Thou relationships are not possible, because they require toleration of gaps and confronting surprises. The ability to face the unknown of the relationship is essential to entertain the tension between what is and what is not.

Bion gets close to Buber's I-Thou relationship when he introduces the ideas of "becoming O" (by which he means connecting to ultimate Reality rather than ordinary knowledge), at-one-ment with O, faith, evolution, emotional turbulence, and the importance of being without memory and desire for the patient in the therapeutic setting. The analyst's capacity for "at-one-ment" with O is related to being receptive to O. His capacity for unification with himself and with the patient's material depends on his confidence in himself as a separate human person, on opening up to faith, tolerating powerful, frightening moments, and on an ability to stay in the present. All of these attitudes are similar to Buber's concept of the I-Thou relationship, in the following ways: The analyst is direct and present as a whole person; he welcomes revelation; he is open to surprise and novelty; and his genuine listening replaces established theories. The analyst holds his ground, or distance, as he "walks the narrow ridge" by experiencing and joining with the patient's raw states of mind. This attitude is made even more frightening when it is not viewed from a causal framework and is boundless.

Bion's outstanding paper on "Caesura" (1977) is profoundly influenced by Buber. Out of ten references, Bion mentions Buber four times. Bion stresses two aspects of caesura – gaps, separation, pause, discontinuity, and continuity in relationships. Bion ends the paper stating that "the analyst needs to investigate the caesura; not the analyst, not the analysand; not the unconscious, not the conscious; not sanity, not insanity. But the caesura, the link"

(p. 57). By this he means that we need to study the gaps, the pauses, the shifts, the between. The discontinuous events of entering the I-Thou relationship provide the driving force for human growth. Stopping personal becoming (a pause of I-It relating) is essential to the process of becoming. Without such a pause, one cannot respond or care for the Thou. Buber states that "we need to remain open to I-It. Remaining open is the presupposition of the religious life. Discontinuity is not overcome, we take it upon us and master it through the realized primacy of the dialogical" (Buber, 1967, p. 742). Buber's articulation of this process is strikingly similar to Bion's notion of transcending the caesura.

What is the "between" that Bion emphasized following Buber? Bion (1978) states that "the relationship between two people is a two-way affair and insofar as one is concerned with demonstrating that relationship is not a matter of talking about analyst and analysand, it is talking about something between the two of them" (p. 12). In a transcript of a recorded interview published in *The Journal of Melanie Klein and Object Relations* (Junqueira de Matos, 1999) Bion states: "In psychoanalysis it's really talking about not you and me but us: the relationship between us. For some reason, I find this is very difficult for analysts to realize" (p. 6). In the same interview, a participant asks Bion how to describe a certain feeling with a patient. Bion answers, "You can't. I can say something about I and You; but the moment I am able to say something about I and You, or You and I, it turns into I and It and You and It - that's quite different. It's restricted, it's restrictive. You've broken up this relationship which is unrestrictive, which is boundless." (p. 19)

In Summary

The between is an ontological occurrence. It takes place not within us, but amidst us. The analyst has to stir his being into the life of the patient. At the same time by holding onto his distance, he has to completely experience the rawness of the patient's existence in the present. He has to be unrestrictive and boundless. If he is able to be this way, there is a chance that the between will unfold and lead to discovery and mental growth; otherwise the between will be experienced in a chaotic, oppressive, and petrifying manner. If the between unfolds in a boundless way, it will confirm the wholeness of both the analyst and the patient. In order for the between to unfold, the analyst has to hold onto his own self-consciousness lightly. In a certain way, the analyst has to forget himself. This forgetting allows the analyst to be involved wholeheartedly. From this perspective the unconscious is between the analyst and the patient. It is the ground of personal wholeness. It is boundless. It is the realm in which body and soul are not separated. Analyst and patient make moments of contact with the unconscious through their undivided wholeness. The unconscious is in the unfolding of the between. One cannot say anything about the unconscious in and of itself. But, in the between, conscious and unconscious can be integrated.

References

Bion, R. W. (1962). Learning from Experience. In *Seven Servants*. New York, Jason Aronson.

– (1963). Elements of Psychoanalysis. In *Seven Servants*. New York, Jason Aronson.

– (1965). Transformation. In *Seven Servants*. New York, Jason Aronson.

– (1967). *Second Thoughts*. New York, Jason Aronson.

– (1976) Emotional Turbulence. In *Clinical Seminars and Four Papers*. Abingdon, Fleetwood Press.

– (1977). *Two Papers: The Grid and Caesura*. Brazil: Imago Editora Ltd.

– (1978). *Four Discussions with W.R. Bion*. London: Clunie Press.

Buber, M. (1957). *Pointing the Way*. New York: Schocken Books.

– (1958). *I and Thou*. New York: Charles Scribner's Sons.

– (1965). *The Knowledge of Man*. New York: Harper and Row.

– (1966). *Hasidism and Modern Man*. New York: Harper Torchbooks.

Friedman, M. (1996). Becoming Aware: A Dialogical Approach to Consciousness. *The Humanistic Psychologist, 24*(2), 203-220.

Junqueira de Matos, J. A. (1999). *Journal of Melanie Klein and Object Relations*, 17, 5-22.

Levinas, E. (1967). Martin Buber and the Theory of Knowledge. In A. Schlipp and M. Friedman (Ed.), *The Philosophy of Martin Buber*. La Salle, IL: Open Court.

Molino, A. (1998). *The Couch and the Tree: Dialogues in Psychoanalysis and Buddhism*. New York: North Point Press.

Pines, M. (1985). *Bion and Group Psychotherapy*. London: Routledge and Kegan Paul.

Schoen, S. (1994). *Presence of Mind*. New York: The Gestalt Journal Press.

CHAPTER 8

Dreams are Alive

Stephen Aizenstat

Introduction

Dreams are alive. Four or five times each night, living images play inside our brains, weaving together ingenious stories. This theater of the night affects our daily experience, shapes our decisions, and largely determines who we are and who we become.

Curiously, a person awakes in the morning claiming: "I had a dream." *Who* had a dream? Conscious ego, the one who calls himself "I"? "I" made up that story because I was scared yesterday when my daughter went too deep into the ocean? Or, because my boss criticized me, or whatever the residues of yesterday's events? Because of these past events, "I" created that dream?

The ego wants, and perhaps needs, to believe that it is in charge, that the conscious "I" is in control. As Swiss psychologist Carl Jung observed, this is particularly true during the first several decades of a human life. In order to sustain the fantasy that the ego is in control, ego has to pretend everything else is static, nonexistent, or at least, less powerful. Each night the unconscious speaks in the language of dreams; each morning ego scrambles for control, announcing: "*I* had a dream."

But, if "I" didn't create my dream, who did? Most psychologists believe that a dream is a product of the human unconscious. But what is the human unconscious that it can construct these ingenious literary productions five times nightly?

Over billions of years life evolved into a variety of forms that we know today, one of which is the human being. We are born out of the essential, organic life process – made of the same stuff as is all life. Human beings are but one expression of nature. The psyche is an evolution of life energy within the natural world, and thus participates in the ever-changing patterns of evolving and dissolving life form.

The unconscious isn't created by "me." The unconscious is born out of the rhythms of life. The dream – one expression of the psyche – is located in these essential life rhythms. Dreams are expressions of a psyche that is grounded in nature. Dreams are alive.

How shocking it is to break through to the awareness that the world is alive, that each organism within the world has a life of its own, interacting with other life forms (like you and me). Perhaps you are lying on a thick green lawn, enjoying the warmth of the sun on your skin. You turn your head. Suddenly, you're eyeball to eyeball with a fly. You brush the fly away only to notice an ant is crawling up your neck. Then, you see a worm emerging from the ground onto your hand. It hits you: *this* is not outdoor carpeting! You are lying in the midst of a living, breathing, changing ecology with millions of creatures crawling around and in and out and getting born and dying, right along with you.

We are not isolated living beings on a static and dead landscape; we are participants, constituent members of a living ecology. Our very existence is dependent upon our interacting intimately with other life forms.

The ego lying on the grass with all the other creatures is confronted with the realization that a human being is just one of the many players in this game of life. This holds true in the psychological realm as well as the physical realm. The person who calls himself "I" is one constituent member of the psyche. Imaginal figures are meandering around day and night, within him and without him, each with lives of their own. The ego is but one of many members of a living ecology of imaginal figures that compose a psyche.

A dream is an event in which some of the many imaginal figures of psyche reveal themselves. In the dream, the ego is relativized, often pictured as one of a cast of characters. Other dream figures (human or not) interact with dream ego, and, in the dream, they have lives of their own, physical bodies of their own, feelings and desires of their own. These images are constituent members of life itself.

A dream is one manifestation of nature revealing herself through image. This revelation can reflect one's personal nature, our collective human nature, and/or the nature of the *anima mundi* – soul of (and in) the world.

The Multidimensional Psyche

In order to conceptualize the different functions of the psyche, psychologists delineate several levels. Most psychologists agree that these levels include the Ego (consciousness), the Personal Unconscious, and the Collective Unconscious. I add a fourth level, the World Unconscious, which will be discussed later in this article.

Because dreams emerge from the psyche, they are shaped by all four of these levels of psyche, in what the alchemists called "a gentle mingling between levels." Although a particular dream may reflect one level more than another, it is important to listen to what the dream may say on each of these four levels.

The children's song tells us: "Row, row, row your boat, gently down the stream, merrily, merrily, merrily, merrily, life is but a dream." By the time a child sings this wise song, he or she will have some awareness of being the rower in the boat. "I," ego, am sitting in my life vehicle, holding the oars, rowing from one attraction to the next.

The rower of the boat, may be aware that the current of the river to no small degree determines where the boat goes. We are born into this life in a stream, a particular stream of forces in our individual life circumstance. This stream can be said to constitute the Personal Unconscious. Freud defined the Personal Unconscious as the repository of the dreamer's unconscious daily perceptions and personal experiences. The Personal Unconscious is structured as to gender, profession, family and other relationships, and personal life history. Most psychologists tend to understand a dream as the voice of the Personal Unconscious, speaking of personal unfulfilled wishes, repressed feelings and experiences.

It is the destiny of a stream to join with other individual streams into a river. In this metaphor, the river, composed of the many streams, represents the Collective Unconscious, a concept postulated by Carl Jung. Jung observed that individuals throughout time and across cultures seem to share universal psychological forms, which he called "archetypes."

The Collective Unconscious can be said to be the psyche of the human species, in which we each experience the nature of our species and its shared patterns of perception. The Collective Unconscious is thought to be universal and transpersonal. The same archetypal imagery that appears in a dream can be seen in the motifs of age-old myths, legends and fairy tales manifest in every culture throughout the history of the human race. Jungian psychologists tend to focus on the dream in terms of the relationship between ego and the Collective Unconscious, hearing the particular archetypes presented and exploring how ego is in relationship to them. From the viewpoint of the Collective Unconscious, psyche is heard in the context of archetypal patterns.

Continuing in this lyrical metaphor, the river eventually joins with the deeper waters of the ocean – the source of life itself. The ocean locates us in yet another dimension of the psyche, one not often assumed by psychologists, but commonly perceived by poets and mystics throughout history as well as in contemporary findings of theoretical physics. In this oceanic place, which I call the World Unconscious, the unconscious is imagined as connected to an implicit order underlying all of reality. The World Unconscious consists of the "subjective inner natures" residing in all the phenomena of the world. Therefore, it is not limited to the personal or collective human condition. At the level of the World Unconscious all the phenomena of the world are interrelated and interconnected. These "inner natures" of the world's organic and inorganic phenomena make up the contents of the World Unconscious and they are reflected as dream images in the human psyche.

A dream heard from the psychological perspective of the World Unconscious gives voice to the phenomena of the world, speaking through the dream on their own behalf. For example, the image of "house" that appeared in last night's dream may be talking about its experience in the world, its plight. Walls may indeed talk, and the tale they tell may be of their own making, located in the World Unconscious – not necessarily a mere projection of the human psyche.

Lest this image of rowing a boat down a particular stream, which joins a river, which joins the oceans, seems too linear a metaphor for the holistic nature of life, it is helpful to remember that at each and every point water evaporates, becomes clouds and fog and eventually rain which falls everywhere. These ever-repeating cycles of nature are the essential rhythms of all phenomena and of our lives. They are the stuff of the World Unconscious and the backdrop of the dream.

The assumption of a World Unconscious is of particular importance to me since I feel that each of us, particularly those of us in the professional disciplines, must be aware of the relationship between our work and our world. As a Clinical Psychologist and dream therapist, I feel obligated to ask myself how my work interfaces with the world. First, it must be remembered that we, as persons, are shaped by the events and things of the world which, in turn, display themselves in the imagery of dreams. We live in continuous participation with world phenomena. From the glow of an electric light to the dark of an overcast winter day, world phenomena echo within us at a sensate as well as a feeling level. To imagine the dream as an occurrence of the inner life only, separate from the world, is a denial of our interdependence with the world. As much as the world is in immediate need of our active re-engagement, we, too, are in urgent need of acknowledging our interdependence with the world. We are always living in intricate relationship with the world. The dreamscape is the worldscape and all the while we are living in it ... as if life is but a dream.

Second, I think it important to remain aware of how the dreamwork that I am doing with my client may, in turn, affect the phenomena of the world. For example, as a therapist working with the dream image of an ancient forest that has been mowed down, it can be imagined that the image, being a manifestation of actual phenomena in the world speaking on behalf of itself, is influenced by the dreamwork taking place between the dreamer and the therapist. By recognizing that the dream image of the defoliated landscape is an expression of the "subjective inner nature" of that landscape in the world (not necessarily tied to the personal psychology of the dreamer), the dreamer and the therapist hear the call of the landscape in its grief and experience its pain. Hearing the psyche of the landscape speak through the dreamwork can engender a sympathetic response to the condition of that physical place in the world. The dreamwork provides dreamer and dream therapist a medium for empathetic relationship between individual psyche and world soul.

The Personal, Collective, and World Unconscious inform one another and are in continuing dialogue. On the one hand, becoming connected to the inner life of our personal experience connects us to a larger sense of self than we knew before. This larger sense of personal self finds participation in the shared stories of the collective psyche, bringing an enhanced sense of belonging to a tribe, and this sense of being part of the shared human experience allows us to experience our species relationship to an even more fundamental process – that of the natural rhythm of life itself. Conversely, the world is always dreaming, and the dreams of the world's creatures and things occasion in us a sense of deep feeling and aesthetic response.

It seems to me that these various levels of the psyche co-exist in the complex nature of reality, and that psychotherapy and dream therapy can and should include all the dimensions of the human psyche. This living ecology of psyche exists at all times, and is always available to us when we learn to be present to it.

Tending the Living Image

The various levels of psyche all express themselves in the form of images. It is through understanding the nature of an image, and learning how to "tend" an image that we can experience the living psyche.

"I" am not in charge of "my" images. Images have lives of their own, and walk around as they choose, not as "I" choose. They inhabit the landscape of the dream, walking its ground, flying its skies, and swimming its seas. Images present themselves in the dream as living entities in an evolving landscape.

Nor do "I" create these images. They are not rooted in my personal psyche. Elaborating on this idea, archetypal psychologist James Hillman says, "Images come and go at their own will, with their own rhythm, within their own field of relations, undetermined by personal psychodynamics. ... The mind is in the imagination rather than the imagination in the mind." Each image has presence, substance, and imaginal body. To experience an image in written description only, as part of a narrative lifted from last week's journal entry, is to miss the living, active, embodied creature that is the image. In "my" dream last week the elephant looking at me had wide flared ears, and its left tusk was broken off at the tip. With respectful distance and caution, I walked around to its rear side, seeing dirt and tiny rocks scattered over its thin-haired rump. Its tail was busy swatting flies from either side of its sagging hind quarters. The dream elephant, like all images, has body and exists in three-dimensional space.

Dreaming is not merely a human production; it is an ongoing activity in which we participate. It is as if the dream is a social event which "I" experience, yet which each of the other figures also experiences from its own point of view. As they interact in the realm of the dream, images affect and change each other. When the elephant, as an embodied image runs into another embodied image, say that of a hunter, it is a certainty that each figure is affected by the presence of the other. To understand the dream is to realize that each image is a participant in a living network of interacting images.

An image that meanders through one's dreamscape does not ask to be captured, tranquilized, dissected, labeled in Latin, and reduced to a statement about one's childhood or present trauma. Nevertheless, this is an all-too-common psychological approach to images, and it creates several problems: 1) In the move to events of the dreamer's Personal Unconscious, the image itself is often lost; 2) Reducing the image to a meaning renders the image dead; and, most problematic, 3) When one affixes meanings or interpretations to an image, one has not addressed the image for what it is. The image is an alive, embodied expression of psyche – present to be experienced, seen, felt, heard.

How can we approach an image to hear it on its own terms?

To experience the living nature of the dream is not, as I have said, a return to the cause and effect methods of making meaning, but rather, requires a certain attitude, an approach I call "DreamTending." To tend a dream is to attend to the dream images in the immediacy of their presentation, as if each dream figure were a guest visiting you for the first time. As host to these guests, you want to get to know them, tend to them. You listen to what they have to say. When you enter the territory of the living image, there are no established trails, no familiar landmarks. The topological maps of ego no longer apply, for one is in a place much larger than ego. The navigational skills so useful and familiar in traditional interpretive approaches to dreamwork must give way to a new, more interactive craft. The causal logic of determinism gives way to the poetic language of metaphor.

To illustrate these two different approaches to dreamwork, let us think about different styles of walking in the wilderness. A person can walk through nature involved in a purposeful activity. There is a destination to move towards, a goal or intention to be actualized as a consequence of taking this nature walk. Nature walk activities might include: exercise; identifying bird species; or, walking in the wilderness with the notion of meditating on a particular life problem. In each of these instances, a person is using the landscape to facilitate a mental activity or a physical process that is located in the person, not in the landscape.

When one walks with such intention, a sense of alert goes through the wilderness. The animals sense the alien intrusion and discontinue their normal motion: they may freeze, get quiet, go underground. The landscape goes into a state of frozen arrest when a person uses it for his/her own person-centered intention.

In a different approach, a person can walk in the natural landscape with the hope of participating in nature's psyche. When walking for awhile, then stopping and listening, one notices the sounds of the birds, the skittering of lizards, the water gurgling in the brook. And it's in that waiting – in the ability to be patient, to be quiet, to allow time, that one experiences the landscape in its normal activity. The poetry that is indigenous to the natural movement of the landscape is heard.

As Ezra Pound reminds: "The leaves are full of voices." In the quiet of deep listening, the landscape reveals itself to the receptive participant. The sense of the poetic that lives between the participant and landscape comes into awareness, into life – each affecting the other, each dependent on the other. The landscape and the hiker are part of an aesthetic realm of experience which informs them both.

These same approaches are also at play in dreamwork. When we dutifully write down the dream, go into the analyst's office, repeat it in its linear, narrative form with the intention of interpreting its meaning, the dreamscape has stopped or become frozen – just like the shutdown of wilderness activity at the arrival of the intruder. However, like the hiker who pauses to be present to the possibilities of the wilderness, a therapist working with a dream can pause, wait, listen, allowing for the natural rhythm, the indigenous nature of the psyche, to again reveal itself. Then the dreamer and the dream therapist can be in correspondence with the natural activity of the dreamscape.

DreamTending is an approach to dreamwork that respects the living reality of the dream. The dream therapist literally shifts his chair from the familiar face-to-face configuration to a somewhat more open side-by-side positioning, as if therapist and dreamer were sitting together to watch a theatrical presentation. Seated beside the client, the therapist is not so immediately locked into the personal responses of the dreamer which – when one is looking straight across at the other – are so tempting to explore at each and every turn. In tending a dream, the therapist is concerned first with evoking the dreamscape, inviting the actuality of the dream into the room to be experienced. The therapist asks the dreamer to tell the dream in descriptive detail in the present tense. In the telling, the dreamer sees, hears, expresses the images as alive and active in present time/space.

To evoke even greater detail, the therapist asks the dreamer to look with increased focus at specific aspects of the image and to describe with particularity the texture, coloration, movement or shape of the dream figure. For example, in the dream image of a giraffe, the dreamer may be asked to mindfully observe this particular giraffe, noticing its unique characteristics. The therapist can encourage the dreamer to look into the giraffe's eyes, into the inner world of this particular dream animal, thus bringing its alive presence even more fully into dynamic relationship with the dreamer. The dreamer is encouraged to physically move his body to interact with the giraffe and to use his sensate functions of smell, touch, and even taste, to more fully experience the living reality of the image. Questions like: "How coarse is the giraffe's coat?" or "Can you smell the giraffe?" not only provide specific detail but also allow the image to reveal itself in the here and now presence of the dreamwork.

The therapist empathetically enters the dreamtime with the dreamer, as well as keeping, therapeutic perspective. The dreamer and the dream therapist become located in the dreamscape, surrounded by it. The dreamer and the therapist enter the living experience of the dream.

The craft of tending a dream differs significantly from the traditional practice of dream analysis in its initial orientation to the dream. Most dream therapists have been trained to ask: "What does this dream mean?" "Why did this happen?" These questions tend to freeze the dream within pre-conceived developmental schema, or within one of a multitude of intricately contrived psychological explanatory systems – however imaginative and erudite they might be. How different this is to *tending* a dream, where the primary questions are, "Who is visiting now?" "What is happening here?"

The simple question "What is happening here?" locates the dreamwork in the immediacy of the present experience of the dream, looking to the image bodies themselves to reveal their purposefulness, their stories. The dreamer looks neither back to whence s/he came, nor forward to some dire or luminous future consequence, but rather down and around, noting what is just so at that particular moment in time in that particular place. To tend a dream is to recognize that in the telling of the dream the dream is already in the room – existing right now as an alive imaginal process. The question, "Who is visiting now?" engages the living presence that exists in animated dream images – images experienced as embodied persons of psychic reality, the entities behind the masks.

When a dream image evokes a memory of a childhood event, for instance, I believe a dream therapist must ask why psyche presents this historical image in a dream *now*. The point is not the historic event itself or how the dreamer felt about it in the past. Something about this past event matters *now*. Something constellated the dynamics of that past event in the first place. What innate image in psyche, what essential life rhythm within that particular dreamer, constellated that past experience? How has that image evolved in its life to the present time? That voice is being felt again, in its relevance to present as well as future experience. The dream therapist can listen to the "root image" of the historic experience, particularly listening to the living expression of the image in present time. In this way of working, the dream therapist is able to stay with the living image, traversing time in the context of the image, rather than using an image only as a vehicle to access, or work through, personal history. Thus understood, the image itself is the primary referent, not the historical incident constellated by the image.

Case Illustration: "At the Water's Edge"

A dreamer, a woman who has considerable experience in working with her dreams, tells me that she has already spent time considering this dream on her own but feels somehow that she is missing something. She has a sense there is something more. Here is the dream as she first related it to me:

I am walking along the edge of a seaside cliff. I walk until I get to the end of the path, and I become stranded. There is no place to go.

After listening carefully to the dream several times, I ask the dreamer to "associate" to the images or the predicament in the dream. Associations are useful in the beginning. They provide personal context as well as give the dreamer the opportunity to tell what she knows about the circumstance pictured in the dream. For the most part, associations are made to current or historic awake-life circumstances and are therefore limited to the contents of the Personal Unconscious. Methods of Association are reductive in that all images are reduced back to personal circumstances. The dreamer reports the following associations:

Well, it reminds me of a place we visited on a family vacation once when I was ten. I used to walk along the edge of the cliff when I needed time to think. That was the summer my parents were fighting so much. I was afraid they would hurt each other. I guessed they would be getting a divorce, and I didn't know what would happen to me. You know, I'm feeling kind of the same way now. With all the turmoil and budget cutbacks at the agency I work in, I'm wondering if I have reached the end of the line as a staff counselor. I am experiencing a great deal of chaos and fear of possible separation.

In addition to asking about the dreamer's personal associations to the dream, I further invite her to consider how certain dream images may reflect relevant material from mythology and/or literature. Amplification relates the dream imagery to the archetypal patterns of the Collective Unconscious and is a prospective approach in that the dream imagery is listened to as it pertains to the emerging process of the dreamer's individuation. Extending the dreamwork beyond personal associations, a process of "amplifying" the images, evoked the following from the dreamer:

I've felt many times that I was on the edge of something which I could glimpse but not see or experience clearly. It's as if I were on a path leading to somewhere important, like a pilgrimage or journey to some important place or "calling." I keep thinking of Penelope being stuck at water's edge at Ithaca – waiting. As a woman, I often feel as if I have been stranded, waiting at the end of a path, waiting for my man to come home, waiting for that which is out of my control.

Both Association and Amplification reveal important insights for the dreamer. Through Association, in working with the material of the Personal Unconscious, the dreamer had the opportunity to honor childhood fears in the presence of a caring therapist and to explore those fears in relation to her current work situation. Through Amplification, in exploring material of the Collective Unconscious, the dreamer became aware of archetypal themes relevant to her life. The universal images of "water's edge" and "waiting" were suggested as representing potentially important inner life struggles, both part of an individuation process now coming into increased awareness.

In both instances, however, the dream images themselves remained frozen, not given the opportunity to reveal themselves as they currently exist and move. In both the reductive (associative) and prospective (amplificative) approaches to the dream, the dream was used as a fixed justification to either summon memories of the past or to forecast a vision of the future. These kind of analytic investigations, however useful, are limited and invariably leave out the here and now reality of the dream experience. Not surprisingly, the dreamer in this instance felt that somehow the dream held something more, something yet to come alive.

On a third telling I asked the dreamer to pause and listen, to become aware how the images of the dream fill the room, to animate the image. Methods of Animation are used to resuscitate the dream, inviting the living vitality of the dream to come forward.

The mud of the seaside cliff, the smell of the water – all of the images – came alive. They became embodied. They had substance. They were visible. And the dreamer was really at that moment *in* the dream work. She was being moved and touched and informed by the images of the dream. As a result she felt a sense of ground, a sense of immediate connection to this natural landscape, and she experienced the pulse of the dreamscape move through her and work through her. She was now located in the dream, and, in turn, the dream had now located her in its activity.

By remaining stationary on the path (as actually pictured in the dream) and by experiencing the physicality of the mud and the marbled rock (as they made their presence known in the dream), the dreamer felt neither the regressive need to retreat backward on the path, nor the fear of what the future held. Both past and future are favored by traditional approaches to dreamwork – regressing into one's past or progressing into the next phase of individuation. Rather, as we *tended* her dream, she felt the immediacy of her present experience, stranded at the end of the path, accompanied by depth of ocean on one side and breadth of the rock face on the other. She felt situated, able to be in the present reality of her dreamscape.

Conclusion

To tend a dream is to allow its activity, its rhythm, to return to its own landscape. To hear a dream deeply allows the dream its presence, its being, and its becoming. And as that rhythm returns and the dream again becomes alive, is it not true that we, at that moment, re-experience our natural place as constituent members in nature's psyche, reconnected to a deeply resonant ecology? Are we not in this experience, re-connected to our essential rhythm – sourced by the very pulse of life itself?

CHAPTER 9

Telling Our Stories:
Making Meaning from Myth and Memoir

Maureen Murdock

People say that what we're all seeking is a meaning for life. I don't think that's what we're really seeking. I think that what we're seeking is an *experience* of being alive, so that our life experiences on the purely physical plane will have resonance within our own inner-most being and reality, so that we actually feel the rapture of being alive.

Joseph Campbell

I have long been fascinated by both memoir and myth. I grew up in an Irish-American Catholic family reading *The Lives of the Saints* where I was raised on the harrowing tales of twelve-year-old virgin martyrs, like Maria Goretti, who was stabbed to death by a rejected suitor and Lucia who had her throat slit for the same reason and was forever immortalized holding her two eyes in a dish. The male saints seemed to survive adolescence somewhat better, so I identified with St. Francis of Assisi who developed the gift of conversing with animals while wandering the countryside, begging for food. These early stories became my childhood myths.

In the 1980s, I was intrigued by the amazing popularity of Bill Moyers' series on the *Power of Myth* with Joseph Campbell. Campbell gathered language, image and story from every culture and religion and wove them together. He offered us a sense of connection with something larger than ourselves. He didn't preach; he presented us with symbols from nature, religion, literature, art and film and he inspired us to look at our own lives as personal myths. He challenged us to understand that myth helps us learn to deal with life as if, in his words, "You were what you really are." In so doing, Campbell touched a nerve about finding meaning.

In the 1990s, memoir replaced fiction as the literary genre that captured the imagination. Last October I opened the *Sunday New York Times Book Review* and noticed there were five memoirs being reviewed: *Iris and her Friends: A Memoir of Memory and Desire* by John Bayley who wrote about his wife, Iris Murdoch's struggle with Alzheimers; *Out of Place* by Edward W. Said, a tale of the author's alienation growing up a Christian Arab in Cairo in an English preparatory school; *The Million Dollar Mermaid*, Esther Williams' raucous tale about swimming through the ins-and-outs of Hollywood; *All Souls: A Family Story from Southie*, Michael Patrick MacDonald's account of growing up in south Boston during integration in the 1970's, and *Faith of My Fathers*, ex-POW and Senator John McCain's ode to his father, grandfather, and to his own character.

Every week, it seems, a new memoir reaches the best seller list or becomes a film. Seven years ago, when I first started teaching writing courses on the art of the memoir, I could barely find a contemporary memoir on the shelf of my local bookstore. What has happened?

What has happened is that we, men and women alike, long to discover who we are. Memoir, like myth, is a quest for meaning. Myth owes its persistence to its power to express or symbolize typical human emotions that have been experienced throughout successive generations. Memoir owes its popularity to its poignancy in portraying these enduring patterns of behavior or archetypal themes in an individual's life.

James Atlas, critiquing the literary memoir in the *New York Times Magazine* in 1996 declared, "Fiction isn't delivering the news! Memoir is" (26). Readers love the stories of real people. They yearn to find commonality, comfort, perhaps even direction. They want to know, "How did *they* get from there to here?" Mary Karr, author of the best selling *Liar's Club* about growing up in an alcoholic family in the South, has said, "People want a window on how to behave. They want to read about someone's life and say, *This is how it was. This really happened.*" (26)

Because we have become such a mobile society, living, in many cases, across continents from our family and loved ones, we yearn for community, consciously or not. Reading a memoir or sitting in a memoir class listening to the stories of other people gives us a sense of perspective about our own life and an entrance into a community. If I can write about some experience in my life and reflect on it in such a way that it touches an experience in *your* life, then we have made a connection, regardless of our difference in race, age, class, or gender. We may not know it at the time, but something happens on an unconscious level to both of us.

People long for connection, for expression, for their lives to have meaning. Memoir, like myth, examines the important questions in life: Who am I? Who do I belong to? What is my tribe? How do I make my way through life? How and where do I fit into the greater scheme of things? Whether our distant ancestors looked to the sun, moon, and stars for guidance, or our contemporary relations pin their hopes and dreams on meditation, SSRI's, or technology, we have always, as a species, yearned for meaning.

Memoirists are our contemporary mythmakers. Myths explore themes such as alienation, abduction, betrayal, separation, death and rebirth. Myth calls us to a deeper awareness of the very act of living itself, our deep inner struggles, our interior initiations into adolescence and midlife, the thresholds we cross from birth to life to death and back again. Myths are stories of our pursuit through the ages for truth, for significance.

Carl G. Jung writes that the prime function of myth is psychological, to reveal the unconscious, to expose the underlying pattern of our lives (Segal 17). A myth asks *why*. Why is this happening? James Hillman tells us that myths do not tell us how; they give us the invisible background which starts us imagining, questioning, going deeper. The power of myth is that it deals with universal questions.

In every society myth makers start with an archetype, an invisible pattern that Jung believed is in our psychic structure from the beginning, for example, the archetype of the hero or heroine. They then make up specific stories that express those archetypes. But the myth makers are inventing only the manifestations of mythic material already existing in the unconscious of you and me taken collectively (16).

Odysseus is either invented or appropriated to serve as a Greek expression of heroism. Luke Skywalker or Horatio Hornblower are invented to serve as contemporary western expressions of the hero travelling the cosmos or the seas. As Robert Segal observes, "The myth of Odysseus is passed on from generation to generation by acculturation, but the hero archetype that it expresses is passed on by heredity." (16-17)

An archetype functions much like a hidden magnet; we cannot actually see the pattern it creates but we are propelled by its energy. A myth is a metaphor for what lies behind the visible world; it gives us a perspective on what is happening. Myth is a way of seeing through things.

Mythologist Joseph Campbell used to say, "With a myth in your mind, you see its relevance to something happening in your own life" (Personal Conversation 1981). You become the mother goddess Demeter grieving for your daughter Persephone who has been abducted into the underworld, or the sun god, Helios who can't understand what all your grieving is about anyway: "Hades isn't such an unsuitable bridegroom, is he?"

Memoir, in contrast, is how one remembers the events of one's individual life. But rather than simply telling a personal incident or story, the memoir-ist both tells the story and muses upon it. The memoirist asks *how?* How did this happen? What were the details? Not just what happened; that's a testimony, a narrative, perhaps even an interesting tale. No, to be successful, a memoir must demonstrate some evolving awareness, some reckoning with oneself, some understanding of how one's unconscious is at work.

When we read a memoir, we participate in the author's struggle to achieve some understanding of the events, experiences, fantasies and dreams of her personal recollection. That means that the author has digested the experience, not just confessed it. In an interview with National Public Radio correspondent Jackie Lyden, author of *The Daughter of the Queen of Sheba*, her memoir of growing up with a mother who was manic depressive, Lyden spoke about the task of the writer who reflects upon her life:

> … the memoir tries to frame an experience that could have been little more than chaotic at the time, albeit with amazing moments of insight and struggle. We have survived, we are at the end of our journey, we want to, like Odysseus, make some sense of where we have gone. (8)

Indeed, memoir and myth share a depth of inquiry. The language of memoir is casual, everyday, direct and conversational. The writer speaks directly into our ear, confiding everything from gossip to wisdom. Memoir deals with the author's personal experiences, opinions, and prejudices and the conscience of memoir arises from the author's sincere examination of these. The hallmark of memoir is its intimacy with its reader. "This is what I did and felt and learned about myself." The question, "What about you?" is unspoken but implied.

The language of myth, on the other hand, is metaphorical. Because it seeks to reveal the unconscious, myth speaks in archetypes which can express themselves only obliquely through symbols, like the sun or the moon, gods and goddesses, monsters and demons, saviors and scapegoats.

Not only does every myth contain multiple archetypes, every archetype contains inexhaustible meanings (Segal 9-10).

Myth is an ordering principle that gives coherence to the way memoirs unfold. A myth is the pattern or blueprint or structure upon which we hang the remembered incidents of our lives. Myth provides the pattern; memoir provides the details. In telling our story we realize the deeper pattern of our lives; we can't go home until we tell our story, where we have been. The past has to have meaning for us to live in the present. Unconscious patterns are always informing the content of what we remember.

In Homer's *Odyssey* (1967), Telemachus searches for his father Odysseus who has been absent for two decades. Throughout his childhood Telemachus was regaled with the tales of his father's great heroism in the Trojan Wars, but he does not yet know him as a father. Odysseus has become a figure of mythic proportions; Telemachus yearns to know the man who is his father; in his search for him he begins his own heroic quest.

When Telemachus meets the goddess Athena on the road disguised as the man Mentes, he asks news of his father. Homer gives us Athena's response:

Your father. But him have the gods hindered on his journey.
The godly Odysseus has not yet died on the earth,
But he is still alive somewhere, held back on the broad ocean
On a flood-circled island, and troublesome men hold him,
Savages, who somehow keep him back against his will.
Well, I will now tell you a prophecy, how the immortals
Cast it in my heart, and how I think it will end,
Though I am not a prophet, and have no clear skill with birds.
Not much longer now surely, will he be away
From his dear fatherland; not even if iron bands hold him.
He will devise how to return, since he has many resources.
But come now, tell me this, and explain it truthfully,
If, big as you are, you are really the son of Odysseus himself.
You resemble him strangely in your head and your fine eyes,
Since we had contact quite often with one another
Before he embarked for Troy, where the other noblest
Men of the Argives were headed in their hollow ships.
Since I have not seen Odysseus, nor has he seen me."
Then the sound-minded Telemachos answered her:
"All right, stranger, I shall speak quite truthfully.
My mother calls me the son of the man. But I myself
Do not know. No one has ever been certain of his father. (I.l. 195-216)

In *The Duke of Deception*, a more contemporary view of the same theme, another author tries to sort out the identity of his father. Memoirist Geoffrey Wolff writes about the con artist who created a mythic portrayal of himself for his young son. Duke Wolff, his father, seemed a flawless specimen of the American clubman: a product of Yale and a one-time fighter pilot turned aviation engineer. In reality, Duke Wolff was a failure who flunked out of a series of undistinguished schools, was passed up for military service, and supported himself with desperately improvised scams, exploiting employers, wives, and finally, his own son. Wolff writes a poignant memoir of his search for the man who he called father after first saying "Thank God!" upon learning of his death.

Well, I'm left behind. One day, writing about my father with no want of astonishment and love, it came to me that I am his creature as well as his get. I cannot now shake this conviction, that I was trained as his instrument of perpetuation, put here to put him into the record. And that my father knew this, calculated it to a degree. How else explain his eruption of rage when I once gave up what he and I called "writing" for journalism? I had taken a job as the book critic of *The Washington Post*, was proud of myself; it seemed then like a wonderful job, honorable and enriching. My father saw it otherwise: "You have failed me," he wrote, "you have sold yourself at discount" he wrote to me, his prison number stamped below his name.

He was wrong then, but he was usually right about me. He would listen to anything I wished to tell him, but would not tell me only what I wished to hear. He retained such solicitude for his clients. With me he was strict and straight with him, and with myself. Writing to a friend about this book, I said that I would not now for anything have had my father be other than what he was, except happier, and that most of the time he was happy enough, cheered on by imaginary successes. He gave me a great deal, and not merely life, and I didn't want to bellyache; I wanted, I told my friend, to thumb my nose on his behalf at everyone who had limited him.

My friend was shrewd, though, and said that he didn't believe me, that I couldn't mean such a thing, that if I followed out its implications I would be led to a kind of ripe sentimentality, and to mere piety. Perhaps, he wrote me, you would not have wished him to lie to himself, to lie about being a Jew. Perhaps you would have him fool others but not so deeply trick himself. "In writing about a father," my friend wrote me about our fathers, "one clambers up a slippery mountain, carrying the balls of another in a bloody sack, and whether to eat them or worship them or bury them decently is never cleanly decided." (10-11)

Both myth and memoir explore the same theme – the longing for the father. In the first, a young man wants to know if the hero who everyone calls his father still lives, thus affirming his own parentage and ultimately his existence. In the second, a middle-aged man discovers that no matter how much he has tried to escape him through geographical distance, education, and professional success, his father lives on in his very cells. The myth provides the pattern; the memoir provides the details.

For a memoir to work it has to have a ring of universal truth to it. There is a universality to memories; they reflect the dreams and desires we all experience. As the 16th century essayist, Michel de Montaigne wrote, "Every man has within himself the entire human condition" (Lopate, xxv). When a memoir is successful, it reflects part of the archetypal journey we all share. When it doesn't, it is at best, a whine or a self-congratulatory slap on the back.

After her book, *Are You Somebody?: The Accidental Memoir of a Dubliner Woman*, was published, journalist Nuala O'Faolain was stunned by the level of response. She admits that she wasn't thinking of her readers when she was writing the book; she was trying to make some sense out of growing up female in twentieth century Ireland in her particular circumstances. But she struck a chord that went far beyond the details of her life. Her readers insisted on her seeing their lives as well.

She recounts that letters came from Trinidad, Australia, China, Rome and even from a trekker's hut in Nepal. The writers offered her images of themselves in notes pushed through her door, in letters to the newspaper where she worked, in correspondence to her publisher. Hundreds and hundreds of people wrote to her from "kitchens and bedrooms and fireside chairs where men and women unknown to me had sat all night – in a sense with me – reading me." Her story, which she didn't think anyone would care about, gave meaning to the disparate events of her life. In allowing others to see her with all of her rough spots, she held up a mirror to anyone who dared look at himself with courage, love, and compassion (190).

"I never envisaged such cherishing." she writes. "When I called my memoir *Are You Somebody?* it was largely to preempt the hostile people who'd say, at my writing anything about myself at all, 'Who does she think she is?' I never imagined awakening something a bit like love." (191)

When we tell our story and tell it well, so that it reflects the universal experience of being human, we become a part of each other. In describing the quest to make meaning from memory, essayist Michael Ventura writes:

> Henry Miller was fond of quoting his friend, Fred Perles: 'The mission of man on earth is to remember.' To re-member. To put back together. To re-attach a lost member. Memories are the most common, and though untouchable, the most tangible experience we have of one another. Although memories are particular and fragmented they are all we have to offer the loved ones with whom we have shared life. (Ventura 28)

My mother has died. When I reach for her in my memory, I remember her veiled pill box hats before Jackie Kennedy made them fashionable, her blue and white spectator shoes perfectly polished the first day of spring, her fierce devotion to the rituals of the Catholic Church, her sheer joy and abandon in dancing the Charleston, her unwavering attachment, even as Alzheimers claimed the greater terrain of her mind, to her girdle.

I am putting her back together like a mosaic and participating in the mission of humanity by passing her on to the future in the only way I can – passing her on as memory. When I write about her and the complexity of our relationship, I try to bring her alive in the most honest way I can – for a moment. This moment. In another moment, I might write something quite different. I learn something about myself and her and the nature of mothers and daughters every time I do.

In her memoir about her relationship with her parents, *Skating to Antarctica*, Jenny Kiski explored the nature of memory: "Memory is continually created, a story told and retold, using jigsaw pieces of experience. It's utterly unreliable in some ways, because who can say whether the feeling or emotion that seems to belong to the recollection actually belongs to it rather than being available from the general store of likely emotions we have learned?

"Who can say that this image is correct, and not an image from a book or film or a picture, another part of one's life, which, seeming to fit with the general story, is pressed into service? Memory is not false in the sense that it is willfully bad, but it is excitingly corrupt in its inclination to make a proper story of the past." (154)

Author Mary McCarthy wrote about the vagaries of memory in her preface to *Memories of a Catholic Girlhood*. She wondered whether some of incidents that she has written about actually happened or if she made them up. She was an orphan and the chain of recollection, the collective memory of her family, had been broken. Her parents died when she was very young so she had no one to correct her recollections, or to say that couldn't have happened the way you remember it because it was impossible.

She gives the example of her own son, Reuel, who used to be convinced that Mussolini had been thrown off a bus in North Truro on Cape Cod during the Second World War. This memory goes back to one morning in 1943 when as a young child, he was waiting with his mother and father beside the road in Wellfleet to put a departing guest on the bus to Hyannis. The bus came through and the bus driver leaned down to shout the latest piece of news: "They've thrown Mussolini out." (5)

Today, she says, Reuel knows that Mussolini was never ejected from a Massachusetts bus, and he knows where he got that impression, but if she and her husband had died that year, he would have been left with a clear recollection of something that everyone would have assured him was an historical impossibility, and with no way of reconciling his stubborn memory to the stubborn facts on record.

Memory, through imagination, can impose a value beyond that of the actual experience. We usually only store in memory images of value. The value may be lost over the passage of time but some trace of the feeling may still remain. Whether it's a feeling of anger over a perceived injustice, longing for a unrequited love, grief over the loss of a loved one, or despair over a betrayal, the feeling lives somewhere deep within us. It is something we hang onto. Poet Patricia Hampl, in exploring the relationship between "Memory and Imagination," writes, "Stalking the relationship, seeking the congruence between stored image and hidden emotion – that's the real job of memoir." (207)

Memory helps us make meaning of our past so that we can live in the present. Myth helps us accept our past and find our future. Myths have the power to activate mythmaking, to engage us in what Joseph Campbell called creative mythology, the conscious reshaping or reanimating of old myths.

In a lecture at Pacifica Graduate Institute, mythologist Christine Downing said, "To allow myths to start us questioning and going deeper, requires on our part that we move to a place of neither belief nor disbelief but a place of make believe." The language of poetry, art, theater, and music exist because the ultimate core of meaning may be circumscribed but not directly described. Myth, too, circumscribes and gives an approximate description of an unconscious core of meaning.

I don't know if contemporary memoir writers are conscious of reanimating and reshaping the old myths, but I think they are truly the myth makers of our time. In *The Color of Water*, African-American writer James McBride explores his quest for his tribe – black, white, Jewish, or Baptist. As a boy growing up in Brooklyn's Red Hook Projects, he knew his white mother was different. But when he tried to ask her about this difference she'd simply say "I'm light-skinned." Later he wondered if he was different, too, and asked his mother if he was black or white. "You're a human being," she snapped. "Educate yourself or you'll be a nobody!"

Failing to receive a satisfactory answer to the question of his own roots, he asked his mother what color God was.

"Oh boy" she sighed, "God's not black. He's not white. He's a spirit.

"Does he like black or white people better?"

"He loves all people. He's a spirit."

"What's a spirit?"

"A spirit's a spirit."

"What color is God's spirit?"

"It doesn't have a color," she said. "God is the color of water. Water doesn't have a color." (50-51)

James McBride asked the question that people of all tribes have been asking throughout the ages. As we know, the answers to the God question have been innumerable: the sun, the moon, Inanna, Yahweh, Yemeyah, the Great Spirit, Quetzacoatl, Jesus, The Black Madonna, a higher power. We carry in our very cells the same questions our forebears carried. We are a people in search of who we are, where we are going, with whom we belong, and what life's meaning includes.

References

Atlas, J. (12 May 1996). The Age of the Literary Memoir is Now. *The New York Times Magazine*, Section 6, 25-27.

Diski, J. (1997). *Skating to Antarctica*. New Jersey: Ecco Press.

Downing, C. (1996). *Lecture*. Carpinteria CA: Pacifica Graduate Institute.

Hampl, P. (1996). Memory and Imagination. In J. McConkey (Ed.), *The Anatomy of Memory*. Oxford: Oxford University Press.

Homer. (1967). *The Odyssey* (A. Cook, Ed. and Trans.). Norton Critical Edition. New York: Norton.

Lopate, P. (Ed.). (1994). *The Art of the Personal Essay*. New York: Anchor Books.

Lyden, J. (1997). *The Daughter of the Queen of Sheba*. New York: Penguin.

McBride, J. (1996). *The Color of Water*. New York: Riverhead Books.

McCarthy, M. (1957). *Memories of a Catholic girlhood*. New York: Harcourt Brace Jovanovich.

O'Faolain, N. (1996). *Are you Somebody?* New York: Henry Holt and Co.

Segal, R A. (1998). *Jung on Mythology*. Princeton: Princeton University Press.

Slattery, D. *Personal conversation*, January 25, 1999.

Ventura, M. (1996). The Mission of Memory. *The Family Networker 20*(6).

Wolff, G. (1979). *The Duke of Deception*. New York: Vintage Books.

CHAPTER 10

Divinities of Marriage

Ginette Paris[1]

In one of her short stories, Colette, the French novelist, describes the following scene: the time is the First World War. The train station is crowded with women anxiously waiting for mail from their husbands at war. Women are scrambling and hustling on the dock through soldiers and luggage. A young woman sidesteps an older matron, who says to her: "Why are you getting in front on me? Don't you think I may be as anxious as you to get news from my man?" And the young woman says: "I am sorry, but please understand: you had your husband for many years ... I am a new bride, we had just married when he was called." To which the older woman answers: "My child, it's obvious that you know absolutely nothing about marriage. Marriage is an initiation with many stages and levels, and you are only on the first one". And the fifty-year-old woman keeps her place on the dock.

What are these stages and levels of initiation Colette is referring to? Her example of the young and old women shows us an approach whereby initiation is linked to *time*. Nowadays, many psychologists propose theories on the *phases* of marital life, showing what each decade may bring in the way of individuation or destruction through marriage. Another approach, which I will use, consists in examining the archetypes at work from the very outset

[1] This paper was first given at *The Dallas Institute of Humanities and Culture*'s Conference on *Marriage, Intimacy and Freedom*. Dallas, October 1-2-3, 1993. It was later presented at a Pacifica Graduate Institute's Convivium, in Santa Barbara, in 1994.

and throughout marriage's duration. As all forms of initiations are linked to suffering, my purpose is to give an image of this suffering: that of a battle between deities, each deity competing for our attention, for a share of the marriage.

Of course I have no remedy to propose because to refuse the torments of the initiation process is to refuse initiation. One can only hope for a finer consciousness, one that transforms psychological distress into soul-making. Let's begin our examination of the suffering involved in any marriage by reviewing three different kinds of challenges: 1) Peleus and Thetis, the difficulties of an *unequal* marriage. 2) Zeus and Hera and the balance of power in this *equal* marriage. 3) Hephaestos and Aphrodite and the drama of *infidelity*.

Let's start with one of the most famous marriages of mythology: Thetis and Peleus. The story of this marriage starts with Zeus who was attracted to Thetis, the wise and beautiful sea-goddess. He is informed that if he mates with Thetis, she will bear a son that would be so formidable that Zeus would find himself dethroned by him. To be safe, Zeus then arranges the marriage of Thetis with Peleus; by marrying her to a mortal, he diminishes the power of her offspring. Peleus, the chosen mate for Thetis, may be the worthiest mortal of his time, but nonetheless he is not of Thetis' class. He is a mortal and she a goddess. We thus have an archetypal image of an *unequal*, unbalanced marriage.

I suggest we look at their problem as one facing almost any couple, at one point or another. Thetis of course, is not pleased with the prospect of bearing merely mortal children. According to one version, she bears several and dips them at birth into boiling water to test whether they have inherited her immortality. But they die because they have inherited their father's mortality. It seems as if the inequality in this marriage causes problems for those children who take after the spouse of the lower status; those who take after the mortal father die while Achilles, who takes after his divine mother, will have a glorious destiny. As such, this is a typical class problem of an unequal marriage. But I am suggesting that this kind of situation will arise in every marriage. We feel this complex each time we feel married somehow below ourselves, which is the case each time one is thinking "Am I good enough for him, or her? Is she, or he, good enough for me?" The competition might be in terms of class, inherited money, education, IQ, charm, whatever the source of the inequality.

One might argue that inequality exists in many lasting marriages: for example, a husband is much brighter and more educated than his wife, but she has lots of money, so they get along. After all, one of the oldest tricks in the history of social climbing is to compensate any social or personal default by something that has value to the eye of the other, be it money, youth, political power or fame, for example. So, what is one to do if one feels inequality in the marriage? Well, a myth never says what to do; it points out where the difficulties will arise. What the myth seems to suggest here is that the problem of an unequal union does not concern the spouses, who have an implicit deal, but the offsprings. Thetis may accept Peleus's mortality, but she cannot tolerate it when the same condition is visited on her son. Of course there are stories of ugly geniuses married to dumb beauty queens whose children inherit the good brain of the father and the great looks of the mother. But the other way around makes for either tragedy or bad jokes. We all know the anecdote about the flirting lady who supposedly said to Bernard Shaw: "Wouldn't it be marvelous if we made a child, with my beauty and your intelligence?" to whom he supposedly answered, "but what a tragedy if it ended up the other way around!"

When at last Achilles is born, Thetis sees that this son of hers has a potential for immortality. She dips the baby in the river Styx to make him immortal. Another account claims that she treats him with ambrosia by day, and places him in the fire at night. She is giving him the kind of education, or initiation, that prepares him to be admitted in the high circle of the gods. This is normal behavior for any parent: we try to transmit to our children our highest values; if these conflict with those of the other partner, we do it secretly, like Thetis, when she is alone with her child. Or we do it unconsciously, by sending subtle messages, frowning here and smiling there, that the child will interiorize. Peleus, happening upon his wife as she is placing his son on the burning coals, gives an indignant cry. I like to imagine him saying something like this: "what are you doing to my son! You are asking too much of him. Let him be as he is. He takes after me and why is that not good enough? Will you kill this one, too, with your ambitions to make our children immortal?" Thetis is so enraged that she leaves her husband and son, breaking the marriage right there and then, and forever returns to the sea, leaving her son Achilles with a vulnerable spot, an unfinished education, a weakness, by which death will come to him. Achilles dies because as a goddess, his mother could not give him all she was capable of.

Let's look now at a second archetypal situation: perfect equality as in the marriage of Zeus and Hera. Their marriage is *the* example of the lasting marriage, perfectly balanced in terms of origin, strength and power. As the majority of mythologists will outline, the fact that Zeus and Hera are also brother and sister is a symbol of their essential equality, rather than a suggestion of incest, as in the Egyptian dynasties. In other words, having the same mother and father means: my family is equal to your family, my worth is equal to your worth, and neither of us will swallow the other. Though Zeus has swallowed or destroyed many sexual partners and past spouses, he will never subdue Hera, his perfect equal. Their union gives a basic image for marriage: *the husband as king, the wife as queen.* The most lasting couple on Olympus presents us with a metaphor where marriage is *the ruling of a kingdom, where marriage is doing what queens and kings do together.* As usually the case in any royal marriage, sexuality, procreation, love – all this is secondary to the ruling the kingdom. For example, the only time we see Hera interested in sexually seducing Zeus, is when she wants to trick him for political reasons. Any woman, and for that matter, any man, who uses sex to get something else, is not interested in sex but in power.

Hera is known as the archetypally jealous wife. What does this mean? That jealousy is inherent to marriage? Yes, maybe. But when one looks closely at Hera's jealousy, one can see that her vengeance is not primarily directed at her unfaithful husband, nor at his many lovers, her rivals. No. Instead, she expresses her anger towards the offspring of these illegitimate unions. Her jealousy is of a kind for which psychology has no word: let's call it the *dynastic jealousy*, if we may. Anything that can rock the domestic boat is seen as an attack on the kingdom. If only we were more conscious of the regal, *dynastic* dimension of any marriage, we might stop interpreting jealousy strictly in sexual terms. Anxiety over losing territory, fear for the survival of one's domestic kingdom, (however small or poor the household), the fear of imbalance in the division of territory between king and queen, are often as important as sexual feelings. But they are less conscious, because marriage is supposed to be about love and affection, sacrifice and devotion, not about power.

The eternal conflicts in Zeus and Hera's marriage are illustrated further on in their progeny. In their son Ares, the fiery god of war, we see Hera's disputatious character, her love for fights and confrontations, her acrimony. Zeus does not like his son by Hera very much, as though he were saying: "this is really *your* son, his very nature is an expression of your rage" or if he talked with a Jungian tongue, Zeus might say: "this figure of war is *your* animus, and look how superior is my anima, for it has created Athena, a divinity of war that always win over Ares." Their parenting is essentially competition: Athena is daddy's daughter, so Hera will strike back by creating, all by herself, her son Hephaestos. But since she is not satisfied with this crippled, misbegotten son, she throws him down from Olympus. Wounded, a creation of a mother that will tolerate only perfection and high standards, Hephaestos answers that blow by becoming a genius and by marrying pleasure-loving Aphrodite, the very shadow of Hera.

To recapitulate: first we had Thetis and Peleus, an image of the *imbalance* of power. Then Zeus and Hera, an image of the *balance* of power. There is not much space for sexuality in these unions. So let's now look into a marriage that does have some sex in it, that of Hephaestos and Aphrodite. It is rather late in the evolution of Greek mythology that Aphrodite finds a husband in Hephaestos, the divine smith. This evolution of the myth may receive many interpretations. Some feminist readings of the myth consider her marriage as a symbol of the loss of freedom women experienced at the classical period. If that is the case, then it must be added that *when* Aphrodite enters the patriarchal marriage, *then* she takes a lover, as if to inform us that there is an aphroditic spirit of resistance to marriage, (above all when the husband has been imposed and is, as Hephaestos is, crippled.)

But Aphrodite's marriage has also been interpreted as a symbol of the importance of honoring sexuality within the *marriage*, rather than as an oppressive patriarchal tendency. Myths, because they do not give the same kind of reassurance or certitude as dogma, are endless sources of discussion and exploration. There are many more equally valid interpretations of Aphrodite's marriage. But myths are nonetheless precise. For example, it is quite clear that Aphrodite, although married, is not a Goddess of marriage: that is Hera's domain. Aphrodite's task is to insure the reciprocal attraction of spouses, without which the marriage would remain cold and sterile.

The problem is that whenever She shows up, trouble is not far behind her as Aphrodite will not be contained within the conjugal bed frame. The reassuring wife whom the Greeks imagined with the qualities of an industrious bee (nourishing, chaste, and humble) is an image in exact opposition to Aphrodite. The men of Ancient Greece expressed in many texts their fear of associating Aphroditic love with marriage. But on the feminine side, the cult of Aphrodite *within* marriage seemed to always have had an important place.

It seems as if whenever a marriage doesn't allow enough room for sexual pleasure, the essential resemblance between Hermes and Aphrodite will emerge. These two divinities will stoop to lying, cheating and conniving to serve the principle they personify. Hermes, a trickster and a liar, was seen by the Greeks as the god of communication. Aphrodite is, in relation to marriage what Hermes is to politics and diplomacy. When the obligation to "tell all" to one's spouse becomes a kind of psychological remote control, the effect is to kill desire. Rather than deepening the relationship, it keeps one fenced in the narrow territory of avowable behaviors. Between a man and a woman, in the realm of attraction and desire, the necessity of "telling all," if it is compulsive, may serve the infantile need to be discharged from responsibility, to be pardoned for everything by a partner seen as "mother" or "father." In those cases, it is not the lover's transparency which prompts the confession, but the need to kill within the egg any illegitimate desire, which would then have to be confessed. At that point Aphrodite whispers lies, so that sexual attraction may continue to filter between man and woman, despite the dominant moral organization. This is after all what she represents. Lies and infidelities sometimes have the same role as disobedience in fairy tales. Marie-Louise von Franz has wisely observed how the fairy-tale heroine often transgresses a "taboo" through disobedience, bringing about terrible consequences. But her disobedience is also the act which brings her to a higher level of consciousness after many trials and sufferings. *I am not saying that fidelity is not good, not sexy. No.* It is quite a natural thing for satisfied lovers to be faithful to one another, without resentment; in fact, this is the very beauty of fidelity and loyalty and faithfulness. This kind of fidelity cannot be *promised*, it can only *exist* and one notices it after the fact, *a posteriori*. When faithfulness is mixed up with control, the confusion fogs the transparency of the relationship even more than unfaithfulness.

Lying is also at times a last resort in averting tragedy, and Aphrodite, as much as Hermes, has more affinity with laughter and frivolity than with the truth, if this truth must be somber and tragic. When Hephaestos catches his wife Aphrodite in bed with Ares, he is furious and calls in the gods to witness his tragic situation. All the gods hasten in to render justice to the deceived husband, only to find Hermes joking about how much he would like to be caught in this kind of act with beautiful Aphrodite.

Paradoxically, by lying and cheating, Aphrodite is true to the principle she serves: eternal attraction between the sexes. In her absence, marriage is indeed a very long power trip. But if you do invite her in your life, her kind of fidelity is towards the sexual drive, not towards the spouse who may or may not inspire it. Her code of honor does not include telling the whole truth as it is generally understood. The shimmering and multivalence of sexual desire prevents her from a legalistic definition of truth.

In conclusion, one of the things wrong with marriage, besides its psychology and its sociology, is its theology: one man, one woman, and one God! It blurs the conscience. It is responsible for the fact that we ask of one man, or one woman, to be all, to be perfect, impeccable. It is responsible for the fact that we still have but one and only sacrament to unite man and woman, and of course it is not enough.

Now that procreation and sexuality are established as two different experiences, why don't we have two different sacraments? One, an intimate ritual, no contract, no witness, a private celebration of the eternal union of man and woman in lovemaking. A ritual as renewable as the sacrament of communion.

Another, a public, communal celebration with official contracts being signed and future responsibilities all precisely cut out, a sacrament that would unite not a man and a woman to one another, as our actual marriage does, but as mother and father, forever linked to the child that is being conceived. Thus it would be clear that the making of a child is a lifelong commitment for which there is no divorce. And it would also be made clear that procreation implies the union of two families, two clans, two branches of ancestors that become forever part of the same family tree.

And why not a third sacrament, one that would acknowledge the Zeus-Hera aspect of marriage with a little more sophistication than the actual standardized marriage contract enforced by rigid laws on divorce settlement. It would clarify not only matters such as inheritances, family names, property titles, scope and limit of the spouses' mutual financial responsibilities, but would also address the more profound aspect of the king and queen metaphor: that of the sharing of powers between a man and a woman of equal strength.

None of these new "sacraments" would spare us from the suffering that is the very essence of initiation into the deep and beautiful mystery of conjugality. They would only get us more quickly into the heart of it because they would spare us the detour of guilt. Our whole psychology, sociology, politics and economics of marriage are still based on a religious view that has become a fantastic guilt generator working day and night. I have never met anyone whose marriage was (and stayed) 'right' in the traditional way. Not even one couple. Am I the exception? That sort of guilt is a moral suffering that leads nowhere. It is like spinning at high speed in the mud, and only getting deeper into it. As Confucius is supposed to have said: when you're in a hole, stop digging! Guilt is digging the hole you set yourself into. I look forward to a completely new theology of marriage yet to come, one that would push us out of our actual muddy patch of thinking and guilt feelings about our marriages, one that would bring back the sacramental dimension in the many ways man and woman are connected.

CHAPTER 11

The Chrysalis Experience:
A Mythology for Times of Transition

Hendrika de Vries

The future enters into us,
in order to transform itself in us,
long before it happens.
Rainer Maria Rilke

From Caterpillar into Butterfly

When I was a little girl living in Amsterdam, Holland, my friends and I often played on the tree-encircled cobblestoned square at the edge of our street. One year there was a large outbreak of furry caterpillars on the old trees around which we liked to play hide and go seek. Now, I don't know how the adults felt about the unusual number of caterpillars, but we children thought it was great fun. Here were all these furry little playthings, these hairy little cats, as I learned later the name caterpillar signifies. We would let them crawl on our hands and stroke them. We even named our favorites.

Then one day, of course as caterpillars do, they began to lose their liveliness and one after the other spun themselves into cocoons. I asked my mother what was happening, and she, being a wise woman, found me a very large open glass jar into which she put a leafy branch holding one of the cocooned caterpillars. For a while nothing much happened. But one early morning she called me to witness the emergence of a trembling exquisite little pale butterfly. I was in awe of the mystery of transformation that had taken place within that now empty chrysalis, that little cocoon, and thrilled by the beauty of this little winged creature.

But, deep down I also felt sad because I missed the furry little caterpillar that could walk on my hand and be stroked. For the rest of my life throughout the numerous transitions and transformational patterns that life would challenge me with, I would always have a little bit of a hard time letting go of the caterpillar stage, the comfort of the old. I have tended to stay in the betwixt and between chrysalis stage of transitions just a little too long before I would be able to open myself to the new life that wanted to take wing.

Imagination is Destiny

James Hillman believes that "The way we imagine our lives is the way we will go on living our lives" (*Healing Fiction* 23). Another way of saying this might be that we create our lives out of our personal mythologies.

We are all mythmakers and storytellers. Even when we are not listening or paying attention to the stories or myths we tell, others are nonetheless aware of them. Even when we are asleep or preoccupied with something else, our stories rise up out of our depths and pop out through our dreams, our Freudian slips, our art, our relationship patterns, our physical and emotional symptoms and oddities, and whisper endless litanies in our heads. We are all, in a very real sense, walking expressions of our personal and cultural myths and stories. As children we clamor for stories, and the stories and characters that touch us the most are the ones that set us on the path to imagining our lives and begin to shape our personal mythology.

Exercise #1: I invite you to think back for a moment to when you were a small child and you were told stories, or if you cannot remember being told stories, perhaps you read stories or saw them on television. Take a moment and recall your very favorite story. Which character did you identify with most? Write it down. Reflect on the behaviors and attitudes of this character. What was this character's role in the story? How did others behave towards him, her, or it? Now think. In what areas of your later life have you noticed similar characteristics in either yourself or in others who you have attracted to you? How does this early identification continue to influence you today, if at all?

Noticing who we identify with in stories, who we hate, who we love, and who we ignore begins to tell us something about our own personal mythology. Personal mythology, Carl Jung reminds us in *Memories, Dreams Reflections*, is not our literal historical life story. (3) It is the mythic infrastructure of preferred archetypal patterns and motifs around which we construct our lives. Thomas Moore in *Rituals of the Imagination* also warns against "mythic orthodoxy" in personal mythology (26). He contrasts the Greek word *mythos*, which refers to myths and fables, with the word *logos*, "which is the hound of truth" (20). The realm of myth is the imagination. As such, myth does not offer facts but gives us a way of imagining events. Moore also points out that myth has a nonlinear, fragmented and unending quality. (21) Mythic stories change over time. The gods and goddesses shapeshift, depending on the context.

We reach our mythic autobiography "not by telling the story of a life, but by telling its stories, over and over again, with all their many versions and contradictions" (26). While the search to know the literal facts of our historical childhood story may be a crucial element in our healing process, mythic imagining helps us reach into ground of our deeper story, the never-ending story of the human psyche or soul.

Psyche in Transition

"Psyche" is the Greek word for soul, which also means butterfly. Why would the ancient Greeks connect psyche and soul with butterfly? In *Words as Eggs* Russell Lockhart questions and explores this linguistic connection in the context of the soul's or psyche's need for concealment and hiding in the process of transformation.

> Consider the life history of the butterfly. The female butterfly lays thousands of eggs which hatch worm-like larvae. These are called "grubs" and are ugly and creepy. How can a beautiful butterfly come out of such horrible stuff? We know what larvae are, but what does the name hide? It is a Latin word, and among its meanings we find 'disembodied spirit,' 'a ghost,' 'a spectre', 'hobgoblin,' 'scarecrow.' A related word meant to 'bewitch' or 'enchant.' Later the larva came to mean 'mask' ... (169-170)

Lockhart goes on to say that "as the larva grows hairs, it becomes what we call a caterpillar which translated literally means 'hairy cat'" (170). When the caterpillar moves into the chrysalis stage, it literally provides a shelter, a hiding place, for the butterfly.

> The change from egg to larva to caterpillar to pupa to butterfly is a magical process of transformation and one into which man's early psyche projected the nature of his own soul transformations. (Lockhart 170)

The symbolic connection between butterfly and psyche alerts us to the need for sacred space during times of transition. It reminds us that a move into the chrysalis experience may be accompanied by inwardness, introversion, a need to withdraw from normal, everyday external activities. From the perspective of the new life that wants to emerge, this is a necessary time out, a time for the psyche to be concealed, hidden, protected, in order that the mysterious alchemical process of transformation may take place.

The pattern of ending and renewal is one of the most powerful mythic motifs in human life. Every transition, even a minor one, is accompanied by the spectres of chaos and emotional upheaval. The more traumatic transitions such as deaths, births, marriage, relational coupling and uncoupling, residential moves, major career changes, life-phase transitions and health issues require intense emotional adjustments.

As we journey into the new millennium, most of us will be experiencing the motif of ending and renewal in our everyday lives at much faster intervals than experienced by any of our ancestors. Longevity, increased global mobility, and scientific and technological advances which require sweeping adaptations and assimilations will challenge many people with radical career and lifestyle changes. Unprecedented ethical and biotechnological health, relational and life-phase decisions will occur at dizzying speeds.

Each of these transitions, depending on the degree, will normally be accompanied by fluctuating emotions of loss, sadness, fear and grief as well as expectations, hopes, desires, and the need for a healthy psychological and spiritual adjustment from one stage to the next.

If imagination is destiny, how do we begin to imagine these transitions in our lives? How can the image of the psyche or soul as butterfly help us start our mythic imagining through our personal challenges of times of transition and apparent breakdown?

Exercise #2: Think back to your own childhood for a moment. How did your family handle transitions? What mythic patterns were used to help you make the transition and make it safe and meaningful? Was there a sacred space where your soul or psyche could hide as it grew into its new form? For the most part, our Western culture has followed the conquering hero's myth to deal with transitions and adaptations. I imagine that for many of you the patterns were those of the lone hero or heroine who lives by the messages: Hang on. Grit your teeth. Grin and bear it. Don't cry. Don't grieve, and for heaven's sakes if you do, don't show your feelings to others. Do not burden others. Do not talk about it. Get over it. Get on with your life. For others, it may have been the mythic pattern of the helpless victim, who projects the hero onto the external world. An example from fairy tales may be the Sleeping Beauty who waits and waits for her rescuer, while she lives in the deathlike sleep of denial and ignorance.

If we take seriously the connection between the butterfly and the human soul or psyche, we might approach our chaotic, disorienting transitions quite differently. If the psyche needs a chrysalis so that it can transform itself before it takes wing into its new life, how could we make that happen? How would that look in our everyday busy schedules? How many of you have had the experience of being told to rest, to take some time out and get used to what is happening? To see who or what it is that is calling you into the future in this state of chaos, or to help you deeply grieve what needs to be let go of?

Transitions frequently demand a cruel emotional deepening into the darkness of reality, and yet paradoxically they can push us into a higher state of being. Is there a mythic story which can set us on the path of imagining our way through the chaos, fear and disorientation of that chrysalis time between one way of being in the world and the next? Since the butterfly is seen by many people as "the universal symbol of natural development and change, symbol of innermost archetypal transformation, a symbol of the spiritual aspect of life that goes back to prehistoric times" (Signell 212), perhaps we can let the butterfly image speak for itself.

The Myth of the Butterfly Goddess

The mythology of the butterfly as goddess lay buried deep in the earth of old Europe for the past five to nine thousand years. But just as we bring to life our personal mythology with the bric-a-brac of storied recollections and imaginings, so in the second half of the twentieth century, Marija Gimbutas, archeologist, linguist, and mythologist brought the mythology of the butter-fly goddess to life. Gimbutas spent some twenty years gathering, classifying and interpreting more than two thousand pieces of symbolic artifacts dug up from the earth of the earliest Neolithic village sites of old Europe ca. 7000-3500 BC. From the ritual objects, painted pottery and richly decorated figurines and potshards, she brought to life the existence of a pre-patriachal, prehistoric old European mythology in which the universe is constantly cycling through ever-recurring transitions. Gimbutas also found a striking absence of warfare images, as if men and women really were able to live in peace and harmony with one another.

In addition, Joseph Campbell in his foreword to Gimbutas' book *Language of the Goddess*, was particularly struck by the contrast between the view in this early mythology of the earth as alive and vibrant with an innate intelligence which she communicates to her creatures through dreams, visions and instinctual knowings, and the much later Genesis myth which would teach that the earth was made out of dust.

The rituals and symbols of this old European prehistoric mythology stress the self-regenerative powers of the cosmos, but to avoid getting caught in "mythic orthodoxy," I will let the story lead us into our own mythic imagining.

The Story

Once upon a time long before human beings had invented the skills of writing and history, the planet earth was in perfect peace and balance with the rest of the universe. There was no warfare, and men and women who lived there lived in love and harmony with one another, and they venerated the cosmos as the living body of their Mother-Goddess-Creatrix within whose living body they and every other living thing partook of her divinity. At least, so the story goes.

In this mythical time, the earth from which all living things came, was not imagined to be made out of dust as people would think later, but was alive and vibrant with her own innate intelligence which she communicated to her creatures through images in dreams and visions.

Time was cyclical and all creatures knew that life gave birth to death and death gave birth to life and that the great mystery of the cosmos was this constant renewal of life, not just human life but all of life and indeed the whole cosmos. The rituals and symbols of the people of this time depicted these self-generating powers of the cosmos in the form of the parthenogetic Goddess whose basic functions were to wield death to one form and bring life to another. At least, so the story goes.

Her images included many of the animals with transformational powers, such as the snake which could cyclically slough off and regenerate its own skin. One of the main epiphanies of this Goddess of eternal regeneration was the form of the butterfly. From the image of the butterfly goddess emerging out of the chrysalis spun by the caterpillar the people learned that life was never constant, but eternally engaged in rituals of letting go of one form and transforming them into another.

Now, we should not project our Western romantic ideas on to this image. This ancient butterfly goddess was not a doting sentimental mother goddess. On the contrary, she could be quite brutal, and her "No" to one form of being was as definitive as her "Yes" might be to another. In between the "No" and the "Yes" there was often the descent into deep dark matter, into the depths of dissolution, disorientation, grief, chaos and perhaps even madness, but this stage she wrapped up tenderly in a safe, dark cocoon or chrysalis.

Of course all that was once upon a time a long time ago. The time came for a new mythic cycle, and great male sky gods such as Wotan, Zeus, and Jahweh swept the earth. The cosmos brought forth new stories and new possibilities, while the butterfly goddess lay buried in the deepest strata of the earth's cocoon.

An Ancient Image for Times of Change and Chaos

But as James Hillman says, you cannot kill a god or a goddess, or an archetype. They will come again in a different form, and the butterfly goddess continues to surface in the psyche, which in Greek of course already means butterfly, and she laughs or perhaps cackles as she hides in fragments of myths and fairy tales, in old European folk sayings, and even in the languages of the old European countries where she was once worshipped. Through the bric-a-brac of linguistic images and traces left behind, her non-sentimental fierceness continues to tell a mythic story of meaning and wisdom. Through this lens we can view the process of transition, chaos and change in our own lives. As one of my clients, a wise and witty woman in her eighties, once told me: the cosmos is speaking to us constantly if we would only listen.

When we start imagining the process of transition through the mythic lens of the butterfly, we are immediately confronted by her demand for sacrifice. After all, the caterpillar is sacrificed to make way for the emergence of the butterfly. One of the fiercest images we have of this aspect hides in the cruel sacrifice-demanding Aztec goddess Itzpapalot, which means butterfly (Neumann 190). Itzpapalot's wings were tipped with the sharp edges of the obsidian warrior knife, yet the mystery remains that this same obsidian element was also the element from which sprang the maize, or corn, the most mythical of all foods and that Itzpapalot was venerated also as the supplier of this corn. "The Great Goddess bears life, the corn, ... and she also bears death, the obsidian knife." (191)

We see this two-fold aspect again in the image of the bronze and golden double-axe of the Minoan goddess and her priestesses. The golden double-axe alerts us to the death-wielding as well as life-giving characteristics of the experience of ending and renewal, or death and rebirth, in life's constant round of transitions and initiations. Marija Gimbutas interprets the Minoan double-axe as a gradual stylization of the wings of the butterfly goddess and reminds us that between 3000 to 1500 BC this image was as prevalent on frescoes and temples of the Minoan goddess and her priestesses as the cross is on Christian churches today. It is not an accident obviously that both of these images are powerful reminders that while there is pain and sacrifice in the process of change, there is also the promise of rebirth into new forms, new attitudes and perhaps even new ways of spiritual and physical being.

This double-edged motif of the chrysalis experience as an integral part of transformation is repeated in the Sumerian myths of Inanna inscribed on stone tablets by ancient mythographers around 1750 BC (Wolkstein 127). These stories and hymns tell of the Queen of Heaven and Earth, Inanna, who must descend into the underworld to meet her underground sister, Ereshkigal. Psychologically we can understand Ereshkigal as the neglected unconscious aspect of Inanna, or mythically we can imagine her as the forgotten caterpillar aspect of the butterfly. Ultimately, they must be seen as two aspects of the same being. In the underworld Inanna is stripped naked and her body is hung on a hook to rot (60) before she can reemerge to claim her full power and wisdom. At the same time, her dark sister Ereshkigal goes into painful labor with herself. (160) According to Samuel Noah Kramer, "it was this 'labor' or call that Inanna had heard from the Great Above" (Wolkstein 161). From this perspective, it is not only the caterpillar which sacrifices itself in the process of transformation but the spirit of the butterfly, who must descend into the dark before she can reemerge in her fullness. The profound implication is that the experience of dissolution, disorientation and chaos in times of transition holds within itself an opportunity for spirit and body to merge into a different, perhaps more complex, state of being.

This view is also upheld by John R. Van Eenwyk (*Archetypes and Strange Attractors: The Chaotic World of Symbols* 158-159), who in a fascinating study of chaos and symbols points out that when the psyche is faced with chaos in times of transitions, she must embrace that chaos in order for the process to have a creative outcome and not dissolve into entropy. This is not unlike Marion Woodman's belief that the ego can stay "splayed in a perpetual chrysalis" (14). Van Eenwyk distinguishes between entropic and deterministic chaos, and uses mythic stories to illustrate his theory that for a painful and difficult challenge in our lives to be turned into a rite of passage or initiation into rebirth or renewal, we must allow the existing order to dissolve into chaos in order for the new form or pattern to appear. (159) He adds:

> This is a rather radical departure from a firmly held belief of nineteenth-century science that has endured up until now. The second law of thermodynamics describes how order dissolves into chaos through entropy. The idea of entropy is often elaborated into a model wherein death becomes the ultimate unraveling. The opposite of this idea is contained in models that refer to renewal, and rejuvenation. In these models, death gives way to a new state of order, to new configurations and patterns that replace – and sometimes improve upon – the old ones. (159)

Van Eenwyk uses the story of Psyche and Eros as an illustration for his theories. The story of Psyche and Eros is said to have been written down by the Latin poet Apuleius around 125 AD (Neumann, *Amor and Psyche*, 153) but the myth probably has its origin some six or seven hundred years earlier in the time of Lao-Tse and Confucius in China, of Buddha and Mahavira in India, Pythagoras in Greece, and Zoroaster in Persia. Then, not unlike our present time, earthshaking changes were taking place in human consciousness (Houston, *The Search for the Beloved*, 15).

In this myth Aphrodite the goddess of beauty and love turns into a death-wielding goddess of initiation as she ruthlessly puts Psyche, a mere mortal girl, through a series of seemingly impossible tests and trials. It is tempting to view Aphrodite as a mere shrew in this story, the jealous mother of Eros who is bent on destroying her female rival in beauty, but that would be missing the point. Aphrodite is one of the most ancient goddesses in the history of mythology. She was originally a goddess of death and rebirth, a regeneratrix like the butterfly goddess of Gimbutas' prehistoric mythology. With the fierceness of that ancient prehistoric force she initiates the human psyche into her divinity. It is not surprising that this tale has been seen by writers, artists, depth-psychologists, mythologists and poets alike as a parable for the journey of the human soul.

We see echoes of the brutal aspect of the butterfly goddess in the image of the witch in popular fairy-tales. If you kill a butterfly, states a Serbian proverb even today, you kill a witch. The witch according to Gimbutas is none other than the demonized prehistoric goddess herself. (275) And even in the fairy-tales, the witch is usually an instrument for character development and even spiritual growth in the protagonists she seems to want to destroy.

> Though beautiful and ethereal, the butterfly is a symbol which arouses fear. ... because she is the dangerous and frightening Goddess. This ancient meaning of the symbol is preserved in etymology. The Breton and Irish *Maro* means "Death (Goddess)" and Lithuanian *More* is "Goddess of Death, Old Hag"; but the Greek, Germanic, and Slavic *mora, mara,* or *morava* mean both "nightmare" and "butterfly"; the German *Mahr* and French *cauchemar,* "nightmare," are further derivatives. (275)

Children frequently suffer from nightmares when families are in transition. Our adult dreams show images of lost purses and wallets, of lost or stolen cars, of water everywhere and houses dissolving like caterpillars in a chrysalis, of journeys downward (like Inanna into the underworld), and of being trapped in strange, frightening and unfamiliar places. Perhaps nightmares come to us when the earth is in transition also. Times of transition, of transformation, have nightmarish qualities which involve feelings of loss, chaos, disorientation accompanied by a resistance to opening up to that which is as yet frightening and unknowable. This is the realm of the chrysalis, of nature in her most mysterious form. This is goddess time, or lunar time, perhaps more the time of the great lunar moth than the daytime butterfly. This is not high noon, the solar time of the hero, or the time of logical progression, but a time of things happening backwards in the dark, when shadows are present and we cannot see our way ahead clearly. It is perhaps also the time of lunacy.

For this nightmarish, lunar, shadowy metamorphosis to take place safely, Mother Nature carefully provides a container, a chrysalis or cocoon within which she decides what has to be let go of and what unlived life is to unfold and emerge. Earlier societies still more closely connected to the cyclical mythology of the body and the earth set aside sacred spaces and provided sacred rituals which symbolically helped the initiate, the individual or group going through the chrysalis experience, to feel held and contained. The masterful teachers of ritual and initiation, Malidoma and Sobonfu Somé address the ritual space which couples still prepare in their tribal Dagara village to deal with the powerful energies of intimacy, conflict and transition. (*We Have No Word for Sex*, audiocassette.)

For the most part we have lost our sacred containers and watered down our rituals. Where today is there time to experience symbolically what the psyche/body feels in the dizzying occurrences of rapid changes and transitions in our contemporary global culture? How do we contain the nightmarish qualities of these escalating fast-paced changes? Where is our safe place, our sacred or ritual space, where psyche can be hidden so that we can grieve that which must be let go of and dissolved, and tend with care the new life that needs to unfold and wants to grow?

Exercise #3 Take a moment to reflect on a conflict you have or have had in your life. What is your sacred space, your chrysalis, where you can go to reflect upon it? Do you have a woman's circle or a man's group, a place of sacred worship and ritual, a room or place set aside where you can journal and set up an altar, or is there a special place in nature where you can go to meditate or pray, and perhaps dance and chant, a place where you can listen to your body as the unknown future presses into your awareness? Make a note to yourself, and if you don't have a safe or sacred space or group, I encourage you to make it a priority to create one for yourself.

The Power of Myth

Mythology helps us with this conscious charting of our interior lives. The problem is that mythic patterns which shape our personal mythology are filtered through the censors of family and cultural attitudes and scripts. Carl Jung was careful to remind his patients that a knowledge of myth was necessary not just to find myths to live by, but also to recognize which outmoded mythic patterns they needed to disidentify from in order to establish a fresh and different relationship to the archetypal energies which source our many stories. He recognized that families and cultures are often the staunch defenders of a mythic status quo which favors one myth over another and concretizes or literalizes myth into historical dogma. When this happens, it is a little like being given the map of Wisconsin and being told that that is the only map there is. That is fine if you happen to be travelling within the state of Wisconsin, but it becomes a real problem if you are travelling in Minnesota. In addition, families and groups will assign roles to individuals which are deeply embedded in mythic patterns and fairy-tale motifs. One sibling is chosen to be the hero or heroine who will slay dragons and make the family proud, while another may be the princess who waits her whole life for her perfect prince to come and rescue her. When we get stuck in these archetypal roles or patterns, we are trapped in the chrysalis because we have lost our access to the rich variety and diversity of the mythic stories that source the healing imagination. We forget that life is dynamic, not static. And what backs up is our unlived life – the butterfly wanting to take wing.

In the chrysalis experience an existing form is dismembered and dissolved in order to make way for the new form. The mythology of the ancient butterfly goddess provides a way of imagining the cosmos as an eternal round of endings and beginnings, of deaths and rebirths. It warns that the experience within the chrysalis is fraught with spiritual crises and painful emotional, psychological and physical sacrifice. The myth also tells us that there is meaning to this experience.

The human need for mythic stories and imaginative play is not simply a desire for entertainment or distraction. It is psyche's yearning for full expression. Perhaps you have identified with the hero, the princess, or some other role long enough, and other characters are clamoring for a chance to star in your myth. Or perhaps the whole script is worn out from all the wear and tear you have been giving it, and it is time to connect with another tale. The beauty of mythology is that it presents a cornucopia of endless stories to guide us through the uncharted territory between ourselves and the unlived life that is calling us. And that is a gift, for as Stephenson Bond writes in his book, *Living Myth*, "the mystery of the psyche is that we are haunted not by what we want out of life, but by what life wants out of us." (117)

References

Bond, S.D. (1993). *Living Myth: Personal Meaning as a Way of Life*. Boston & London: Shambhala.

Estes, C.P. (1992). *Women Who Run with the Wolves*. New York: Ballantine.

Feinstein, D. & Krippner, S. (1997). *The Mythic Path: Discovering the Guiding Stories of Your Past – Creating a Vision for Your Future*. New York: G.P. Putnam's Sons.

Gimbutas, M. (1989). *The Language of the Goddess*. London: Thames and Hudson.

Hillman, J. (1983). *Healing Fiction*. Barrytown, New York: Station Hill Press.

Houston, J. (1987). *The Search for the Beloved*. Los Angeles: Jeremy P. Tarcher, Inc.

Jung, C.G. (1965). *Memories, Dreams, Reflections*. New York: Vintage.

Lockhart, R.A. (1983). *Words as Eggs: Psyche in Language and Clinic*. Dallas: Spring Publications.

Moore, T. (1983). *Rituals of the Imagination*. Dallas: The Pegasus Foundation.

Neumann, E. (1990). *Amor and Psyche: The Psychic Development of the Feminine*. Princeton, NJ: Princeton.

Neumann, E. (1974). *The Great Mother: An Analysis of the Archetype*. Princeton, NJ: Princeton.

Signell, K.A. (1990). *Wisdom of the Heart: Working with Women's Dreams*. New York: Bantam.

Somé, M. & Sobonfu. (1994). *We Have no Word for Sex: An Indigenous View of Intimacy*. Oral Tradition Archives.

Van Eenwyk, J.R. (1997*). Archetypes and Strange Attractors: The Chaotic World of Symbols*. Toronto, Canada: Inner City Books.

Wolkstein, D. & Kramer, S.N. (1983*). Inanna Queen of Heaven and Earth: Her Stories and Hymns from Sumer*. New York: Harper & Row.

Woodman, M. (1985). *The Pregnant Virgin: A Process of Psychological Transformation*. Toronto, Canada: Inner City Books.

CHAPTER 12

Look Out: Three Occasions of Public Excitation

James Hillman

"How mean a thing a mere Fact is,
except as seen in the light of some
Comprehensive Truth."
S.T. Coleridge

"Vision is the art of seeing the invisible."
Jonathan Swift

The occasion today and tomorrow invites adventure. We are trying to turn psychology inside out. We are looking for the inside outside. This move attempts to deliteralize the idea of psychology as an examination of human subjective processes inside our minds, our feelings, our 'behaviors, our relationships because this idea of psychology leaves the world out there abandoned, deserted, only sociology, economics and science, quite disemboweled of soul.

Strange to realize, shameful to admit, that a whole century of psychology has been devoted to this illusion. We psychologists who believe ourselves so smart have located all the invisibles – spirits, demons, complexes, energies, syndromes, archetypes, moods, dreams, feelings and fantasies – only inside us humans. How swollen we must be to contain all these invisibles. What pretension, what anthropocentrism, what imperialism! The most ordinary indigenous person anywhere knows there is an inside out there and that invisibles inhabit things and places and creatures, and cannot be held within our human bodies.

So my companions and I are not breaking new ground so much as returning to very old ground, the ground of the planet, its life, its soul.

For my part I want to mention three writers whose thought gives impetus and direction to what I have to say. First, Norman O. Brown, who offered his method of fragments in *Closing Time* and *Love's Body*. A method I love and also find in Giambattista Vico and Heraclitus, but I have never been able to practice it. Today I shall try, here and there, to break with my own propensity to the rhetoric of narrative.

Second, Robert Jay Lifton, who sets the task: We must awaken, he says, from what he calls "psychic numbing," and which I call an-aesthesia, so as, Lifton says, borrowing from Buber, "to imagine the real." We try to imagine through and beyond the real. We call something "real" mainly because we do not recognize that beyond its familiarity, it is also fantasy. The task is to see through to the soul's intentions, and this is an aesthetic move towards essence that feels delightful, beautiful. Lifton repeats the old cry of the teacher, from Socrates and the cave to David Miller and the playful, from Krishnamurti to Freud: – what else is going on besides what you are blind to and therefore call real. In the gross is the subtle; the gross *is* subtle, *shtula* holds *suksma* in its embrace; *suksma* wraps *shtula* in its evanescent light.

A method from Nobbie Brown, a direction from Robert Lifton, and, third, a motto from Jean Paul Sartre: A Frenchman no less ... : "... essences and facts are incommensurables, and one who begins his inquiry with facts will never arrive at essences." [J.P. Sartre, *The Emotions: Outline of a Theory*, N.Y. 1948]

Furthermore, besides fragments, this inquiry shall try something else I have never ventured before: to focus on immediate actual occasions of public excitation. They are *Kosovo*, *Littleton* and the *President's impeachment for perjury*.

How active can one get! Stop, Look, and Listen! Hear the whistle blowing, cross the trestle coming. ...

So, to Kosovo:

Saddam Hussein, Khomeini, Quaddaffi, Castro, Ho Chi Minh, North Korea, – now Milosevic. We bombed, we blitzed, we invaded, we mined harbors, we blockaded, embargoed, froze assets. Gunboat diplomacy. Force. And these enemies: *They did not go away!*

The primary mistake of warfare: Underestimating the enemy. How does the American mind estimate the enemy? Facts: comparative firepower, tonnages, numbers of men under arms, vulnerability of command and control, technology. What about estimating the will to win, the stubborn capacity to endure, the importance of honor, and honor above death. What about cultural pride, national ambition? Human networking at subsistence levels versus high-tech networking? What about the sustaining strength of the enemy's history, its myths?

We seem to have no means for taking the measure of the enemy's madness except in terms of our own madness. We define power in our terms, and poverty too. (We shall come back to poverty.) We do not imagine the reality of the other as a *psychic* fact, a *psychic* force, only their material facts, their material force. There is a reasoning of the blood, of the grandfathers and ancestor spirits. There is always a desire to sacrifice life for them. There are spirits in the land living on spilled blood and always asking for more.

But we who have never fully landed, only one or two generations here, or dragged here in chains, do not understand the power of place. Nor can we understand the magma of hatred, the Furies and Titans waiting to rise at the slightest shift in the tectonic plates of ethnic proximities. We euphemize the potential volcanic fires with happy solutions: "diversity," "melting pot," "tolerance," "folk culture". ... What do we know of the passionate ecstasy of revenge? Do or die patriotism? The brutal reality of the return of the repressed?

We cannot estimate a culture of death, what strength it harbors. So we can easily deal it out, but not take it in. War without woundings. Not one death may mar our campaign. No wounded. In the victory parade down Fifth Avenue in New York after the Gulf War, veterans in wheel chairs were not allowed to take part, to be witnessed or remembered. How account for the underestimation?

First, demonizing the victim assures us of righteousness. The enemy is already slotted, labeled: Bad. Evil. War criminal. No further imagining necessary. Second, since our technical style of warfare requires no sense of the physical actuality, we can push the button and pull the lever without emotion. "Hey, No Problem." Smart bombs, dumbed people. No emotion means also no imagination. Third, we project rather than imagine. We project onto the enemy our kind of mind. Anyone in his right senses in the USA would at once realize the folly of a one-sided war that wipes out control centers, infrastructure, communications, transportation, power, utilities. ... Let alone the rising insecurity and disruption of consumption. To suffer all this merely for the idea of a remote, impoverished part of the country populated largely by non-Christians! Of course Milosevic will capitulate: we would. We project our mind's values and reasons instead of imagining their mind's values and reasons.

Our estimations are made by the impoverished American imagination of an impoverished American culture. Impoverished? Our notions of poverty are confined to the statistical economics of the poverty line: annual income, minimum wage, number of amenities like cars, fridges, TVs, computers. A poor way of seeing things. Our assessments are impoverished and so we underestimate, we under-value the power of culture because ours is under-developed.

So long as the United States cannot imagine the non-American components of the world's society, who do not believe as we do, value as we do, measure as we do, we are imaginatively incompetent, and therefore morally unjustified in policing the world. Old ostrich isolationism may serve the world better than the spread under the flag of righteous nobility of our impoverished fundamentalism of faith and fact.

Now to Littleton, to Columbine High. *Nomen est omen*: Columba = dove; columbine, a dove-like plant. The dove of peace and the holy spirit. Columbus, our "discoverer," that intrepid missionary who brought the Bible, genocide and extermination to the Carib people. Founder of our New World. What do our mentors say: Imagine the real. Search for essence. To find the essence, imagine the boys – their minds, their desires, their lives, their world.

Instead, we collect the facts and discuss practical measures of prevention. Why did the SWAT team take so long to enter, allowing one student to bleed to death? How did the boys smuggle all that equipment into the school? Smart kids: resourceful, inventive. We track the guns, the ammo: where bought, how, when; track the internet: how to make pipe bombs; reconstruct the entire incident: collect every bit of shrapnel from the pockmarked walls; lay out the timing minute by minute – map out where each person was, what they saw, heard, did. Interviews, records, photographs, lists ... interview everyone, follow every lead. Like a thick American biography of genius – all the evidence, no understanding. Like Starr's Report: know ye the facts, the whole mountain of them, and ye shall know the truth. And *blame*: the movies, TV, the parents, the gun lobby.

Another kind of facts: facts of atmosphere, of culture, of language, of architecture. In what cosmology did the boys live; what ideology fed their souls, what passion was eating at their hearts? Architecture? William Hamilton, *New York Times* May 6, 1999:

Designers of the newest American suburbs say they have largely ignored or avoided one volatile segment of the population – teenagers. ... three dozen urban planners, architects, environmental psychologists ... and experts on adolescent development agreed that community planning and places for teenagers to make their own are missing.

Architecture: that Georgia boy who, soon after Littleton, shot up his school, resided in an exurban brick fortress of a house on an acre and a half lot of a subdivision called Hanover Square (why are they never called Montezuma Heights, Senegal Bend or Bratislava Court?) "where the lawns are lush and manicured as putting greens." [David Firestone, *N.Y. Herald Tribune*, May 22/23, p. 3] Price range: two hundred thousand to half a million.

Architecture: Lawrence Diller, M.D. reports: The United States produces and uses ninety percent of the world's Ritalin. "Attention Deficit Disorder in adults is now statistically as common as severe clinical depression or drug abuse." "ADD diagnosis and Ritalin remain overwhelmingly a phenomenon of white, suburban, middle-and upper-middle-class children." "The Ritalin explosion ... a warning to society that we are not meeting the needs of our children." [*Future Survey* 21:3/116, March 1999]

Dream House in exurbia. The American Dream, the American Home: site of poverty, madness and a gun case. Children in their private rooms. Columbine High had high density classrooms. Local taxpayers had recently turned down a tax increase that would have lowered the ratio of students to teacher. Imagine the buildings of schools: the cafeterias, the food, the corridors, surveillance monitors; materials and design: Modernist Institutionalism – like a government administration block, like a clinic, like a social service center, like the blown up building in Oklahoma City.

Adolescent protest. Violent rioting of teenagers goes back three hundred years, even in East Coast Ivy League schools. *Litima*, as it is called by the Gisu people of Uganda, is a red force in the soul that teenage boys are meant to express by running wild through the village, and setting fires, doing damage. It belongs to a cosmology, and is watched over by elders. Read Michael Meade: *Litima* is "the source of the desire for initiation and of the aggression necessary to undergo radical change." [*Men and the Water of Life*, Harper, San Francisco, 1993, p. 234]

Where can they carry on today? Where is the supportive ideology, the larger cause that cries out for truth, envisions beauty and demands justice? Where is Berkeley, today? And the riders and marchers in Alabama? Where is Woodstock, and the outraged milling crowd of Chicago '68? Tiannamen

Square, a dead stop. That calamity echoes far beyond Chinese internal politics. Shoot down the youth. Imprison the youth. Fail the youth. Expel the youth. In Texas (G. W. Bush's state), one in 6 ninth graders fail to become sophomores. Cut them loose, drop them out from learning and exploit them to consume.

Search and Destroy. Fail and Expel. For any local school system to show statistics of improvement, simply constrict the sample from all children age 14 to only those in school, then, further, to only those in regular classes. Omit from the facts those in special education and those disabled who are already not in school. Remove the bottom, the top rises, looks better. Improved scores prove the educators' success. And the others? Disappeared from the facts. We have our own *desparacedos* in the United States.

Outsiders. The Littleton boys were outsiders. Some considered the Georgia boy an "outcast." Cast out of what? Outside is where art begins and revolution, sparks of new consciousness. *Litima* remains, charging the interior soul, but no place for it in the clean well-lighted place. *Litima* without social context – the lonely outsider without vision, sullen rage without beauty, despair without solace, inventive intelligence and meticulous planning focussed on a pathetic, senseless target.

Senseless? The world took notice. Whether they knew it or not, they died for their *un*reason – more than our volunteer soldiers are allowed to do for our noble reasons. In the year 1996 of a calendar we call our Lord's. In Japan, Germany, Great Britain & Canada *together* hand guns murdered 364 persons – 1 a day. In the United States, also in 1996, handguns killed 9,390 people – roughly 26 a day. Gun as ultimate hard core fact. Not just access to guns – but why do they want them so? Why are *we* so afraid of them, and *they* not?

Every year the suicide rate for American teenagers rises; every year the suicide rate for American little children rises. What percent are in prison, on probation, in juvenile court? Left back, in special ed.? The anxieties, the pressures – and for what? William Bennet would throw the *Book of Virtues* at them. I say read Michael Meade, or Shakespeare.

Shakespeare? In many expensive colleges, you can major in English and graduate without having had to read one piece of Shakespeare. In the state of Arizona, poetry is no longer on the school curriculum, anywhere. Orwell's world revived in Phoenix: poetry eliminated. Instead, a computer for every kid from first grade on, courtesy of the generous corporations. And what is poetry but fact condensed, transformed to essence; imagination seized in the act of creating itself.

Cut the arts budgets, the high school bands, pay more to the coaches;

install more technology, more armed guards, demand higher math scores. A culture of poverty.

About math – let me get started! Our national testing stresses math – not foreign language, not history, not the arts and drama. Drop-out and repeating due largely to math failures, math resistance. The student body divides between those who can do math and those who can't or won't – and the division is racist, genderist. … The math requirement fosters a large underclass of school drop-outs, a sociological, psychological, political disaster. An unreflected residue of 19th century worship of science and a carryover of models of thinking that have no bearing on the actualities of today's life or the poverty of its culture.

Yet, as we sit here, a new national curriculum and test is being devised – aimed to bring US eighth-graders in line with math levels in forty nations. Our eighth-graders placed only 27th. This won't do, won't do at all! We'll lose our competitive edge, or such is the thinking of the silent majority, read "numbed" for silent, and epitomized in the national math committee headed jointly by the Republican Governor of Wisconsin and the CEO of IBM.

Math is the "bellweather of future achievement in school," says the newspaper report. Math is "the bane of many a student," also says the report. What's in the symptom? That is the question of psychological activism: what's at the essence of this factual paradox that math is so important and math is so resisted? What is the soul of the American eighth-grader saying that is not being said by other kids elsewhere in the world? Is the math resistance a resistance to a math-based culture, whereas elsewhere, perhaps, the eighth grade soul is less impoverished, better nourished by its culture?

Why so honor math; unquestioning? What kind of thinking does math teach? Pure fact, free of value, free of ambiguity, free of psyche, either true or false, right or wrong, easy to test and easy to score, perfectly fitting our fundamentalist literalism. … Math, beyond one year of combined basic algebra and geometry, should be an elective like any other foreign language. It has been established – factually – in the State of North Carolina that students who get much music in schools do better in *all* their scores, language and math, too. Plato was right. He pushed music. Ancient Greeks played music – even before battle. Manly as guns.

Sean Altman, composer, recommends an "all out music awareness juggernaut" in the schools. "Any overheard schoolyard conversation," he says, "is evidence that nothing excites kids more than music. Musicians, even more than athletes, are the heroes of youth." [NY Times, OP ED, 6/19/99] "No student should be able to graduate without having experienced live, in-school renditions of the 11 Indispensable Post-Renaissance Compositions:" from the Brandenburg Concerto No. 5 and the Ode to Joy, to Hound Dog, Yesterday, and Free Bird.

Gresham's Law in music. The bad drives out the good. Kids deprived of an education of their musical interests and tastes and talents are left impoverished, with only commercial crapola and psychic numbing. Impoverished imagination lowers the capacity to discriminate, to tell fantasy from action, reinforcing the Christian notion that there should be no *distinction* between what we imagine in mind and what we do in action. and I say unto you everyone that looketh on a woman to lust after her hath committed adultery with her already in his heart." Matthew's report of Christ's words (5:28).

The boys made no distinction in mind between fantasy and action. Again and again the commentators piously declare we will never understand the mystery of this tragedy. No reason for it. They come up with nothing. *Nihil.* (But a kid in Georgia glimpsed something and set off to do the same.) No reason for it, but know what to do about it, say the authorities: Act with authority. Parenting as surveillance; watching over becomes watching. Counseling as inquiring. School uniforms. More curfews, more groundings, more pharmaceuticals. No more Doom and Quake on the Internet; interiorize the doom and quake. Cold War brought home. Parental spying on concealing kids.

The Rolling Stone reports the facts of kid harassment. Freak hair, piercing and tattoo, secret slang, black colors in any form: look out. Look out especially for the clever ones, the computer nerds. But doesn't the future of the economy require just these very nerds who prefer to do homework than socialize (the Georgia boy)! Weed out the exception before he kills. "... kids who already felt like outsiders are being made to feel like killers as well." [*N.Y. Times*, Carey Goldberg, May 1, 1999, p. A 11]

Is this adult retreat from imagining the real, from the poetics of tragedy, not part and parcel of the impoverished imagination that produced the boys? Denying the possibility of penetration to the essence exposes the culture's nihilism, its *absence of essence*. And the boys in the fire-light of their *litima* exposed it, exposed us, more sensitive in their desperate way to the culture than the commentators who would explain them.

What did the boys especially target? Their aim, their intention? Jocks. Compeers of color. What does this suggest to you? These are the contemporary insiders, for jocks and blacks and Latinos have a style, a culture, a language, a recognizable identity that confirms their *being*. The two boys tried to find theirs in Mafia identification, a sub-culture, and vicious yes, but one that requires honor, blood-truth, loyalty, initiation. The boys of suburban white culture were outside of *being*, searching to *be*.

Celebrity, the short cut to being. Celebrity and celebrity-cognates. A woman of Littleton said, "I always wanted this town to be famous for something – and now it is – but then I realized what I was saying." Look out, and into the other. See the void in the imagining heart of the most powerful, wealthy, technically progressed people on earth. Forget family psychology; the boys had families, lived in private houses, good ol' fourth-of-July-white-church-green lawn-small-town-USA, Littleton: *nomen est omen*.

Forget psychology of progressive development, of genetic determinism.

Read Brett Easton Ellis: *American Psycho*, the psychology text of our time and our people. Read Phillip Roth: *American Pastoral*, the case study of the good exurban father and the killer exurban daughter.

The boys as avatars of awakening from psychic numbing. In their fire-power, the power of fire. Demanding initiation, a call to the culture of no problem, have-a-nice-day, enjoy, smile. How many more horrors will it take for us to see Columbine as it has become: the dove holds a pipe bomb in its beak. Littleton a space made sacred by dead children. Their deaths as sacrifices to implacable Gods who ask for more from the white nation that occupies this originally Indian land. Shiva too is a God, and there is a God in every disease.

To look out is to look into. Activism looks to the facts; *psychological* activism inquires into essences. In the President's case, facts and essence fall apart, that is, when facts are narrowly defined. "I did not have sexual relations with that woman" – clearly denies the facts, contradicts the facts. The facts made perjury of his statement.

As at Littleton the Republicans collected the facts.

Why stop at the facts?

Essentially, he did not have sexual relations with that woman. They did not join in flesh, consummate their passion. He withheld himself; "unrelated." He may have abandoned his judgment but not his psyche. Sexual relations is a psychic phenomenon, of the soul. It is more than hanky-panky, messing around, making out, heavy petting. Sexual relations has always meant true scoring, a home run. Clinton and Lewinsky didn't get past third base.

Let me bear witness: I know analysts who have played sexually with their patients, patients who have played sexually with their analysts. They kept a barrier, a frame, by not having sexual relations. No coitus. Psychic reservation ritualized in the style of actions.

Those analysts and the President follow a more subtle tradition in keeping with Clinton's old-fashioned Southern style, one that is also common in Ireland, France and Italy, and probably in many other lands whose habits of desire I am less familiar with. There, mothers may even instruct their daughters: you may mess around genitally in all sorts of methods and procedures without losing virginity. In Ireland a hand-job, a blow-job, even anal penetration did not impugn virginity. These forms of pleasure are not sexual relations, merely genital contact.

In France there is a term for this person who enjoys sex without sexual relations: a *demi-vierge*. Statistical Fact: in 1991 a researcher of the Kinsey Institute asked 599 Indiana students whether "they considered oral sex to be sex." 59% of them did not. When this report was published in the prestigious *Journal of the American Medical Association*, its editor, George Lundberg was fired. Establishment America does not want to know even the facts.

The old definition of rape required penetration; the classic grounds for Catholic dissolution and annulment of marriage depended not upon whether there had been genital contact, but upon coitus. Coitus as consummation, not orgasm. D.H. Lawrence, as obsessively occupied with sexual complexities as anyone writing in the twentieth century, adamantly insisted that only full nude bodies conjoined constituted sexual relations. All else – partial gropings, partially unclothed, underwear (thongs) and other come-on's – is merely pornography. Did the President lie – or stick to the essence?

To Barr, Starr, Rogan, and Mr. Hyde (*nomen est omen*) Clinton lied because facts are concrete particulars: sexual means *genital*, relations means *contact*. Genital contact equals sexual relations. *Eo ipso*, perjury. Yet, the *lack* of sexual relations is just what Lewinsky whined about.

Fact: the first paragraph of Lewinsky's handwritten document submitted by her lawyer to gain for her immunity says: "Ms. Lewinsky had an intimate and emotional relationship with President Clinton beginning in 1995. ... Ms. Lewinsky and the President had physically intimate contact. This included oral sex, but excluded intercourse." [*The New Yorker*, Nov. 15, 1999, pp. 73-74.] The damning fact of the damned spot on the blue dress is concrete evidence of the lack of sexual relations. That spot is factual evidence not of Clinton's lying but of his essential truth.

Starr said "I am in pursuit of the truth." What truth? Truth as defined by fact. The prosecutors collected the facts like at Littleton: where, when, how, what, how long, how often. Dates, Times, Positions, Body Parts. Bits of Shrapnel. Their inquiry never penetrated to essentials; thus Starr's inquiry remains moralistic and prurient both. Starr, a *demi-vierge*.

Truth: which truth, whose truth? Of Hermes, of Venus, of Zeus, of Juno????? When we swear to tell the truth, the whole truth and nothing but the truth, the whole truth goes beyond the factual truth. The whole truth is full of holes; like an undersea gelatinous membrane, its edges waver. It deconstructs itself even as it fills itself out with embroideries, avoidances, and factual lies. I touched this, I did that, but I did not have sexual relations – that is the whole truth. Deep inside that bastion of the secular state, the White House, you can find a myth. Remember Virgil's tale of Dido and Aeneas? [*Aeneid*, p. 4.]

Aeneas, son of Venus, warrior king on his way from ruined Troy to found the new city and empire of Rome, paused to dally a while in Carthage, where he was received by its Queen, Dido, whose first move in her seduction was to take Aeneas' little son into her lap. Venus had transmuted this boy into Cupid, so that the connection between the lovers is via the little boy. What do we say now? Infantile sexuality, polymorphous perverse foreplay, Clinton's immaturity?

The tale of these lovers ends disastrously. After much Virgilian description of her desperate hots for him, Dido and Aeneas meet in a dark cave to consummate their passion. The meeting is all pre-arranged as a political compromise between Juno and Venus, Juno favoring Dido, Venus Aeneas, who is after all her son. So the two humans unite in the grips of their personal passions. Actually, in the grip of their respective inhuman divine protectors. For Dido it means marriage. For Aeneas it is desire in a dark cave. One among others. Venus, goddess of promiscuity.

In each other's arms, but each in his and her myth. Not sharing the same fantasy. What did Lewinsky want from Clinton further down the road? Marriage. Juno can even get at Valley girls. Then, to cut this short (which one should never do with a myth), Aeneas is called by his patron, Jupiter, via Mercury, to continue his task, set sail on his ship of state, found Rome, leaving a disconsolate Queen, as Shakespeare writes: "… stood Dido with a willow in her hand/ Upon the wild sea-banks, and waft her love/ To come again to Carthage." (*Merchant of Venice*, 1596 5.1, ll. 9-12)

Shakespeare took it lightly. Dido didn't. She remains eternally deserted, caught in hell forever, bitter, betrayed. Hope of personal relations through impersonal sex destroyed. "He didn't really love me; just used me." The typical complaint stemming from Juno's vision of Venus. Read the *Aeneid* Book IV to compare the details of emotion in the White House with those in Carthage.

This devotion to fact-finding, this faith in fact, that fact leads to truth, that those who do not bear with this truth are liars, smart-asses, perverts, even evil, is the myth that dominates our activism. The myth of facts cannot contain the psyche's propensities for more inventive modes of understanding. When the plane blew up over Long Island Sound, every bit large and small was fished from the sea and assembled in a giant hangar to establish the facts of the disaster; still there remained fantasies of a military missile having struck it, a supposed secret kept from the public and denied by officials. Somewhere there is an undiscovered essence.

Years after, perhaps forever after, the Warren Report stated the facts of the Kennedy assassination, the report confirmed and reconfirmed, yet there remains a host of other fantasies. Facts do not hold the richness of the mind's conjectures. Intelligent complexity is its meat. The myth-making psyche with its inquiring nose, its hankering after the suspect, its delight in the fantastic and beautifully absurd, its affinity with the underworld – no, the psychological mind cannot be laid at rest by facts. What is this American faith in facts? This blindness to essence? Why can't we imagine the real? Whence American literalism?

In other times there was little ability for measurement of men and material. Greeks, Romans, Persians decided political questions – even the decisive battles – by inviting the Gods to display their intentions by oracle, haruspicy, portents, and the motions of birds. Thermopylae, the victories of David, Caesar in Gaul, Agincourt (celebrated in Shakespeare's *Henry the Fifth*), Napoleon's defeat at Moscow, the defeat of the Spanish Armada, Grant held back in Virginia, Hitler at Leningrad all show in various ways that estimation by fact does not assure victory. Even more, these events show that faith in the force of facts can lead to ruin.

What lies at the psychological essence of American activism that so hates jocks and darks that it will blow them, and everyone else, away, so hates the evil criminal of Belgrade that it will take out a civilization's infrastructure, that so hates the President that it will ruthlessly, blindly, and righteously shake the foundation of the Republic?

The canker that distorts our American vision of liberalism, tolerance and justice is our Biblical literalism. One of the inspiring ancestors of this Pacifica Graduate Institute, Joseph Campbell, said: "The Bible, it's simply a bad book." And Joseph Campbell knew a thing or two about books, especially books of myth. How could he make such an offensive statement? Especially since that very book, those very Gods, are now held up as cures for our societal disorder. Bob Barr of the Judiciary Committee wants the commandments on the wall of the classrooms; prayer in schools; return to faith in the Bible as fact. Therefore, Clinton's perjury was more than legal misdemeanor. It was a sacrilege. Do we not swear on the Bible?

Joseph Campbell must have meant that the Bible tends to take itself literally and that's why it is "bad." It too often announces itself as fact, historical fact. It suffers amnesia that its tales are just that, tales, extraordinary stories, images of indelible power, truths of many sorts. But somehow, somewhere – and probably David Miller knows better than anyone among us how and when and where – that is, the facts, – these marvels collapsed, the imaginative air of fantasy squeezed out of them. No longer stories to be pondered, imagined, but facts to be believed. The spirit gone, only the words remain; the word become fact; literalism the faith; that faith, the American myth.

To put it another way from another viewpoint, that of Michael Ventura: At the end of an epoch: enantiodromia. The virtues turn into vices, vicious. Though the words retain the former virtuous intention, they become hollowed out, so that the acts coming from the words become vicious. This is not merely classical hypocrisy – far more, far deeper. It is the good intentions themselves that produce bad effects. The better the intentions, the shorter the road to hell.

At a time of enantiodromia the Devil and Christ change places. The truth-seeking Special Prosecutor and Judiciary Committee; the school authorities and good willing community in Littleton; NATO against genocide – all in the name of the good – yield destructive results. Inescapable enantiodromia.

No matter in which way we as Americans bring psychology into the public arena, our acts will be governed by our myths. All things are full of Gods, said Euripides, including our acts, and the God in our acts is the God in our disease of literalism, The Biblical God. Whatever constructive vision we aspire to must be accompanied all along by deconstruction of our own motives, our own subjectivity, our biblical righteousness. For we are each and all, willy-nilly, like it or not, children of the Biblical God. It is a fact, the essential American fact. If the Bible is fundamental to our kind of consciousness, then we must read it, learn it, know it and see through it.

Closing Time. That's all folks. No summary, no conclusion. There can be no closure since we are right in the middle of it all. No armistice resolves Kosovo; no re-opening of Columbine High ends its devastating witness to our civilization; Starr and Hyde may themselves fade, but the State is ever after cursed by those oily phantoms.

References

Altman, S. (1999, June 19). Op Ed. *The New York Times*.

Diller, L. (1999, March). *Future Survey 21*(3), 116.

Firestone, D. (1999, May 22/23). *New York Herald Tribune* p. 3.

Goldberg, C. (1999, May 1). *The New York Times*, p. A11.

Hamilton, W. (1999, May 6). *The New York Times*.

Meade, M. (1993). *Men and the Water of Life: Initiation and the Tempering of Men*. San Francisco: Harper.

The New Yorker. (1999, November 15). *The New Yorker*, pp. 73-74.

Sartre, J.P. (1948). *The Emotions: Outline of a Theory*. New York: Carol Publishing Group.

Shakespeare, W. (1596/1965). *The Merchant of Venice*. (Kenneth Myrick editor). New York: New American Library.

Virgil. (19/1961). *Aeneid* (D. Lewis, Tran.) London: Hogarth Press.

CHAPTER 13

'A Myth is as Good as a Smile!'
The Mythology of a Consumerist Culture[1]

David L. Miller

Introduction: *"Archetypal Activism"?*

The phrase "archetypal activism," under whose aegis we are gathered, has problems:
- The word "archetypal" refers to the deep self, to complexity and fundamental ambiguity, to plurality and polymorphous structures, to depth, to the fact that things have more than one side, many sides, like the many gods of mythology. The logic of the term is that of metaphor.
- The word "activism" refers to some ego or egos taking a stand, a singular stand, at least for the moment, acting in the everyday surfaces, one-sidedly, like the monotheism of the religions noted for law, for morality and for ethics. The logic of this term is literal.
- If an activism attempted to be authentically archetypal, it could not and would not act.
- If an archetypalism took a stand and acted, it would no longer be archetypal.
 Archetypal activism is an oxymoron. It doesn't refer to any physical behavior in the real world. The phrase makes no sense. It is non-sense. There is

---

[1] A different and much abbreviated version of this presentation was published by *The Salt Journal*, 2/1 (1999): 64.

no such thing as "archetypal activism." Putting the words "archetypal" and "activism" together in the same phrase is like comparing apples and Thursdays, or peanut butter and chess.

James Hillman has said that the archetypal idea of *anima mundi* compels activism. He has also written that we always behave a fantasy. It would be hard to quarrel with these points. But when we behave, what we behave, for the moment, is one of the many fantasies or archetypes of a complex life and world. When reflection on the soul of the world turns into a particular activism, it is no longer, for the moment, archetypal. It is egoic, not deep. It is not plural. It is some monolithic singularity. It is not aesthetic. It is willful. If it is called "archetypal," it only means that archetypalism has in this moment become a monolithic perspective and point of view. It then is one more dogmatism and ideology along side all the other fundamentalisms: archetypal fundamentalism. We laugh when Yogi Berra says, "If you come to a fork in the road, take it," because we know that no one can do that. One cannot simultaneously enact singularly a multiplicity. "Archetypal activism" is a laugh!

When "archetypal activism" is claimed for some behavior, it is often a rationalization, an attempt to sanctify, a defense of, one's own acting out of a particular singular ideology. It is my so-called soulfulness over against your so-called lack of soulfulness. The phrase "archetypal activism" has the same problem as the phrase "religious ethics."

To use words this way and to claim that they mean something is to act like Humpty Dumpty, who, in *Alice in Wonderland*, said that words mean "whatever I want them to, neither more nor less." But Alice knows better. She knows that language has its own force and meaning, that it plays with us, not we with it. It is well to be as sensitive to language as one is to people, because language is where people's meaning resides. Violence to and violation of language is ugly and it makes for dysfunction. It was not for nothing that Confucius called for a rectification of names in China when violence and war and immorality had erupted everywhere.

The title of this conference was chosen after I agreed to be a part of it. So now I am in the awkward position of speaking on behalf of something that I do not understand, something that I do not believe in, and something that, by my lights, in principle cannot be made understandable. Nevertheless, a promise is a promise. I agreed to speak and so I will. But what am I to do? And how am I to do it? I am committed to speak and I have nothing to say.

The situation is neither unique nor unusual. And there is an "on the other hand" to what I have so far said. One is often caught between a rock and a hard place, as between activism and archetypalism, between ego's perspective and the perspective of a deeper self. It is not for nothing that poets intentionally construct oxymorons in order to awaken sensibilities to paradoxical truths of everyday existence. Perhaps poets did not write about apples and Thursdays or peanut butter and chess, but surely they did write phrases like ...

– Loving strife
– Joyously shuddering emotions
– Thunderous silence
– Deafening silence
– Sweet sorrow
– Cruel kindness
– Laborious idleness
– Frozen flame
– Pointedly foolish (i.e., "oxy" = shape + "moron" = dull)

In *A Midsummer Night's Dream*, just before the performance of the play within the play, Theseus uses several oxymorons in a row: hot ice, tragical mirth, brief and tedious, wondrous strange snow, for example.

Voltaire called oxymoron a figure of speech with a lot of truth in it. So it may be that there is truth in the phrase "archetypal activism" precisely because of its impossible nonsense, because of its oppositionalism.

So, the question becomes: How does one respond appropriately to an oxymoron, to the juxtaposition of two oppositional truths, each of which needs to be honored, and for which there is no third position? i.e., two truths like archetypal and activism, each of which in itself is very important. How does one speak to the poetry of the idea of "archetypal activism."

In the Jewish tradition there is a way prescribed. When a rabbi, a teacher, is confronted with a question about an ultimate matter, about something that is a mystery, about a point of the Law that is puzzling, a question about the coming Messiah, the rabbi is supposed to respond according to the formulaic structure which says, "On the one hand. ... On the other hand. ..."[1] So, I will follow this old spiritual advice in these remarks.

---

[1] Milka Ventura observes, for example, that "people used to rabbinical literature are acquainted with the expression [*devar 'aher*] and know its worth as a deterrent against hermeneutic dogmatism. No interpretation can be all-encompassing. There is always another possibility, a *devar 'aher*, (a different word), a different point of view. Apparently it contradicts the previous one, but in fact it adds depth to it by shifting the perspective." ("Biblical Women Who Move Out," *Spring 63* (1998): 81)

I. On the One Hand ... The World is Godless and Mythless ... Perhaps too much so!

I begin with a picture ... two pictures, actually. Picture this:

– The location is at Bayreuth in Germany. The years were 1976 to1980. It was the Wagner festival's performance of *The Ring Cycle*. Wolfgang Wagner, grandson of the composer, appointed Pierre Boulez as conductor and Patrice Chéreau, aged 30, as director. Here's the picture. In the opening scene, the Rhine daughters were represented as three prostitutes cavorting around a hydro-electric power dam on the Rhine. Industry is the modern myth. Capitalism is the mythology. It is not a German romantic, storybook, mythic world. According to Linda Hutcheon's report on this remarkable postmodern production of the *Ring*, the audience booed. They didn't like it that people might go to the theatre and not escape reality, but escape illusion, the illusion that the myths are still alive. It gets worse in the second picture. (Hutcheon, 1994)

– The place is still Bayreuth, but now from 1988 to1992. Daniel Barenboim was conductor and Harry Kupfer, then an East German, was director. The conceit was that *Götterdämmerung*, the twilight of the gods, refers to the ruin of the world ecologically and nuclearly. Environmental disaster reigns. An utterly bare, empty stage is lit up every ten feet or so by side lights. The sets show modern ruins, twisted girders and the torn-up concrete, that is, a landscape after a nuclear bomb or meltdown or some chemical disaster. Brünnhilde's cave becomes a mine shaft. Everyone wears plastic. Wotan's eyepatch is sunglasses. The gods carry lucite suitcases and spears, and they are capitalist consumers of the first order, as are those who believe in them. This is a world without redemption, especially without redemption through the aestheticization and mythologization of Wagner's music. (Hutcheon, 1994)

The artists who invented these two stage productions of Wagner's *Ring* had intuitive sensibility. There is something right about their portrayal of the twilight of the gods and the idols. Mythic productions are irrelevant, on this view. Poets for a century have been in agreement about this. Remember Eliot's *Wasteland*. Five additional examples will make the point that Eliot's hollow men and the dive bombers in place of angels of *Four Quartets* are not isolated or idiosyncratic images:

– Yeats' *Second Coming*:

> Turning and turning in the widening gyre,
> The falcon cannot hear the falconer;
> Things fall apart, the center cannot hold;
> Mere anarchy is loosed upon the world. (Yeats, 1970, 184-85)

– Aiken's *Time in the Rock*:

> We need a theme? Then let that be our theme:
> That we, poor grovellers between faith and doubt,
> The sun and north star lost, and compass out,
> The heart's weak engine all but stopped, the time
> Timeless in this chaos of our wills –
> That we must ask a theme, something to think,
> Something to say, between dawn and dark,
> Something to hold to, something to love. (Aiken, 1936, 2)

– Arnold's *Dover Beach*:

> Listen! You hear the grating roar
> Of pebbles which the waves draw back, and fling,
> At their return, up the high strand,
> Begin, and cease, and then again begin,
> With tremulous cadence slow, and bring
> The eternal note of sadness in
>
> … … …
> The Sea of Faith
> Was once, too, at the full, and round earth's shore
> Lay like the folds of a bright girdle furl'd.
> But now I only hear
> Its melancholy, long, withdrawing roar,
> Retreating, to the breath
> Of the night-wind, down the vast edges drear
> And naked shingles of the world.
>
> … … …
> … we are here as on a darkening plain
> Swept with confused alarms of struggle and flight
> Where ignorant armies clash by night. (Arnold, 1959, 972)

– Stevens' *Loneliness in Jersey City*:

> The steeples are empty and so are the people. (Stevens, 1997, 191)

– Stevens' *A Mythology Reflects its Region*:

A mythology reflects its region. Here
In Connecticut, we never lived in a time
When mythology was possible. ... (Stevens, 1997, 476)

The mythlessness and godlessness of the world is observed also by the artists of image as well as by the artists of the word. Giorgio de Chirico, the Italian painter, wrote: "Schopenhauer and Nietzsche were the first to teach the deep significance of the senselessness of life, and to show how this senselessness could be transformed into art. ... The dreadful void they discovered is the very soulless and untroubled beauty of matter." (Jaffé, 1964, 293). Similarly, in *On the Spiritual in Art*, Kandinsky wrote: "Heaven is empty. God is dead." (Jaffé, 1964, 295) These artists find their work now to be "the search for explanation knowing that there is none," as Helen Vendler put it, writing in the *New York Review of Books* recently about the contemporary Belgrade poet, Charles Simic. Mythological consciousness from traditional times and peoples seems greatly removed from the computer and consumer culture of today.

In the early sixties, Rollo May and Joseph Campbell and I were invited more than once by radio and television in New York City to have public conversations explaining the *Time* magazine cover: God is Dead (Easter issue, 1963), as for example in a long interview-discussion on WNYC and a Sunday on NBC's "The Open Mind." The topic given us to discuss always was the same: namely, what is the "mythology" of this latter-day world? What are the "myths" of a mythless time?

In Santa Barbara, back in the early eighties, and on numerous occasions in Dallas, James Hillman said about *anima mundi* something to the effect that it will do little good to do psychoanalysis with people in the privacy of the analytic hour if they have to return to a world that is lacking in feeling and sense. The point is still the same. It will do little good to educate students in ancient myth, romantic fairy tale, religious narrative and vision, if people have to return from their lessons in the protected groves of academe to a world of mythlessness, soulessness, technicity, violence, money, warring ideology and hate ... which is indeed what is out there.

Let me quickly give four reports of our world, two by culture critics, one by a philosopher, and one by a Jungian

– Walter Rathenau, who was murdered in 1922, in Germany, had the view that mechanical production has long since overshot the elementary goals of food, clothing, self-preservation, and the protection of life. In continually expanding circles of production and consumption, it creates new desires, a measureless hunger for commodities that is increasingly directed at artificialities. Mechanical production has elevated itself to an aim in itself. Labor is no longer an activity of life, no longer an accommodation of the body and the soul to the forces of nature, but a thoroughly alien activity for the purpose of life, an accommodation of the body and the soul to the mechanism. (Sloterdijk, 1987)

– Hermann Rauschning, writing in Vienna, thirty years later, and still forty years ago observed that advertising, the media, social institutions, the state, and the military are great promisers of meaning, but in fact they are the principle agents who "broadcast unconscious nihilism behind a façade of apparent order and forced discipline." (Sloterdijk, 1987, 440) His sentiment was prophetic of our own time.

– Peter Sloterdijk, in *Critique of Cynical Reason*, describes compellingly a postmodern disenchantment with Enlightenment optimism about progress. He writes that there are "massive currents of ... antidemocratic and authoritarian ideologies that knew how effectively to organize the public sphere; an aggressive nationalism with a desire for revenge; an unenlightenable confusion of stubborn conservatisms, displaced petty bourgeois, messianic religious sects, apocalyptic political views, and equally realistic and psychopathological rejections of the demands of a disagreeable modernity." (Sloterdijk, 1987, 10) This philosopher's description is echoed by a Jungian analyst.

– Wolfgang Giegerich, in *The Soul's Logical Life*, among many other writings, (1998, 1993, 1988) has noted that the present day economy makes the industrial revolution look harmless. We face now a rationalization of industry through continuous downsizing and restructuring wherein workers become transient material, human being becomes superfluous, the pursuit of profit is the highest good, there is not individuation, but globalization, that is, the elimination of personal identity and the subjugation of everything individual under the one great abstract goal of profit maximization. Profit must increase, but I must decrease. The logic of money rules. Electronic and information technology, computer, cyberspace and internet pervades. It is not that we are at odds with certain myths, but today we have broken with the status of soul that made myths possible in the first place. Now, to talk of gods is a "glamorizing jargon." When we try to live in soul and in myth, "we live in a superterrestrial world of ideas, cocooned in irreality, and psychology does its best to help install and envelop human existence in this bubble." But this bubble bursts easily in the face of Littleton, Colorado, or Kosovo, or when the doctor announces to you that you have terminal cancer, or when your wife or husband takes a lover or is abusive. Working in and with mythology is anachronistic, atavistic, regressive. Gods are lifeless relics. They are the result of learning, not of religious or mythological experience. Giegerich is echoing Jung who saw this godlessness. Religious and mythic symbols have been squandered, he wrote; spiritual dwelling has fallen into disrepair, and we should not go in for mummeries (*Collected Works,* Vol. 9.i. § 27-31). (Giegerich, 1988-1998)

Since the waning of the middle ages, the gods have been in retreat, and so have mythologies. Already in the 14th century Chaucer's "Wife of Bath's Tale," made the point (and I am indebted to Wolfgang Giegerich for calling my attention to this text):

> When good King Arthur ruled in ancient days
> (A king that every Briton loves to praise)
> This was a land brim-full of fairy folk.
> The Elf-Queen and her courtiers joined and broke
> Their elfin dance on many a green mead,
> Or so was the opinion once, I read,
> Hundreds of years ago, in days of yore.
> But no one now sees fairies any more.
> For now the saintly charity and prayer
> Of holy friars seem to have purged the air;
> They search the countryside through field and stream
> As thick as motes that speckle a sun-beam,
> Blessing the halls, the chambers, kitchens, bowers,
> Cities and boroughs, castles, courts and towers,
> Thorpes, barns and stables, outhouses and dairies,
> And that's the reason why there are no fairies.
> Wherever there was wont to walk an elf
> Today there walks the holy friar himself
> As evening falls or when the daylight springs,
> Saying his mattins and his holy things,
> Walking his limit round from town to town.
> Women can now go safely up and down
> By every bush or under every tree;
> Here is no other incubus but he,
> So there is really no one else to hurt you

And he will do no more than take your virtue.

(Chaucer, 1981, 299)

The world is not ensouled. It is not animated, spirited. There are no fairies, goblins, little people, angels. And religion is suspect, too, if you want to hold onto your virtue!

Giegerich recalls the story of Jung meeting a chief on a visit to East Africa in the twenties. The chief told Jung that after the coming of the white man, no one dreams, and so no one knows from dreams what is going on in war, in the herds, in the weather, etc. Now one doesn't need dreams, because there is the District Commissioner. (CW 10, paragraph 128) Now there is globalization whose logic is money. We all live under the District Commissioner.

The World is Godless and Mythless ... perhaps too much so! This is on the one hand.

II. On the Other Hand ... The World is Full of Gods & Myths ... Perhaps too much so!

Forty-two years ago this nation responded forthrightly to a wake-up call in education.[1] Sputnik was the alarm. It constituted a clarion call, a mandate for scientific and technological education. In October of 1957, the first of Soviet Russia's spacecraft was launched, not only on the horizon of the planet, but also in the consciousnesses, of Americans everywhere. And America responded. For a third of a century, more than two educational generations, this nation heeded the implicit mandate of Sputnik. The United States achieved superiority and strength in science and technology, able to respond to the needs of the world and to its needs. But the times have changed.

As Carl Rowan observed not long ago, the Berlin Wall has been smashed into asbestos-bearing souvenirs. The Warsaw Pact nations have packed it up and surrendered in the Cold War. Our once-nightmarish enemy, the Soviet

---

[1] An earlier version of the paragraphs which follow were presented at the National Museum of Natural History of the Smithsonian Institution in Washington, DC, on the occasion of the inauguration of the Joseph Campbell Foundation (December 14, 1992). They were published in the Joseph Campbell Newsletter.

Union, is dismembered and in turmoil. And yet there is still much to be faced that is disturbing.

I already mentioned Kosovo, but this is only one site of ethnic cleansing, and there is not only ethnic cleansing. There is unbounded nationalism in China, and warring religious fundamentalisms in South Asian India, especially in Kashmir and Sri Lanka; Japanese/Korean tension builds in East Asia; nor need I mention South Africa, the Middle East, and Ireland. Even in Europe, there seems to be more divisiveness in the attempt to unite than before when union was unimaginable. Furthermore, there is Neonazism, not only in Germany and France, but in northern Idaho and Washington State. Perhaps even closer to home, the memory of recent right-wing warrings in Georgia (Olympic Park), Florida (Birth Control Clinic), Oklahoma (Federal Building) and continuously on the web continue to scar the imagination. It would seem that there is savage intolerance everywhere. Strange to say, a Peace Institute in Santa Barbara not so very long ago estimated that eighty percent of present ideological conflicts are motivated mythologically and religiously: it is a case of terrorism in the name of my god against your god.

It would seem that the gods are alive and very well, not to mention doing a lot of damage. There are in our world many activisms claiming to be based upon many so-called archetypes, but only one at a time, a singular one which will allow no others.

America is experiencing in these post-modem, postcold-war times a second wake-up call, a clarion call, a mandate that is at least of the magnitude of Sputnik. Nor now are science and technology what is needed, though these too are always important. Now what is crucial, crucial for the survival of our race and planet, has little to do with information and data, with sound bites or megabytes, not even with kilobytes and gigabytes. We now need to know and think through the myths that divide, and understand the mythology that unites. For myth--the stories remembered, beloved, and believed by young and old, male and female, from long ago and from yesterday, north and south, east and west--such stories (however out of date) are vessels which carry the ultimate signification of what is, at its lowest and highest, most human. Myths are not sound bites, not even megabytes of meaning, they are plots emplotting connections. Myths display narrative structure and extension, giving image and character to life, imagining ways to go on; webs of connection spun by mythic tales out of variety and difference, weaving diversity and plurality in multiple modes, a multicultural tapestry, a texture of the thousand faces of one planet, the masks of all the wonderful modulations of divine variety. Mythology gives the understanding we now so desperately need if we are to survive at the end of this millennium in order to experience richly the next one. At least, mythology can give understanding if it can be thought through.

We have no choice, for mythology there will be, with its ideology and theology and philosophy, for which many will kill. Our only choice is whether or not to educate our youth and ourselves in that which divides and separates, so that it can be also the weave whereby we begin to imagine and discover the threads which unite and connect. Mythology can be an antidote for literalism, humorlessness, overseriousness, fundamentalism, dogmatism, and hate.

It is this insight that James Hillman has been helping us with since the sixties. Again and again he has told us, not so much to look at myths, as to look mythologically. Psychologizing, or seeing through, he has been arguing, is to see one thing in terms of another. This is not only to see things in terms of myths and mythology, but to move the marbles and to remythologize all life.

Hillman has seen and has shown that mythology now, its serious study, is not an "elegant ornament," a luxury, like an earring, as a former Vice President once said in Des Moines about humanistic education. It is now an urgent necessity. Like Joseph Campbell, Hillman already knew the importance of the archetypal for an activism from which it so differs. He and Joseph Campbell knew this when Sputnik had our nation's attention.

Campbell was alluding to the holocaust when he wrote in 1959, forty years ago: "Clearly, mythology is no toy for children. Nor is it a matter of archaic, merely scholarly concern, of no moment to modern men [and women] of action. For its symbols (whether in the tangible form of images or in the abstract form of ideas) touch and release the deepest centers of motivation, moving literate and illiterate alike, moving mobs, moving civilizations ... . The world is now far too small and our stake in sanity too great for any more of those old games ... by which tribesmen were sustained against their enemies in the days when the serpent still could talk." (Campbell, 1959, 12)

Campbell and Hillman sensed the need for myth when we were responding to Sputnik with science. Their work turns out to have been that of voices crying in a developing wilderness of mean-spiritedness. Pacifica Graduate Institute is continuing their work of mythological education with felicity and grace. It is in the nick of time. People are hungering and thirsting for an understanding that mythology and its study can make possible, a rich fabric woven out of multicultural diversity, not to mention the humor, imagination, and love myth promotes. We are now called by our *postmodern* crises to education in mythology just as surely and just as crucially as the Sputnik of a *modern* time called America to education in science and technology. The world of activisms is giving us an archetypal wake up call.

The American poet, e. e. cummings, once wrote: "… a myth is as good as a smile …" (cummings, 1954, 294). Well, perhaps it really is. And if it is, in this day and age especially, we could all of us use a few more smiles. Indeed, we can ill afford less.

The world is full of mythology, People are dying of it. The world is full of gods, perhaps too much so. We had better study this if were are to survive, or smile. This is the "on the other hand."

III. Two Mythic Hands and One Real Body

What are we to do with these two hands? … the right one not knowing what the left one is about, and vice versa. The world is godless and mythless, perhaps too much so; and the world is full of gods and myths, perhaps too much so. How can these be the two hands of one body politic? What we seem to have here is two mutually exclusive and equally valid opposite standpoints.

One person has discovered how the two can be one. Eric Harris got the two hands together in his one body in Littleton, Colorado. His activism hand experienced a world without meaning, without sense, without myth or ritual. It was a world of slick suburban architecture, a slick suburban school, slick jocks and slick cheerleaders being mean to him. But his archetypal hand experienced a world of myth in internet gothic games of doom and apocalypse, and he and his friend created the ritual to go with the virtual reality of cybermyth, a ritual in the face of his world's lack of a ritual of initiation into adulthood, a ritual killing in the face of the lack of the "killing" of the child in traditional cultures' rituals of initiation. In Eric Harris, there was too little myth and too much myth, at the same time. It is no wonder that Jung wrote that the Gods now are sicknesses. Eric Harris was a living oxymoron. He was an archetypal activist. He was attempting archetypal activism, not knowing that it is poetry and not literal behavior. It is a figure of speech to give truth and vision, not a defense of whatever it is that I want to do, that some "I" wants to do.

Harris' archetypal *activism* was not *archetypal* activism because it was literal. But poetry and a poetic life is not so simple. The poetic problem with getting the two hands together can be seen in an ambiguity in the Latin motto of Pacifica Graduate Institute.

Pacifica's motto – *anima mundi colendae gratia* – does not mean what it says it means in the advertising for this conference. It does not mean "for the sake of tending the soul in the world." The word "in" is a mistake. Let me take a moment to explain this, since it is – as we have seen in Colorado – by no means a merely academic matter.

The translation "for the sake of tending," *colendae gratia*, is fine. But *anima mundi* cannot mean "soul in the world." The word *mundi* is genitive and must be translated "of the world," not "in the world." The word "in" would require the dative case, and it would imply that I possess something called soul and that the world does not, and that I am going to put some soul that is in my control into the world that I imagine to be soulless. But *mundi* is not dative in form. It is genitive.

This, however, is not quite the end of the matter. There is one more wrinkle in the language that could lead to troubled understanding. The genitive – the case used to explain the relation of one noun to another – is unstable. Usually, the genitive indicates possession, as in *libri Ciceronis*, "the books of Cicero," *Alexandri canis*, "the dog of Alexander," *potentia Pompei*, "the power of Pompey," or *perditorum temeritas*, "the recklessness of desperate people." These are all possessive genitives, sometimes called subjective. On this model, *anima mundi* means "soul of the world," and it implies that soul is possessed by the world, its soul.

But all genitives are not so straight-forward. For example, there is ambiguity in the phrase *odium Caesaris*, which means the "hate of Caesar" and could mean the hate of Caesar by other people or Caesar's own hatred of others. The latter is possessive and subjective, but the former is an objective genitive. It is like the phrase *amor patris*, "love of a father," which could mean some child's love for her or his father, or it could mean the love the father has for the children.

In spite of the possible ambiguity in the Latin of Pacifica's motto, it is easy to see that the subject matter makes things clear. There is no possibility of a parallel between the objective genitive, the love towards a father, and *anima mundi*. It is not possible to say and make sense of the phrase the soul towards the world.

This is not a scholarly quibble of grammar. Get this wrong and it changes the way one studies myth, the way one sees and lives in the world, the way that one thinks and senses and feels and intuits. It is the difference between split off or being full participant. Get it wrong and it could lead me to believe that my task is to put soul or meaning into myth and world. This is what Saint Paul called "spiritual pride." It is, in simple terms, human arrogance over against world and gods.

I am sensitive to this, perhaps too much so, since I myself made this mistake publicly in my book *The New Polytheism*. In the first edition (1974), I seemed to be suggesting that people behave (*ethos*) the patterns (*mythos*) of the stories of the gods and goddesses. For example: I had written "Activism is the work of Heracles" and "Urbanization bears the imprint of Athena" and other such things. I was roundly criticized in reviews for these literalist mistakes, and properly so. This is like writing the words "archetypal activism."

So in the "Introduction" to the next edition (1981), I tried to correct my own inconsistency. Here is what I wrote:

> Myths do not describe or prescribe actions. They do not symbolize univocal behaviors. Rather, they express articulately in ways that we often are not able, our feelings or thoughts, our consciousness or sense, concerning any behavior. Oedipus, for example, is not some particular moral or ethical activity, say, between the persons of Father, Mother, and Son. Oedipus is not something sociological at all, or at least not in the first instance. He is more psychological. He is the epiphany that comes to pass when one, anyone at all, a Father or a Mother or a Child, either Son or Daughter, interprets or feels, wittingly or unwittingly, a sense of self or relationship in terms of an intimate, family-like triangle in which love and hate figure prominently at the same time.

> The same would be true for other complexes, other figurings of the gods. Archetypal perspective makes *mythos* of *ethos*, not morality out of ancient myth. Each myth has many behavioral manifestations, and every behavior is susceptible of being felt and known in plural perspectives. We do not behave the gods; rather, their behaviors are our senses, our meanings. (Miller, 1981, 16)

This is what I said fifteen years ago. So, fifteen years ago I tried to make myself very clear about my views regarding what some might call "archetypal activism."

What I then was and also now am trying to say is that the study of myth is crucial. It gives us a way to think, a way to think about the myths of our time, the myths which are literal bombs in Kosovo, killings in Littleton, ecodisaster, plastic briefcases, cell phones during lunch, blue sun glasses when the sun is not out, and – above all – money as Giegerich says, the economy as Hillman says, or as Clinton said: It's the economy, stupid! These are the religions, the myths, the dreams that we should be studying and trying to understand. But to do this, to find the *anima mundi*, the soul of the world, in these matters, we will likely need to adjust our notion of soul, since technology, e-mail, and global capitalism are not, I suspect, what we thought soul meant.

We have to face the fact that those who are against myth, those who think our study of myth silly and irrelevant, may be more relevantly mythic than those who are for myth that is disconnected from our experience in the world. Those who are against myth are embodying the world's mythology, the soul of today's world in the proper genitive sense, the *anima mundi*. It is our work – as Pacifica's motto says – to tend them and their experiences and views.

For Eric Harris, myth was relevant to everyday life, relevant in a deadly literal way, like it was for the terrorists who blew up Pam Am 103 over Scotland with thirty-five of my undergraduate students aboard. For these people, who committed these atrocities, myth was relevant to life.

For me, on the other hand, the study of ancient myth is irrelevant to contemporary culture, which is why *I* study it, so that I may see and feel the myths of our world: the spirituality and poetics of business, global politics; the narratives and images that unconsciously inform and shape lives and cultures.

I study myth because it is irrelevant to life in the world today. I study it to try to get a clue to the mythlessness, the absurdity, the irrationality, the meaninglessness. It tells me something about what I am, because it tells me what I am not. One can study old mythologies not to learn mythology but to learn to see everything mythologically, and to learn a different way of thinking, a mythopoetic way, a different insighting of the present world.

The world is archetypally activist. We can learn from it where and what the soul of the soulless world is. The world thus gives us who study myths the agenda. We don't give it our agenda from the good old days or from the pie in the sky wish fulfilled future.

It is easy to study the myth of myth, fairy tale, and literature. Anyone can do that, if the effort were worth it. But it is difficult to study the myths of mythlessness, the myths of world. It is easy to pit soul against world; it is hard work, difficult, to find the soul of the world, the soul of money, consumerism, capitalist exploitation, global relativism, violence in schools, rape warfare, ethnic cleansing, military solutions, classism, sexism, racism, hate, drug rape, binge drinking, all the craziness and pathology. On the one hand, world is without soul. On the other hand, I wonder what is the soul of being without soul,

Some people seem to study myths and the world by bringing their so-called soul with them and laying it on the world, like a trip, like a warm fuzzy Linus blanket, a pair of rosy glasses, like a sugar coating for a bitter pill. Then they think that they have found soul in the world. But that's not it. That's fake soul and fake world. Real *soul* of the world is the soul of the *world*.

Conclusion

It is like Picasso's *Guernica*, a portion of which appears on the advertising brochure for this conference. Guernica was a village in northern Spain which was victim to the first instance of saturation bombing. It was a case of Germany and Italy helping a fascist Spain defeat a loyalist government that was leftist. The bull is a symbol of fascism and the naked light bulb indicates that god is dead and that the only light now comes from naked technology and science The theologian, Paul Tillich, referred to Picasso's painting as the most religious art-work of our time. He might also have said most mytholog-ical. Tillich wrote about this painting saying that it depicts "pieces of reality, people, and animals in a way so as to make the piece-character of our reality most horribly visible." (Tillich, 1956, 138) The painting is a piece of soul because it shows the soul of pieces ... soulfully.

My work is to study old dead myths in relation to our live world, which is also dead. My worry is that when gods go away, they don't really leave. My wager is that they go underground, and return as demons. Mythology then is like a computer program running in the background, like an antivirus program, except in the case of mythology the program may be the disease rather than the cure. However, like an antivirus program, unconscious mythology only surfaces when something is wrong. It is the return of the repressed, as Freud said, or gods casting shadows, as Rilke said. *Von den Göttern ein Schatten fällt.* (Rilke, 1942, 28) Heidegger referred to this as "traces, of the gods," *die Spuren.* (Heidegger, 1972, 250) *Éperons,* wrote Derrida, "traces," when speaking of Nietzsche's madman declaring the death of myth. (Derrida, 1979) One important work today is to track the traces of the gods who have gone, tracing those tracks in the here and now. As the poet, A. R. Ammons, put it:

... the gods from the high wide
potentials of aura, of encompassing nothingness, flash into
concentration and descend, taking on matter and shape, color,
until they walk with us, but divine, having drawn down with them
the reservoirs of the skies: in time the restlessness that is in
them, the overinvestment, casts the shells of earth to remain with
earth, and the real force of the gods returns to its heights
where it dwells, its everlasting home: these are the mechanics
by which such matters carry out their awesome transactions:
if the gods have gone away, only the foolish think them gone
for good: only certain temporal guises have been shaken
away from their confinements among us: they will return, quick
appearances in the material, and shine our eyes blind with adoration
and astonish us with fear: the mechanics of this have to do with
the way our minds work, the concrete, the overinvested concrete,
the symbol, the seedless radiance, the giving up into meaninglessness
and the return of meaning: but the gods have come and gone
(or we have made them come and go) so long among us that
they have communicated something of the sky to us ... .

(Ammons, 1974, 48)

The gods may well have communicated something of the sky to us, but they also still astonish us with fear, not only for the damage that they do in Kosovo and Colorado, but also for the havoc they wreck in a person's heart and soul. It is because I am afraid of the lively dead gods that I study and teach mythology at Pacifica Graduate Institute. I do it because I have two hands and not one.

References

Aiken, C. (1936). *Time in the Rock*. New York: Scribners.
Ammons, A.R. (1974). *Sphere: The Form of a Motion*. New York: Norton.
Arnold, M. (1959). Dover Beach. In R. Aldington (Ed.), *The Viking Book of Poetry of the English Speaking World* (Vol. Two) (p. 972). New York: The Viking Press.
Campbell, J. (1959). *Masks of God: Primitive Mythology*. New York: Viking Press.
cummings, e.e. (1954). *Poems 1923-1954*. New York: Harcourt Brace and Company.
Derrida, J. (1979). *Spurs: Nietzsche's Styles*. Chicago: University of Chicago Press.
Giegerich, W. (1988). Effort? Yes, Effort! *Spring*, 184.
Giegerich, W. (1993). Killings. *Spring 54*, 6, 12-14.

Giegerich, W. (1996). The Opposition of 'Individuation' and 'Collective' – Psychology's Basic Fault. *Harvest: Journal for Jungian Studies, 42*(2), 7-27.

Giegerich, W. (1998). *The Soul's Logical Life: Toward a Rigorous Notion of Psychology.* Frankfurt: Peter Lang.

Heidegger, M. (1972). *Holzwege.* Frankfurt: Vittorio Klostermann.

Hutcheon, L. (1994). *Irony's Edge.* New York: Routledge.

Jaffé, A. (1964). Symbolism in the Visual Arts. In C.G. Jung (Ed.), *Man and His Symbols* (pp. 230-271). Garden City, NY: Doubleday.

Jung, C. G. (1957-1978). *The Collected Works of C.G. Jung* (Vol. 10). Princeton, NJ: Princeton University Press.

Miller, D. (1981). *The New Polytheism.* Dallas: Spring Publications.

Rilke, R.M. (1942). *Sonnets to Orpheus* (M. D. Herter Norton, Trans.). New York: Norton and Co.

Sloterdijk, P. (1987). *Critique of Cynical Reason.* Minneapolis: University of Minnesota Press.

Stevens, W. (1997). Loneliness in Jersey City. In *Collected Poetry and Prose* (p. 191). New York: Library of America.

Stevens, W. (1997). A Mythology Reflects its Region. In *Collected poetry and prose* (p. 476). New York: Library of America.

Tillich, P. (1956). Existentialist Aspects of Modern Art. In C. Michalson (Ed.), *Christianity and the Existentialists.* New York: Scribners.

Yeats, W.B. (1970). The Second Coming. In *The Collected Poems of W.B. Yeats* (pp. 184-185). New York: Macmillan Co.

CHAPTER 14

Yes, Indeed! Do Call the World

The Vale of Soul Making:

Reveries Toward an Archetypal Presence[1]

Robert Romanyshyn

[1] The title of this paper is an affirmation of the vision of the poet John Keats. In a letter to the George Keatses dated April 21, 1819, he says "Call the world if you please 'The Vale of Soul-Making,'" and then adds that "Then you will find out the use of the world" (1988, p. 549). This paper affirms that vision because it argues that the task of an archetypal activism is to open the aesthetic depths of the world, not by becoming politically active but by being a witness, as is the poet, for what is otherwise marginalized by the collective follies of the age. These aesthetic depths are the occasions where the timely and the timeless meet. Evoking these depths, we find the true use of the world, which is to be distinguished, I believe, from the mind's preoccupation with how the world – and ourselves – is, or might be, useful. The true use of the world is its purpose, and our task as depth psychologists is to be attentive to how the world addresses us, attentive to what it wants of us. I find this same appeal in a poet like Rilke, a theme which is developed in the body of this paper. I find it too in artists like Cézanne and Van Gogh. They open these aesthetic depths of the world, the ways in which the world wants to see itself, become itself, continue its creation. In this regard, would we dare ask if Van Gogh's "Starry Night," for example, is useful. It would be an absurd question, which would not only miss the point of the task of the artists, but would also imprison this work within categories which destroy its soul. Depth psychology is particularly prone to this temptation when it seeks to become useful.

The original paper was accompanied by a video presentation with music and voice over narration. To arrange for a showing of this production piece the author can be contacted at *Romany@pacifica.edu*

"They also serve who only stand and wait"[1]

"... and what are poets for in a destitute time?" This question is posed by the nineteenth century poet Hölderlin in his elegy "Bread and Wine." Considering it, Martin Heidegger, perhaps the single most important philosopher of our century, says: "We hardly understand the question today." That assessment seems quite right to me. We live, Heidegger says, "In the age of the world's night, {when} the abyss of the world must be experienced and endured." (1975, pp. 91-92)

If you are fond of words, as a depth psychologist must be, if you love words and hear within them the ancient songs and rhythms of the soul, then abyss cannot fail to attract your attention. It is the place of the deep, the bottomless pit of the sea. The abyss – *bathus* – is about depth and the word is kin to grief – *penthos* – and passion and suffering – *pathos*. Within this constellation, where words are like the stars of the soul, the abyss is the depth to which we are led by the suffering of grief over loss. If the poet has something to do with calling us to attend to the abyss, then the poet in this capacity has something to do with calling us to experience and endure the deep, stirring waters of grief and suffering.

But what have we lost and why should we need to be called to the abyss and to attend to this place of grief and suffering? In *The Soul in Grief: Love,*

---

[1] The quote is the last line of Milton's sonnet "On His Blindness." (1998, p. 84, l. 14). Although I had initially misremembered the source, my inquiries about it have proven quite fruitful. The quote, which arose from some unconscious layers of the psyche, is a fitting one for this article for three reasons. First, blindness is a kind of abyss, and the major theme of this paper is what is asked of us at the abyss. Second, Milton's response is entirely in keeping with the reply to this question offered in this article. At the abyss, we are asked to be a witness, and it is this posture which defines for me the character of an archetypal activism. Archetypal activism is not about doing. It is about a way of being, a style of presence, the presence of the witness. The witness is one who also serves by standing and waiting. For additional comments on the witness see "On Angels and other Anomalies of the Imaginal Life" (Romanyshyn, in press). Third, after his blindness, Milton dictated to his (reluctant?) daughters "Paradise Lost." It seems most fitting to me that it is this epic work which arose from the depths of his blindness. Another theme of this paper is that loss is the spur of the soul's awakening, the moment when, beyond the concerns of ego, one is called to be a witness for what has been lost, marginalized, or otherwise neglected individually and collectively. For a more detailed treatment of this issue, the reader is referred to The Soul in Grief: Love, Death and Transformation (Romanyshyn, 1999). I want to thank Prof. Glenn Arbrey of The Dallas Institute for Humanities and Culture for his help with this citation, and for the historical background which he provided concerning this sonnet.

Death and Transformation (1999), I described how personal loss can be an opening to a larger, shared, collective sense of loss where we encounter the archetypal figure of the Orphan. In this encounter we come face to face with our deep sense of homelessness, and we discover within ourselves the gnawing hunger which we have for a lost sense of the Divine, and for the lost sense of the sacred in the ordinary. Grief is in this respect a homecoming, and this journey toward home begins, and can begin, only at the abyss, at that place where all the props of ego consciousness have fallen away and we stand naked and alone in an alien world under a darkened, winter sky.

But is not the abyss all around us on a daily basis? Do we not everyday see stories of suffering and violence, of war and deprivation? What is this strange indifference that we so often adopt in the face of these countless tragedies? Have we become so numbed to suffering and loss, and so familiar with the absence of the Divine in our world, that only some deeply moving personal loss can awaken us to the dismal fact that we are blind men and women stumbling in the darkness of the world's last nights toward oblivion?

Something seems terribly awry about the times in which we are living. The evidence of the abyss is visible, but the response that we give to it seems dangerously flawed. Do we need to be called to the abyss because we have lost our capacity to grieve? Have we forgotten how to feel and be touched by the world's suffering? Heidegger tells us that the abyss is the complete absence of the ground which frames us as mortal beings and gives us our place within the scheme of creation. Have we, in spite of all our intelligence and magnificent achievements, forgotten our place, forgotten who we are, where we come from, what we are *here* for? There are moments when I think that we need a planetary day of mourning. There are moments when I believe that the experience of grief at the abyss, and our willingness to endure it, is a necessary one if we are to return to our senses. There are moments when I dream that at the abyss our human tears of grief are mirrored in the face of a pathetic God who weeps for us.[1]

Breathing at the Abyss: Language and the Soul of the World

But what does it mean to return to our senses? In the face of this question, I now trust only the poets. Neither the politicians nor the psychologists – with rare and wonderful exceptions – neither the theologians nor the philosophers – again with rare and wonderful exceptions – linger at the abyss. Only the poet does, and only the poet who begins to see only when night comes, who begins his work as Rumi says, "When merchants eat their big meals and sleep/ their dead sleep, we night-thieves go to work." (1994, p. 40) Rilke is such a poet, a night-thief, a poet for a destitute time. At the abyss he wonders:

> Are we, perhaps, here just for saying: House,
> Bridge, Fountain, Gate, Jug, Olive tree, Window, –
> possibly: Pillar, Tower? (1939, p. 75, ll. 32-34)

Imagine that! Are we here for speaking the words of the world, here for the sake of being its witness, for being, perhaps, possibly on occasion, its voice? When we speak are we speaking up for the things of the world, giving voice to their desires, breathing with them in a con-spiracy of dreams? Is this our vocation, which we have lost, and for which we silently grieve, as do the things of the world?

Gaston Bachelard, the great French master of reverie, says that poetry helps one breathe better (1969, p. 50). This claim is not just extravagant nonsense, a mere aesthetic diversion. Something of great value is present in these words, something we have lost, something we no longer remember of ourselves and about our place within the order of creation. Breath is life; it is soul, the anima mundi. When we breathe we exchange ourselves with the world around us. On the in-breath, in the moment of inspiration, we not only take in the world, we are also nourished by it, in-spired by it. And then at the pause, so slight and so subtle, in that briefest of moments before the ex-piration, when we give back to the world what it has just given to us, an alchemy occurs. Sound becomes word, rhythm becomes song, and the world blossoms into a new kind of beauty. On a bit of moving air, on this so fragile,

---

[1] This notion of a pathetic God, a god of compassion who out of deep loneliness empties himself into creation, is movingly described in *Alone with the Alone: Creative Imagination in the Sufism of Ibn' Arabi*. (Corbin, 1969) I cite this work because it is a pathetic God whom we meet at the abyss, and not the almighty God of power. Indeed, this latter God is, I believe, the one who authors the abyss, who is responsible for our abysmal moments. It is this God image, working itself out in the psyche, which is responsible for the "slaughter of the innocents" portrayed in the video portion of this paper. At the abyss we are called to be compassionate. "To become a Compassionate One is to become the likeness of the Compassionate God experiencing infinite sadness over undisclosed virtualities ..." (p. 118) One of these undisclosed virtualities is our participation in the divine, a remembrance of our spiritual heritage. In the face of suffering we find the compassion which can move us to tears, and in the tears of ourselves and the other we find a mutual mirroring of the Compassionate One who dwells between, around, and amongst us. But why must such moments depend so often on being at the abyss?

slender, invisible thread depends the continuing act of creation. Rilke says it this way:

> For the wanderer doesn't bring from the mountain slope
> a handful of earth to the valley, untellable earth, but only
> some word he has won, a pure word, the yellow and blue
> gentian. (1939, p. 75, ll. 29-32)

For Rilke, this work of giving voice to the world is heartwork. It is a descent into the depths, a move from the visible to the invisible, to that subtle realm of the imaginal which halos the visible. In these depths a reversal takes place, and we realize that we are called into speaking the world, that we are in-spired to be who we are by something other than ourselves, that we are made by the world, that the world truly does breathe its life into us, as it happened so long ago, at the beginning of time, when the breath of the Divine was breathed into mortal clay. Is it not curious, then, that it is at the abyss that we recognize that human life is truly a vocation and that the task of a human life is to be responsive to a destiny which calls one to be in service to the world? In a moment like this, we might even realize that we owe our very being to something which, as wholly other, often beckons as holy and divine.

We are drawn to the abyss when we no longer experience the presence of the Divine in the world. At the abyss, in the depths of grief and suffering, we meet the gods who have taken flight from the world. Mark Strand, a contemporary poet, captures something of the melancholy mood which attends the moment when we realize this hunger in ourselves to be called and addressed by an Otherness which is more than ourselves. In a poem entitled "The Night, The Porch," he writes:

> To stare at nothing is to learn by heart
> What all of us will be swept into, and baring oneself
> To the wind is feeling the ungraspable somewhere close by.
> Trees can sway or be still. Day or night can be what they wish.
> What we desire, more than season or weather is the comfort
> Of being strangers, at least to ourselves. This is the crux
> Of the matter, which is why even now we seem to be waiting
> For something whose appearance would be its vanishing –
> The sound, say, of a few leaves falling, or just one leaf,
> Or less. There is no end to what we can learn. The book out there
> Tells us as much, and was never written with us in mind. (2000, p. 10)

The book out there was never written with us in mind! A simple sentence, and yet one which has the power to disrupt our ordinary ways of thinking and being. In spite of what we might wish to think or believe, the sun does not shine for us, nor do the stars glow in the midnight sky with us in mind. With this reversal do we not become, at least for a moment, strangers to ourselves, and, indeed, is this not what we desire – more than season or weather, what we desire is the comfort of being strangers, at least to ourselves.

To be strangers to ourselves! Why should this be? Why do we long for this? Perhaps this emptying out of ourselves is the necessary first step to becoming available to the Divine which calls us, a first step in becoming open to something as simple as the sound of just one leaf falling, or even something less than that. In emptiness something so simple can feel like a blessing, and can betray within itself some hint of the sacred. Once, at the abyss, in the depths of the winter time of mourning, I saw a spider's web haloed by the bright light of the full moon, and I knew that spiders' webs are silver stars woven on the earth.

There is a sense of great weariness in Strand's poem, as if he is giving voice to some ancient, tired place in the soul which has been too burdened by consciousness. Have we finally reached a point where we can admit that we are exhausted by what we know, by the ever increasing on-slaught of information, by our theories and systems of knowledge, which now too often seem bankrupt and too thin to water the soul? In a few simple lines the poet e.e. cummings gives us a memorable image of our deep hunger to be nourished by something more than what we know. He writes:

> since feeling is first
> who pays any attention
> to the syntax of things
> will never wholly kiss you; (1926, p. 35)

Beyond meaning we long for presence. Beyond knowledge we long for something more direct and immediate with the world, for something as intimate as a kiss. When I look at Van Gogh's "Starry Night" I know that he was kissed by the stars. And then I return to the poets, to Cummings again, and say "Yes!" to these words:

> While you and i have lips and voices which
> are for kissing and to sing with
> who cares if some one-eyed son of a bitch
> invents an instrument to measure Spring with?

since the thing perhaps is
to eat flowers and not be afraid. (1926, p. 29-30)

With the help of the poets, I am suggesting that an archetypal activism must start with a way of being present. Such presence is an enantiodromia, a reversal of direction, a turn from doing first to being. This reversal is a humiliation of our consciousness, a humbling of our minds which returns mind to nature, which soaks mind in the humus of the anima mundi, the world soul.

This turn about is an abysmal moment, a moment when we are brought to the edge and reminded of our hubris. It is a painful moment and one which more often than not invites grief for what we experience as absent in our lives. The danger in such a moment is that we will become busy and active in an effort to fill that absence, that we will substitute in the place of grief an activity born of fear. Already early in this century, Rilke knew this temptation and called for a change in direction:

Here is the time for the Tellable, *here* is its home
Speak and proclaim. More than ever
the things we can live with are falling away, and their place
being oustingly taken up by an imageless act. (1939, p. 75, ll. 43-46)

This world calls for our participation, and now more than ever, Rilke says, because we are in increasing danger of losing touch with it by acting in an imageless way. We are stuffed with our ideas about the world, and overloaded with facts about it. But we are poor when it comes to the images which dress our actions and engage us in the world, those images which bubble up from the depths of the soul and animate our encounters with the world, so that even something as simple as the arc of a leaf as it floats in the wind can inspire a sense of simple beauty. Something in us longs to be touched again by these simple aesthetic moments of the world's epiphany, longs to sense the world before we make sense of it. Something in us longs to be awakened from our anesthetic sleep.

The Call of Beauty

So "… what are poets for in a destitute time?" The great Russian novelist, Dostoevsky, once said that beauty will save the world. Hearing this claim, we should not think of beauty as what is merely pretty or handsome; we should not debase this claim by imagining beauty in terms of our modern impover-ished vocabularies, which would equate, for example, the beautiful with the beauty pageant. Such a reduction would forget what Rilke cautions us to remember about beauty, that it is "nothing/but beginning of Terror we're still just able to bear ..." And if this coupling of Beauty and Terror, which silences us into a state of awe-ful contemplation – not unlike the figures of old experienced when they met an Angel – should not be enough, then Rilke adds in the next line: "and why we adore it so is because it serenely/ disdains to destroy us." (1939, p. 21, ll. 4-7)

Poet and novelist are telling us that Beauty is not our creation, that Beauty is the radiance of the world's holy darkness, a wonderful phrase which I borrow from my good friend Charles Asher. Beauty is an archetypal experience, and hence one which overwhelms us in the moment. So, if we ask again what are poets for in a destitute time, then we might say that they are here for the sake of Beauty.

It is a wonder to me that it is at the abyss that we meet Beauty, at the turning points of the soul, in the depths of passion, suffering and sorrow. It is a wonder to me that Beauty can blossom from grief, as can love. It is as if only the storms of some powerful, tumultuous feeling can shake us from sleep and awaken us to the world's invisible Beauty. It is as if we need earthquakes of the soul, moments of love and loss, to rouse us from some ancient slumber.

Plato, in one of his most enticing fables, (1989, p. 844) provides a context for why this moment of Beauty and its Terrors must be an abysmal moment, must carry an archetypal power, a numinous charm. The soul, he tells us, drinks from the forgetful waters of Lethe, as it approaches this life. We are, as it were, born to forget. And yet, for some, for the poets for example, a dim remembrance of that other place remains. So Wordsworth, paraphrasing Plotinus, says,

> Our birth is but a sleep and a forgetting:
> The Soul that rises with us, our life's Star,
> Hath had elsewhere its setting,
> And cometh from afar:
> Not in entire forgetfulness,
> And not in utter nakedness,
> But trailing clouds of glory do we come
> From God, who is our home:
> Heaven lies about us in our infancy! (1994, pp. 139-145, ll 57-65)

For Plato, Beauty is the first moment of *an-amnesis,* of waking from forgetfulness, the first way in which we recover the sense of who we are, where we come from, and what we are here for. Kathleen Raine, a poet herself, and the world's foremost authority on William Blake, captures this power of beauty and our need for it in our lives, in her classic essay, "The Use of the Beautiful." She writes:

> We are haunted by the presence of an inaccessible
> knowledge, and by a sense of estrangement from some
> place or state native to us; the paradise of all
> mythologies, once and forever known, but lost. Of this
> Paradise all are native, for it lies within ourselves,
> forgotten or half forgotten. (1967, p. 171)

Musing upon the beauty of a Botticelli face, Kathleen Raine adds that to experience such beauty is a "homecoming." But again the caution, the warning, which is always there: "though the way from this world to that is long and we may well fear the journey."

The poet in a destitute time leads us to the abyss, and there we join hands with Beauty and all its Terrors. In its presence we are transformed through grief over the loss of our birthright as creatures, all of us, who belong to that holy darkness of creation. We are awakened to the mysterious depths which haunt each moment of experience, and begin a journey to that other place where, as Keats noted, "Beauty is truth, truth Beauty." (1988, p. 344-346)

The Rose Which In Its Blooming, Already Begins To Fade

What is the Truth of Beauty at the abyss? It is the realization of the transience of all that we love and experience. Beauty belongs to the figure of Death; it is, if you will, Death's Bride. The poet John Keats expresses this companionship poignantly as a lament in his "Ode to a Nightingale." Hearing the song of this bird, he is led to contemplate the sorrowful difference between its beauty and our own feeble condition:

> Fade far away, dissolve, and quite forget
> What thou among the leaves hast never known,
> The weariness, the fever, and the fret
> Here, where men sit and hear each other groan;
> Where palsy shakes a few, sad, last, gray hairs,

Where youth grows pale, and specter-thin and dies;
Where but to think is to be full of sorrow
And leadened eyed despairs,
Where Beauty cannot keep her lustrous eyes,
Or new love pine at them beyond tomorrow.
(1988, pp. 346-348, ll. 21-30)

We grow old, we grow sick, and we die, and it is a moment like this one, a moment when one hears the simple and passing beauty of a bird's song, that we are most awakened to our condition. And in such a moment, what are we called to do? The poet at the abyss says, "Do nothing!" Only experience and endure the moment, and in this learn to love the beauty of the world in its passing. Thinking of Orpheus, that great poet whose words were so powerful and moving that they persuaded the gods and goddesses of the underworld to release his beloved Eurydice from death, Rilke asks what monument should we raise to the poet. No monument, he says. Let it be only the Rose which in its blooming already begins to fade. No monumental action, no heroic activity – only the simple witnessing of this simple presence, and one which remembers that Orpheus failed.

The poet is the true activist who dares to whisper that there is nothing to do, that there is nothing we should do. He or she is the true revolutionary, the true philosopher who inverts the relation of knowledge and being, of the mind's meaning and the soul's presence. In this respect, the poet is the one who awakens our aesthetic sense-abilities, the one who teaches us to feel again. Aesthetic in its root sense means "to sense", "to feel", and particularly to sense in the sense of hearing. Hearing, moreover, is kin to the word "obey". What the poet asks of us, then, is that in a destitute time we hear and obey the calls of Beauty and its Terrors, that at the abyss we feel again the depths of each moment, of each encounter, that we dare to love, even in the face of loss, all that appeals to us and makes its claim upon us.

An archetypal presence begins in this place of being touched and moved by the holy darkness of the Divine in all its beauty and its terror. It begins as a way of being, and not a way of doing. It is a way of being which is responsive to the aesthetic, that is the felt and experienced demands of the other. It is about responding to the call of the other, in whom the Divine shines through, about responding because we have first listened, about being response-able, able-to-respond, because we have heard. Being first about who one is before being about what one does, archetypal activism is about character. It is about courage too, the courage not only to feel the pains of loss and grief, the sorrows of the world's dark night, but also the courage to stand at the abyss as a witness, not a judge, for what asks to be seen and spoken. Archetypal activism is the natural ethics of the soul.

At the abyss, the poet is the one who challenges us to stop for a moment, and to take stock of who we are before we act or do, to experience and endure in the experience, to stand at the edge of the abyss and all its horrors and wait. To wait even without hope, for hope would be hope for the wrong thing, as T.S. Eliot cautions. But to endure the waiting, which perhaps is made only a little more bearable by these words of another poet, John Milton who says: "They also serve who only stand and wait." (1998, p. 84, l. 14)

References

Bachelard, G. (1969). *The Poetics of Reverie* (D. Russell, Trans.). New York: The Orion Press.

Corbin, H. (1997). *Alone with the Alone: Creative Imagination in the Sufism of Ibn' Arabi*. Princeton: Princeton University Press, Bollingen Series XCI.

cummings, e.e. (1926). *100 Selected Poems*. New York: Grove Press.

Heidegger, M. (1971). *Poetry, Language, Thought* (A. Hofstadter, Trans.). New York: Harper & Row.

Keats, J. (1988). Ode on a Grecian Urn. In J. Barnard (Ed.), *John Keats: The Complete Poems*. New York: Penguin Books.

Milton, J. (1998). Sonnet XVI. In J. Leonard (Ed.), *John Milton: The Complete Poems*. New York: Penguin Books.

Plato. (1989). The Republic. In E. Hamilton and H. Cairns (Eds.), *Plato: The Collected Dialogues*. Princeton: Princeton University Press, Bollingen Series LXXI.

Raine, K. (1985). The Use of the Beautiful. In *Defending Ancient Springs*. West Stockbridge, MA: The Lindisfarne Press.

Rilke, R. M. (1939). *Duino Elegies* (J.B. Leishman & S. Spender, Trans.). New York: W.W. Norton and Company.

Romanyshyn, R. (in press). On Angels and Other Anomalies of the Imaginal Life. In K. Raine (Ed.), *The Temenos Academy Review*. Ipswich: Golgonooza Press.

Romanyshyn, R. (1999). *The Soul in Grief: Love, Death and Transformation*. Berkeley: North Atlantic Books.

Rumi. (1994). *Say I am You* (J. Moyne and C. Barks, Trans.). Athens, Ga.: Maypop.

Strand, M. (2000). The Night, the Porch. In *Blizzard of One*. New York: Alfred A. Knopf.

Wordsworth, W. (1994). Ode: Intimations of Immortality from Recollections of Early Childhood. In J.O. Hayden (Ed.), *William Wordsworth: Selected poems*. New York: Penguin Books.

CHAPTER 15

Seeding Liberation

A Dialogue Between Depth Psychology

and Liberation Psychology

Mary Watkins

Depth Psychology and the Liberation of Being

Over the past thirty years since my initial love affair with depth psychology – particularly Jungian and archetypal psychology – I have periodically wondered about what it was that so seduced and intrigued me. Was it its acceptance and valuing of inbreaks of the imaginal, of depression, of pathologized images and experiences, all of which frightened me as a young woman? Was it the impassioned deconstructing of cultural and psychological ideas beneath this acceptance that appealed to my fierce desire to see beneath the taken-for-granted? More recently I have thought that this long marriage between myself and depth psychology has been possible because I found in depth psychology a basic orientation to being that seeks to allow *what is* to be present in its animation and its difference. It is a desire for the liberation of being.[1]

---

[1] This paper is half of a longer presentation given at a Pacifica Graduate Institute conference, Mythologies of Soul, Spring 1997. The other half, previously published, traces the effort toward liberation in the methods of Freud, Jung, Reich, Winnicott, and existential-phenomenology (see Watkins, 2000).

In depth psychology our habitual point of view, the "ego," is held suspect, and seen as partial and prejudiced. The various methods of depth psychology – Freud's free association, Jung's active imagination, Reich's body work, Winnicott's play, dream work, working the transference – attempt to have us listen into the margins of our experience for thoughts, images, and bodily knowings that hold alternative perspectives and insights. The stance is one of listening and humility, a practiced vulnerability to being wounded, questioned, brought up short. Such listening allows the diversity of psyche's voices to come into audible range. There are various rewards for this intentional bracketing of the Western ego's desire to control, dominate, define. For one, there is a simple relief in dropping the pretense of being in control, when, in truth, we are not. In addition, when the ego opens its straitjacket, the realms of imagination, nature, and other people regain their animation. Differences and peculiarities become immensely interesting, rather than nuisances or threats to be avoided.

Van den Berg (1971) argues that the historical emergence of a strong, bounded, masterful ego constellated the co-emergence of what in depth psychology is called the dynamic unconscious. The logical rationality of the ego pushed emotion, intuition, and image into the shadows of the margin. The "discovery of the unconscious," which characterizes the modern birth of depth psychology, is a radical commentary on the partialness of Western culture's ordinary ego viewpoint. This discovery calls us out of an identification with ego consciousness and into dialogue with what has been pushed to the margins of our awareness. Through such hosting and dialogue, we become more aware of the diversity and multiplicity that characterize psyche. Unconsciousness is understood to be created by the repression and oppression of this diversity. An ego which cleaves to its own point of view – without seeing it as such – is contrasted with what Jung called "a non-ego centre" that can acknowledge multiplicity and be deepened and tempered by relation to it.

In a similar vein, Fromm (1976) argued that the rise of capitalism and industrialism created a cultural shift from an emphasis on being to having. Such a transition entailed a further strengthening of the colonizing ego, its desires for control and mastery, and its silencing of the voices of those it marginalized. This strengthening was won by disassociating from the broader base of psyche, body, nature, community, and the spiritual, until the autonomy of the ego became seen as a goal. Movements of mind that support such an ego involve copious comparisons between self and other, meticulous monitoring of issues of sufficiency, inferiority and superiority, a heightened critical and judgmental capacity, scrupulous maintenance of power, control and autonomy. They also lend themselves to depressive, narcissistic, and obsessive-compulsive states of being. Fromm imagined the cultural unconscious (1960) as including all that one's culture excluded in its ways of perceiving, understanding, and acting. For Fromm, making the cultural unconscious conscious entailed a radical process of being able to see how one's identity is created by identifications with cultural norms, and to actively question these – indeed, a liberatory process. What are the processes by which this can be accomplished? How does such a project effect our views of selfhood, development, psychopathology, and healing?

To address these questions, over the last fifteen years my interest in liberation has led me to the work of liberation theology and psychology. Paulo Freire, Gustavo Gutierrez, Ignacio Martin-Baro, Sulak Sivaraksa and others have become my teachers from the South, and it is through their perspectives on liberation that I have a beginning sense of how depth psychology could more fully embody its own deepest desire for liberation. Turning to such teachers is a move to further encourage depth psychology to turn not only to the marginalized voices of individual consciousness, but to the marginalized voices within our culture, and outside of our culture. Just as attention to what has been excluded is healing on the individual level, attention to the voices excluded from our psychology, and our culture that gives rise to it, can be liberatory. The processes by which an unconscious is created on a cultural level are similar to those on the personal level. Identification with dominant ideas and practices, where power is coalesced, push to the margins all else. It is only through practices of concerted contact with what has been marginalized that dominant points of view can be challenged/critiqued, avoiding the very partialness depth psychologists are so leery of intrapsychically.

Liberation psychology, birthed from the inspiration of liberation theology, argues that psychology itself requires liberation before it can be a clear force for liberation. To aid this process I would like to compare and contrast several central ideas of depth psychology with ideas within liberation psychology/theology, in an effort to "see-through" (Hillman, 1975) some of the ideas/practices most familiar to depth psychologists. My aim is twofold: to critique how depth psychology can be practiced to mitigate against liberation, and to suggest how through several key re-visionings underlined by liberation psychology it could practice more deeply and broadly as a psychology for liberation. I have chosen Jung and Hillman's work as a place to bridge from toward liberation psychology, seeing in their ideas an anticipation of ways of holding psyche and culture together in our awareness, ideas, and practices.

Individuation

Jung's stated telos for psychological work was individuation, an idea I would like to compare to liberation, the telos of liberation psychology/theology. Jung focused on the emergence of individuality out of collectivity. For him, individuation "is the process by which individual beings are formed and differentiated; in particular, it is the development of the psychological *individual* as a being distinct from the general, collective psychology" (Jung, 1971, § 757). I read "collective" here as the culture(s) one is residing in psychologically. Jung understood the power of a culture's dominant ideas over the individual and saw that simple identification with these norms provided no critique of them, no interest or power in resisting them, no moral center apart from them.

The goal of individuation is the recognition of and relationship with the Self, a center of organization and imagery apart from the control of the ego. The method of individuation is acute attention to "the exploration and experience of the archetypal symbols and figures in dreams, visions, active imagination, and everyday life" (Hopcke, 1989, p. 63). Jung felt that the imaginal would bring forth what had been cast aside in the culture and by the dominant viewpoint of the ego. Personally he was drawn to a method of exploration that was largely practiced alone, allowing images and visions to arise, trusting that through dialogue and interaction with them that the one-sidedness of conscious thought and experience would be ameliorated.

Jung's focus on the individual and on individuation went hand-in-hand with a deep distrust of the group (see Colman, 1995), and even a fear of psychic contagion between analyst and analysand. For the latter reason he never even had patients do active imagination in the presence of the analyst. For him, consciousness could best be developed by a focus on the individual, hosting imaginal experience that arises at the margins. It was only this process – individual by individual – that could lead to a more conscious group.

> Hence every man is, in a certain sense, unconsciously a worse man when he is in society than when acting alone; for he is carried by society and to that extent relieved of his individual responsibility. Any large company

composed of wholly admirable persons has the morality and intelligence of an unwieldy, stupid, and violent animal. (Jung, 1953/1966, § 240)

Once the individual is thus secured in himself, there is some guarantee that the organized accumulation of individuals in the State. ... will result in the formation no longer of an anonymous mass, but of a conscious community. The indispensable condition for this is conscious freedom of choice and individual decision ... (Jung, 1954/1966, § 227)

Jung was working out a psychology that deeply acknowledges interdependence, and yet he was doing so in a culture that was highly individualistic (see Watkins, 1992). This created a strain in his work, one he himself acknowledged. While he could see that the same attitude he was advocating for internally needed to be used externally, he was not clear about how one could become conscious while in relationship.

The present day shows with appalling clarity how little able people are to let the other man's argument count, although this capacity is a fundamental and indispensable condition for any human community. Everyone who proposes to come to terms with himself must reckon with this basic problem. For, to the degree that he does not admit the validity of the other person, he denies the 'other' within himself the right to exist – and vice versa. The capacity for inner dialogue is a touchstone for outer objectivity. (Jung, 1960, § 187)

There are moments in Jung where he tries to underline the interdependent nature of being and the necessity for individuation to surmount individualism and to take place in relationship. At the end of Jung's life he was clear about a felt-sense of interdependent being:

Yet there is so much that fills me: plants, animals, clouds, day and night, and the eternal in man. The more uncertain I have felt about myself, the more there has grown up in me a feeling of kinship with all things. In fact it seems to me as if that alienation which so long separated me from the world has become transferred into my own inner world, and has revealed to me an unexpected unfamiliarity with myself. (Jung, 1961, p. 359)

While much of his earlier work reflects the alienation he refers to here, there are significant points – particularly in his seminars on Nietzsche's Zarathustra – where he makes needed clarifications (see Perry, 1987).

... and there really could be no self if it were not in relation: the self and individualism exclude each other. The self *is* relatedness. ... You can never come to yourself by building a meditation hut on top of Mount Everest; you will only be visited by your own ghosts and that is not individuation: you are all alone with yourself and *the* self does not exist. The self only exists inasmuch as you appear. Not that you *are*, but that you *do* is the self. The self appears in your deeds, and deeds always mean relationship.

Individuation is only possible with people, through people. You must realize that you are a link in a chain, that you are not an electron suspended somewhere in space or aimlessly drifting through the cosmos. You are part of an atomic structure, and that atomic structure is part of a molecule which, with others, builds up a body. (Jung, 1988, p. 795, 103)

These passages help reorient now common mis-uses of dream work, active imagination and inner dialogue that actually create a Mont Blanc situation of unconsciousness. I take it from the above that he did not intend this. The absence of a method to be able to ferret out the cultural ideas we have identified with, however, is largely missing in Jung, as is emphasis on how consciousness arises in and through relationship. How can one see-through collectivity unless there is an effort to look closely at the ways culture has become embedded in the psyche?

Psychopathology

To the extent that depth psychology unconsciously uses an individualistic paradigm of the self, it obscures the larger sociocultural context that gives rise to individual suffering (see Watkins, 1992). Too often in the practice of depth psychology the individual's issues/pathology are contextualized primarily within the local family situation and, at times, in universal/archetypal context. This leaves an individual suffering pathology unable to ferret out the ways in which their individual situation speaks to larger configurations that also create suffering for others. Most often psychotherapy is limited to working out personal solutions/accommodations to much larger cultural issues, without affecting or even clarifying consciousness about the larger context.

Depth psychologists would do well to carefully study the epidemiological evidence that reveals the impact of each of the following on the increased incidence of psychopathology: poverty, the effects of Western capitalism on third world countries, urbanization, population mobility, family fragmentation, poor and inadequate housing and education, gender inequities, racism, homophobia, torture, rapid social change and social disintegration, war, genocide, forced migration, unemployment, failures of social and community support structures (Kleinman, 1988). The fact that "most mental disorders have their highest prevalence rates in the lowest socioeconomic class" (Kleinman, 1988, p. 54), where there is least access to healthcare, should give some weight to liberation psychology's "preferential option for the poor." Cross-cultural studies of psychopathology allow us to see that the Diagnostic Statistical Manual's "character disorders" are in fact cultural disorders, limited as most of them are to our culture and similar Westernized nations: paranoia, schizoid, antisocial, borderline, histrionic, avoidant, dependent, obsessive-compulsive, narcissistic. In addition, dysthymic disorder, anorexia, and agoraphobia may not be valid categories for many other societies (Kleinman, 1988). That the cultural differences provoked by gender profoundly impact mental health is amply displayed by the greater frequency in women of the following "disorders": borderline, histrionic, dependent, agoraphobia, major depression, panic disorder, somatization disorder, somatoform disorder, conversion disorder, pain disorder, dissociative identity disorder, anorexia, and bulimia.

In addition, the course and prognosis of various disorders is directly effected by cultural context. The most stunning example of this is schizophrenia which is eight times more prevalent in cultures where there is limited social belonging and a high sense of fatalism due to poverty and abusive working conditions (Shulman, 1997, p. 70). Despite American psychopharmacological sophistication, sufferers of this psychopathology in America endure a course of the illness that is more severe and chronic than similar sufferers in third world countries like India, where the disorder is seen as acute (not chronic), where the individual is not taken from the community and from work (Kleinman, 1988).

If, as depth psychologists, we keep psychopathology at the heart of our concern, but widen our conception of its cause and expressions to include culture, then to address psychopathology, to be in dialogue with it, our attention turns to world and community as well. The symptom as it appears in the individual points us also toward the pathology of the world, of the culture. When we are not able to follow the symptom into the culture on which it comments, we misinterpret its protest, and negate its voice. Perhaps we can see this most clearly in extreme examples. In China and Brazil during periods of political oppression and chronic hunger, neurasthenia was seen as a biological condition and treated with drugs, silencing the protest of the body and the mind (Shulman, 1997).

Listening into much of the suffering that I hear in the consulting room, I concur with Hillman (1992):

> My practice tells me that I can no longer distinguish clearly between neurosis of self and neurosis of world, psychopathology of self and psychopathology of world. Moreover, it tells me that to place neurosis and psychopathology solely in personal reality is a delusional repression of what is actually, realistically, being experienced. This further implies that my theories of neurosis and categories of psychopathology must be radically extended if they are not to foster the very pathologies which my job is to ameliorate. (p. 93)

Context for Liberation Theology / Psychology

It is too easy for us to forget the power that Old Testament ideas and stories still hold for many of us. The story of Exodus, of the Jews' struggle to liberate themselves from the dehumanizing and oppressive experience of being slaves, has inspired efforts toward liberation throughout the world. In America's history, we hear this influence in Puritan writing as they described their movement as "an errand into the wilderness," likening their bid for freedom to the early Jews. Despite Christianity being the religion of their oppressors, African slaves in America heard in Exodus the promise of a god who was on the side of the enslaved, helping them in their efforts toward liberation (Cone, 1972). Black gospel songs echo the words of Moses:

> When Israel was in Egypt's land,
> Let my people go;
> Oppressed so hard they could not stand,
> Let my people go;
> Go down, Moses, way down in Egypt's land,
> Tell ole Pharaoh
> Let my people go

We also heard the use of the Exodus story in the fight against apartheid when South African church leaders met in Soweto in 1985 to draft the Kairos Document. This document used the Bible's description of oppression as being crushed, degraded, humiliated, exploited, impoverished, defrauded, deceived, and enslaved (Ellis, 1987) to depict their current circumstance.

In 1968, at the Second General Conference of Latin American Bishops at Medellin, Colombia, liberation theology was initiated with an invocation of the Exodus story – an invocation that united faith and social liberation. For Gutierrez, the founder of liberation theology and a Peruvian priest, faith in God requires our acting on behalf of justice, because God is seen through the Book of Exodus as encouraging and desiring liberation from oppression (Ellis, 1987).

What are the poetic images in Exodus that have quickened the thirst for freedom over time? In Exodus, the beginning of an attempt to become liberated is likened to entering the wilderness. One leaves behind the security of oppression and takes on the uncertainty of being neither a community of slaves nor a community of the emancipated. In Exodus, Moses learns that liberation is not immediate. It is a process filled with challenges, doubts, and backsliding. The thing that orients the process is utopic imagining.

> To enter the wilderness one must carry close to the heart an image of the land of milk and honey.

> A land wherein thou shalt eat bread without scarceness, thou shalt not lack anything. (Deuteronomy 8: 7-9)

> Isaiah, Micah, and Joel imagine the new Jerusalem, thusly:

> And my people shall build houses and inhabit them; and they shall plant vineyards, and eat the fruit of them; They shall not build and another inhabit; They shall not plant and another eat. (Isaiah 65: 21-22)

> They shall enjoy the work of their hands. They shall not labor in vain. (Isaiah 65: 22-23)

> They shall sit every man under his vine and his fig tree; and none shall make them afraid. (Micah 4: 4)

> And it shall come to pass afterward, that I will pour out my spirit upon all flesh; and your sons and daughters shall prophesy, your old men shall dream dreams, your young men shall see visions; and also upon the servants and upon the handmaids ... will I pour out my spirit. (Joel, 2: 28-29)

In South and Central America, community work led by followers of liberation theology and the related work of the radical pedagogist of the oppressed, Paulo Freire, laid the foundation for the emergence of liberation psychology articulated by Ignacio Martin-Baro. In 1989 a United States government-funded Salvadoran death squad murdered Martin-Baro, a Jesuit and a psychologist. His "crime": a call for the creation of a liberation psychology. He was working to create the outlines for a psychology of liberation, inspired by liberation theology – a psychology that by its focus on liberation could be a force for justice, peace, human rights, psychological well-being, and humanity. What kind of light can the ideas and practices of liberation psychology and theology shine on depth psychology? How might their dialogue together enable depth psychology to more fully realize its liberatory impulse?

Individuation / Development / Liberation

Third World liberationists have rejected the term "development" to characterize cultural or economic progress, for too often it implied adopting an economic and cultural system that required their oppression or their neighbor's. The Third World has directly witnessed that the "development" of one may result in the underdevelopment of others, where in their experience inequality has been generated by others' economic growth (Goizueta, 1988, p. 5). Economic underdevelopment is understood to be a result of dependence, not interdependence. Dependence is defined as "the assimilation of one nation or region within another's sphere of influence to such a degree that the development or lack thereof is governed, controlled, and determined by the development of the latter" (Goizueta, 1988, p. 7). Dussel argues that "it is necessary to be able to undertake *one's own path of development*, different from the European (because up to the present we have been the other face of the same system, but the exploited, dominated, dependent face)" (in Goizueta, 1988, p. 230). To take one's own path requires uniting interior with community changes in consciousness. One has to be able to recognize and articulate one's own interests, aspirations, and hopes. What has been silent and unspoken needs to enter into dialogue with others in order to move toward desired transformations.

Liberation was chosen as a better term for the goal of cultural change, for it is relational, based on a paradigm of interdependence. The liberation of one is inextricably tied to the liberation of all. This is true on the psychological level, as well as on the material level, where oppression and domination in a culture are mirrored in the skewed and polarized dynamics of psyche. To think in terms of liberation points us toward the roots of suffering in both psyche and world, not just the manifestations. Perhaps liberation is also a better term for psychological development in a perspective that strives for the acknowledgment of such interdependence.

Liberation is a holistic term that urges us to consider economic, political, socio-cultural, spiritual, and psychological liberation together, and in community. In its holism it helps us to resist thinking that one could be psychologically liberated or individuated while economically or culturally enslaved or curtailing of the freedom of others. As psychologists it urges us to look at how psyche reflects these other levels of human existence. The Thai liberationist Sulak Sivaraksa outlines that there are four levels of freedom that are indispensable for the realization of peace and happiness: physical freedom, social freedom, emotional freedom, and intellectual freedom. He would argue that these are interdependent, not achievable in isolation from one another.

Liberation means to set free, to emancipate, to release from bondage, captivity or slavery. The Chinese characters for liberation mean to let go, to release, to untie. In Mahayana Buddhism, liberation is seen as freedom from conventional views of reality (Queen, 1996, p. 9), as it is in depth psychology and liberation psychology. In both Greek and Sanskrit, liberality – meaning both generosity and freedom from prejudice – is *desire* (Hyde, 1979, p. 35). It is this link between liberation and desire that implicates the imagination. Liberation attempts to move what *is* toward what is *desired*.

Individual Work / Group Work

Liberation psychology values the coming to awareness through dialogue within a group, because it is in the group that we can most clearly see that much of what we have thought of as individual fate, virtue, failure, and suffering is shared beyond the individual. Such insight links individuals so that they can work together to address the cultural conditions that impact their well-being. In the group it is easier to see how the culture has gotten into our hearts and minds, into our intimate relationships – as partner, as son/daughter, parent, and friend. To focus on what are the problems of the people or of a group helps us orient to suffering that arises more broadly.

Instead of directing the participants' attention to search for personal 'causes' of a feeling, such as fear, worry, anger – in Freire's method of developing critical consciousness the leader (called the animator) asks questions to help raise to awareness the relationship between the feeling and the cultural reality one is in. Change is directed first and foremost not toward individual change, but to cultural change that will ultimately effect the participants. Freire argues:

> I don't believe in self-liberation. Liberation is a social act. Liberating education is a social process of illumination. … Even when you individually feel yourself *most* free, if this is not a *social* feeling, if you are not able to use your recent freedom to help others be free by transforming the totality of society, then you are exercising only an individualist attitude toward empowerment or freedom. (Shor & Freire, 1987, p. 109)

Martin-Baro calls this psychology's critical error: "to change the individual while preserving the social order, or, in the best of cases, generating the illusion that, perhaps, as the individual changes, so will the social order – as if society were a summation of individuals." (p. 37)

Liberation psychology argues that psychological work within a group is necessary for the development of critical consciousness. This difference between individuation and Freire's "conscientization" is central to understanding what liberation psychology can contribute to depth psychology.

It is important to note, however, that the composition of the group that is required for critical consciousness is radically different when one is working with those who have been oppressed and silenced by the dominant culture(s) as compared to those whose roles foster domination. In the former, the sharing of the group with those who suffer the same context helps members clarify the connections between their psychological life and their cultural life. Those who have enjoyed colonizing situations, often employing silencing techniques (consciously or unconsciously) need a group context where sociocultural differences are encountered. Such encountering demands that one's usual stance of speaking and holding power is bracketed, allowing others to speak who bring awareness from the margins. Relying solely on intrapsychic confrontation in an upper-middle class, white population isolates the individual from more radical challenge of their standpoint. In some ways Jung intuited this, and in his travels tried to encounter other ways of being – African, Native American. In his writings from these forays, however, one is struck by how little dialogue actually occurred and how much projection ensued.

The Self / The Other

In general, depth psychology focuses on the development of the self; analytical psychology on the arising awareness of the Self. If this Self/self is conceptualized in Cartesian terms, it will be imagined separate from the wider world. Within this framework, "the other" becomes most likely an intrapsychic other, a dream image, the analyst, or a close friend or family member. There is a sustained focus on interiority, locating processes of development and individuation as occurring within the individual, and through the dyad of therapist and patient. One can work on one's own "development" without regard to the other, even while acting in ways that use the other or impede the other is his or her own development.

Liberation psychology links interior with exterior, shifting the focus to community and inter-relatedness, from "self" to "the other," underscoring the self's encounter and treatment of the other. Development from this perspective has to do with how I interact with the other, and with otherness. The self is seen to be in chains if the other – person, nature, group – is only a means to my own gratification – objectified, appropriated, de-animated, de-humanized.

Development goes hand-in-hand with releasing the Other from objectification, so that he or she becomes the center of his or her own world, rather than determined by another's (Goizueta, 1988, p. 68). Such a release of the Other is also a liberation of the self. Perfection does not consist in a "realization of *my* 'potential-being,' but in a love that first loves the Other: love-in-justice" (Goizueta, 1988, p. 72). The process is one that involves listening and serving.

In oppression, the capital of one group builds itself by deplenishing the capital of another. In oppression, need does not draw resources but continues toward utter depletion. There is a rigid boundary between groups: one being valued, the other denigrated; one being used as a tool for the other. Instead of witnessing the thoughts and feelings of the other, these are attributed to, projected upon, the other in ways that serve the ends of the self: "Negroes prefer slavery because they are well cared for."

A focus on liberation requires that we carefully look at how otherness is experienced and related to. A focus only on the self is insufficient and misleading. In a psychology of liberation, the term "the Other" is as crucial as the term "the Self." Openness to the revelation of the Other is as necessary as openness to the liberation of one's own thoughts, feelings, and images. Focus on allowing the other to freely arise would turn depth psychology toward a more penetrating study of the silencing of the other, violence, the stranger, to the psychology of hate and love, racism and prejudice, dehuman-ization, greed, injustice, poverty, the abuse of nature and animals. This openness to the revelation of the Other is an act of liberation (Goizueta, p. 68).

"Seeing-through" / The Development of Critical Consciousness

The work of liberation in depth psychology involves giving attention to two related areas: the margins and reflection on the ideas of the ego. Hillman (1975) calls the latter "seeing-through." It is by bracketing the ego position and moving toward the margin, that one can begin to see-through the identifications of the ego. Hillman makes it clear that ideas we are not able to see-through dominate us, and sustain our unconsciousness. The impor-tance of such seeing-through has been echoed by many in depth psychology such as Freud, Jung, Adler, Horney, Sullivan, Fromm, but their advocacy for seeing-through cultural ideas has often been forgotten or neglected.

Freire also focuses on seeing-through the cultural ideas one is identified with that create and sustain the day-to-day reality one lives in. His method of working with groups oppressed by cultural realities linked the gaining of literacy with becoming able to decode the sociocultural world one lives in. Such decoding paved the way for imagining desired transformations and action on behalf of them. This decoding is at the same time a shift in how one sees one's self.

Freire describes that initially we experience the problems we suffer as inevitable and normal. In this "magical" stage, we sense that things are being caused by factors beyond our control, and thus our acting is futile. We experience ourselves as impotent, without the power to comprehend or to change our circumstances. Next, we begin to see the problems we suffer, but understand them to be caused by single individuals: ourselves or some evil or deficient other. There is not yet an understanding of how an unjust and oppressive social system creates oppressors. In the third stage, critical consciousness, "the individual has an integrated understanding of the socio-political system, enabling him/her to relate instances of oppression to the *normal* functioning of an unjust and oppressive system" (Alschuler, 1997, p. 290). One can now reject the oppressor's ideology and seek to transform the system in collaboration with others. What was previously seen as personal problems are often now seen as community problems, and often as class problems. Only at this point is collective action used to transform the context. This progression is possible through dialogue, Freire says, "reflecting together on what we know and don't know, we can then act critically to transform reality" (1987, p. 99). "Libertory dialogue is a democratic communication which disconfirms domination and illuminates while affirming the freedom of the participants to re-make their culture." (1987, p. 99)

In American culture we can cite many recent examples of such linking of what is suffered as a personal problem to cultural issues that require profound redressing: from suffering post-traumatic symptoms of sexual abuse by a particular father to questioning patriarchal prerogatives and the use/ abuse of the feminine; from suffering a crippling sense of personal inferiority to insighting the reproduction of racism in a society that gives rise to it; from being a medical patient dealing with a disease to growing into awareness of its link to unacknowledged environmental pollution and degradation of various kinds. This path between symptom and culture needs to be tread by depth psychologists, as surely as the path between symptom and family dynamics, archetypal patterns, and neurochemistry.

Liberation psychology critiques depth psychology for not adequately understanding and articulating the relationship between sociocultural/economic structures and individual suffering. The focus on intrapsychic dynamics and the dyadic transferential relationship between patient and therapist often neglects the relationship between cultural and individual pathology and healing. Indeed, the underlying paradigm of self in American culture would have us each think we are individually responsible for our shortcomings, gifts, pain, pathologies, and health. A more contextualized view of self would seek to articulate the interrelations between what we have cordoned off as internal/private and what we take to be public/ social.

> ... psychology has for the most part not been very clear about the intimate relationship between an unalienated personal existence and an unalienated social existence, between individual control and collective power, between the liberation of each person and the liberation of a whole people. Moreover, psychology has often contributed to obscuring the relationship between personal estrangement and social oppression, presenting the pathology of persons as if it were something removed from history and society, and behavioral disorders as if they played themselves out entirely in the individual plane. (Martin-Baro, 1994, p. 27)

When depth psychology operates within the cultural paradigm of radical individualism, development is largely seen as the individual differentiating out of the collective. This interpretation of depth psychology reinscribes the heroic ego as on its own in a hostile world. Its psychology is implicitly based on upper-middle-class experience. Part of this experience is the negation that culture and economics have critical impacts on development. Martin-Baro says that when working with the well-to-do,

> social context is thus converted into a kind of natural phenomenon, an unquestioned assumption before whose 'objective' demands the individual must seek, individually and even 'subjectively' the solutions to his or her problems. (1994, p. 37)

When this is the case, psychological suffering that arises from a given social order can not be deeply addressed, as its roots are not clearly seen. Psychotherapy can act then as a palliative practice, and also as one that perpetuates blindness about some of the causes of suffering – and thus the possible redressing of such suffering.

Desire / Creative Imagination / Annunciation

The second part of the process of developing critical consciousness Freire calls "annunciation": a process of conceiving a more just social order. Here utopic imagination is central. How do members of a community most desire their community to be? Imaging what is desired is the link between critical consciousness and creation, action that attempts to nurture and bring into reality the desired.

Depth psychology's focus on creative imagination has ordinarily taken us in one of two directions: the personal or the universal. Relatively lacking has been a sense of how the cultural shapes images and conveys the historically conditioned to our inmost being. It has anticipated the contents of the imaginal with its interpretive designs – bad breasts, phallic towers, anima figures, puer voices, Hera figures – rarely inviting awareness of the cultural through the imaginal. We know from dreams and fleeting images that it comes unbidden anyway: images of war, nuclear accidents, rape, racism, holocaust imagery, the death of nature. These inbreaks are rarely met by the creation of a space in which what is deeply desired in our world can come forth imaginally. Such desire is restrained by hopelessness, apathy, complacency, fear of failure and a depth psychology that too often continues to see us as apart from the world, a depth psychology that makes little room for cultural desire.

In depth psychology, consciousness and action, imagination and action have been sundered, depriving imagination of some of its creative and transformative power. Freire (1989) charges us to hold reflection and action together, to avoid a non-reflective activism on the one hand or a detached and universalizing reflection on the other. Perhaps a participatory action form of research brings us closest to this ideal, as self-and-other-in- community is imagined, reflected upon, and enacted to achieve creative practices of liberation.

Coming Home

As I have worked clinically within the theories and practices of depth psychology, I have been moved by how their methods and manner of listening release from bondage images, memories, thoughts, and desires, that radically decenter one's identity. I am left, however, with the clear sense that depth psychology – to the degree that it has remained in a collective, Cartesian world – has over-focused on interior liberation without sufficiently insighting how inseparable the interior is from the so-called exterior, or how psyche cannot be isolated from the culture, economics, and politics that in part form it. To work toward a psychological liberation without such awareness can actually subvert that very goal.

In retrospect, the myopic quality of depth psychology's desire for the liberation of being should not have surprised me. Any theory that creates a radical path from the cultural norm inevitably also bears the mark of the culture it is departing from. It conserves as well as creates. It is hard to see this from within the culture, as any culture naturalizes its practices and ideas, making them seem universal and normal. While we can never completely look in on the culture we are part of from an outside position, being in dialogue with the viewpoint(s) of another culture(s) is an excellent way for us to begin to see more deeply into our own. It is such dialogue that I want to practice here, as I hold together the liberational impulses and insights of depth psychology and liberation psychology/theology.

While depth psychology can be seen as an effort which radically challenges dominant cultural paradigms of selfhood and reality, it may also be seen as reflecting, conserving, and perpetuating aspects of the cultural status quo that contribute to human suffering. At this point it is a confusing mixture of oppressive and liberatory practices and theories. It is a mixture which perhaps the lens of a psychology of liberation can help us clarify, so that liberation on one level of existence does not mitigate against but supports liberation on other levels.

Cushman (1995) argues that when we question why in our time the interior or the psychological has been chosen as the backdrop for human concern and activity, we discover that it has allowed us to retreat from disappointment and disillusionment about the lack of community and tradition that we suffer from. I would add that this retreat to the psychological has also buffered us from our feelings of impotence and ineffectuality in creating the kinds of communities and social order that we most deeply desire to be homed by, and that we already know are more conducive to psychological well-being.

Our excursion through Exodus to liberation psychology/theology in South and Central America returns us back to our everyday practice and theory within depth psychology. Can we see the link between psychological liberation and economic, political, and spiritual liberation, and will depth psychologists know that each of these domains essentially forms psyche and needs our attention? If our ear for psychopathology can hear the symptom speak of such things as poverty, social fragmentation, the injuries of violence and prejudice, the desecration of the material and natural worlds, then we must follow its voice and heed its commentary. It would place our work both in the consulting room and in the world that surrounds it.[10]

If we have colluded in silencing utopic imagining by cordoning off the private from the public, the inner from the outer, we must take down the dividers and bear the pain of seeing what is desired next to what has been sadly created or destroyed. We learn from our Southern neighbors that this work with the cultural unconscious is best done together rather than alone, so that we can begin to hear the resonances between our experiences, and find the collective energy to address the contexts we share. At the same time, we must challenge our perspectives by placing ourselves in the company of others whose experiences bring into focus our assumptions and practices.

Alongside Jung's sense of our work as an *opus contra naturam*, a work against nature, we can see it as a work against culture, the unconsciousness

---

[1] Pacifica Graduate Institute has begun a Ph.D. program in depth psychology that has – among other areas of attention – precisely this focus of creating a bridge between depth psychology and cultural work; a bridge between psychological and ecological/sociocultural/economic understandings. Its hope is to assist students in creating collaborative community fieldwork and research that broadly imagines liberation. Participatory action research and other dialogical models are used as means of collaborative intervention and assessment.

of culture about its dominant ideas, their shadow, the suffering in them. If we do not see that depth can also be between self and Other, then the verticality and interiority of the way we have imagined depth becomes a hideout, mitigating against the effort of consciousness it is supposedly supporting.

Returning from this journey to liberation psychology, I cannot help but remark on the multiple threads that link liberation psychology and depth psychology: the acknowledgment of multiplicity, the listening into what has been marginalized, the use of dialogue as the principal methodology (see Watkins, 1999), the careful attempt to see-through dominant ideas, the valuing of the free-arising of being, the knowledge of the potency of image and story and the necessity to engage them, the effort to liberate from domination. These are pathways to depth and to the ongoing process of liberation. When depth psychology draws itself near to liberation psychology with these threads, it emerges from its unconsciousness about its cultural origins. It gains a way of working in groups toward critical consciousness. Its polarizing splits between reflection and action and image and action are healed. Further, the complexity of forces that forge the psyche are more deeply acknowledged. The imagination, instead of being relegated to personal exploration and to being a preserve of images to shelter one from a forbidding world, is recognized as the potential power it is to bring into being what is most deeply desired. The lens of liberation rescues depth psychology from the paradigm of radical individualism, from which much of our psychological suffering issues. It reconnects the individual with community, culture, and nature, further grounding depth psychology in a psychology of interdependent being.

The dialogue between depth psychology and liberation psychology sews back together the personal and the collective with the cultural and the ecological. It begins to correct the myopia in depth psychology which has distorted our perception of causes and our vision for healing. It is not for me to say how depth psychology might enrich and critique liberation psychology. But if depth psychology is to move toward engagement with the life of the community, it would be well-served to learn from those already there who share its fundamental sensibilities. Through this joining of hands and of visions, possibilities for liberation may indeed be seeded.

References

Alschuler, L. (1997). Jung and Politics. In P. Young-Eisendrath & T. Dawson (Eds.), *The Cambridge Companion to Jung*. New York: Cambridge University Press.

Colman, A. (1995). *Up from Scapegoating: Awakening Consciousness in Groups*. Wilmette, IL: Chiron Publications.

Cone, J. H. (1972). *The Spirituals and the Blues: An Interpretation*. New York: The Seabury Press.

Cushman, P. (1995). *Constructing the Self, Constructing America: A Cultural History of Psychotherapy*. Reading, MA: Addison-Wesley.

Ellis, M. H. (1987). *Toward a Jewish Theology of Liberation*. New York: Maryknoll.

Freire, P. (1989). *Pedagogy of the Oppressed*. New York: Continuum.

Fromm, E. (1976). *To Have or to Be*. New York: Bantam Books.

Fromm, E. (1960). Psychoanalysis and Zen Buddhism. In D.T. Suzuki, E. Fromm & R. de Martino (Eds.), *Zen Buddhism and Psychoanalysis*. New York: Harper.

Goizueta, R. S. (1988). *Liberation, Method, and Dialogue: Enrique Dussel and North American Theological Discourse*. Atlanta: Scholars Press.

Hillman, J. (1975). *Re-visioning Psychology*. New York: Harper & Row.

Hillman, J. (1992). *The Thought of the Heart and the Soul of the World*. Woodstock, CT: Spring Publications.

Hopcke, R. (1989). *A Guided Tour of the Collected Works of C. G. Jung*. Boston: Shambhala.

Hyde, L. (1979). *The Gift: Imagination and the Erotic Life of Property*. New York: Vintage Books.

Jung, C.G. (1921/1971). Psychological Type. In *The Collected Works of C.G. Jung (Vol. 6)*. Princeton: Princeton University Press.

Jung, C.G. (1953/1966). Two Essays on Analytical Psychology. In *The Collected Works of C.G. Jung (Vol. 7)*. Princeton: Princeton University Press.

Jung, C.G. (1954/1966). The Spirit in Man, Art, and Literature. In *The Collected Works of C.G. Jung (Vol. 15)*. Princeton: Princeton University Press.

Jung, C.G. (1960). The Structure and Dynamics of the Psyche. In *The Collected Works of C.G. Jung (Vol. 8)*. Princeton: Princeton University Press.

Jung, C.G. (1961). *Memories, Dreams, Reflections*, New York: Vintage Books.

Jung, C.G. (1988). *Nietzsche's Zarathustra, Notes of the Seminar given in 1934-1939*. J.L. Jarrett (Ed.). Princeton: Princeton University Press.

Kleinman, A. (1988). *Re-thinking Psychiatry*. New York: Free Press.

Martin-Baro, I. (1994). *Writings for a Liberation Psychology*. Cambridge: Harvard University Press.

Perry, J. W. (1987). *The Heart of History: Individuality in Evolution*. Albany: State University of New York.

Queen, C. & King, S. (Eds.). (1996). *Engaged Buddhism*. Albany: State University of New York.

Shulman, H. L. (1997). *Living at the Edge of Chaos: Complex Systems in Culture and Psyche*. Einsiedeln: Daimon Verlag.

Shor, I. & Freire, P. (1987). *A Pedagogy for Liberation: Dialogues on Transforming Education*. Westport, CT: Bergin & Garvey.

Sulak Sivaraksa. (1992). *Seeds of Peace: A Buddhist Vision for Renewing Society*. Berkeley: Parallax Press.

van den Berg, J. H. (1971). Phenomenology and Metabletics. *Humanitas, VII*, 3, 279-290.

Watkins, M. (1992). From Individualism to the Interdependent Self: Changing Paradigms in Psychotherapy. *Psychological Perspectives, 27*, 52-69.

Watkins, M. (1999). Pathways Between the Multiplicities of Psyche and Culture: The Development of Dialogical Capacities. In J. Rowan & M. Cooper (Eds.), *The Plural Self: Multiplicity in Everyday Life*. Thousand Oaks, CA: Sage Publications.

Watkins, M. (2000). Depth Psychology and the Liberation of Being. In R. Brooke (Ed.), *Pathways into the Jungian World*. London: Routledge.

CHAPTER 16

The Presence of Absence:
Mapping Postcolonial Spaces

Helene Shulman Lorenz

This is the map of the forsaken world.
This is the world without end
where forests have been cut away from their trees.
These are the lines the wolf could not pass over.
This is what I know from science:
that a grain of dust dwells at the center
of every flake of snow,
that ice can have its way with land,
that wolves live inside a circle
of their own beginning.
This is what I know from blood:
the first language is not our own.
There are names each thing has for itself,
and beneath us the other order already moves.
It is burning.
It is dreaming.
It is waking up.
      (from "Map" by Linda Hogan in *The Book of Medicines*)

The Map of the Forsaken World

These powerful images by Chickasaw poet Linda Hogan ask us to consider two opposed experiences, one visual and one embodied or tactile. The theoretical maps of the modern scientific worldview present us with a visual space where every location is transparently known on an abstract space/time grid. The world is classified according to fixed hierarchies of binary opposites: latitude and longitude, center and periphery, progress and stasis, order and chaos. Here is a mythology that stresses uniformity and coherence, an undifferentiated universe where natural laws apply in every local arena. This way of thinking is a dissociative strategy, that is, a seeing from nowhere. It is perfectly mirrored by the conventions of modern perspective drawing that organize space as if viewed by a single individual standing outside the scene. In Hogan's poem, this is the space in which "forests have been cut away from their trees." In such an environment, much in us and the world is exiled from consciousness as we look far into the distance.

Every culture must have normalized routines of behavior and thought; but many also have periodic public rituals of disorganization and renewal. In carnival, pilgrimage, and public theater spectacles, alternatives can be reimagined and named. As the European and American press and public entertainment industries become frighteningly more monopolized by giant corporations, our public discourse has become highly controlled. Alternative constructions are largely confined to private and local spaces. What we know "from our own blood" where "beneath us the other order already moves," is happening outside dominant media reporting. Local situated knowledges offer discontinuous images that might yield counter-narratives and counter-histories of place and self. Always incomplete, sedimented in our bodies, memories, and communities, these "maps" represent a fragmentary and potentially conflicting repertoire of performances of intuition, feeling, story, fantasy, ritual, dream, poetry, song, myth, and symptom that have been preserved in spite of having been covered over and marginalized by modernist narratives. These possibilities for knowledge continue to live both in personal and social environments as alternatives which resist official histories. The more they are disowned, the more energy they gather. They are capable of "waking up."

It is possible to understand both world and self through these two different mapping strategies. James Hillman identifies these modalities in his essay "Peaks and Vales." For Hillman, they are the realms of spirit and soul: "the one abstract, unified, concentrated; the other concrete, multiple, immanent." In the Eurocentric discourses of the last several centuries, there has clearly been an overemphasis on spirit, which Hillman compares to climbing up a mountain peak.

> The peaks wipe out history. History is to be overcome … spirit seekers first of all must climb over the debris of history, or prophesy its end or its unreality, time as illusion, as well as the history of their individual and particular localities, their particular ethnic and religious roots … (Hillman, p. 62)

Hillman suggests that the antidote to an overspiritualized worldview is to go down into the "vales", into all that local, tactile, imaginal and embodied history fossilized in symptom, affect, and fantasy. Here we reclaim a different kind of place in the world, where differentiation emerges out of generalities, just as in the evolution of the species. In this process of differentiation, there is a co-development of the individual and the environment. As new perspectives and "healing fictions" are brought into dialogue with official history, more creative possibilities for life may emerge. We have to "see through", live with, and embody contradictory perspectives and antagonistic opposites in ourselves and the world in order to give birth to new energies.

It is probably no accident that abstract and universalist perspectives that seek to "wipe out history" became dominant during the five hundred years of European colonial expansion. Conquest, land-theft, slavery, and genocide do not fit easily into heroic narratives of national destiny. When these brutalities are not publicly named and mourned, a habit of dissociative thinking is hardened into a cultural complex. Educated within it, we may learn to disown all that is disruptive, bloody, bodily, and disorienting in both personal and social experience by climbing up to the peaks of a universalist discourse. The instinct of depth psychology to go into the vale is as much a social as a personal therapy.

These Are the Lines the Wolf Could Not Pass Over

Those of us educated into the one-sided and dissociative way of thinking in Western official history, must imagine ourselves and others through this lens to some degree. C.G. Jung repeatedly stressed the dangers inherent in the modernist worldview, which he called collective consciousness.

Looked at from the standpoint of modern consciousness, the position of medieval man seems as deplorable as it is in need of improvement. But the much needed broadening of the mind by science has only replaced medieval one-sidedness ... by a new one-sidedness, the overvaluation of 'scientifically' attested views ... nowadays the backwardness of psychic development in general and of self-knowledge in particular has become one of the most pressing contemporary problems. (Jung, 1978 p. 220)

This one-sidedness, which is institutionalized in educational and religious institutions and the legal system in Europe and the United States, places enormous pressures on each individual, according to Jung.

The larger a community is and the more the sum total of collective factors peculiar to every large community rests on conservative prejudices detrimental to individuality, the more will the individual be morally and spiritually crushed, and, as a result, the one source of moral and spiritual progress for a community is choked up. Naturally the only thing that can thrive in such an atmosphere is sociality and whatever is collective in the individual. Everything individual in him goes under, i.e. is doomed to repression ... Society by automatically stressing all the collective qualities in its individual representatives, puts a premium on mediocrity, on everything that settles down to vegetate in an easy irresponsible way. Individuality will inevitable be driven to the wall. This process begins in school, continues at the university, and rules all departments in which the state has a hand. (Jung, 1966, p. 153)

If Jung is correct about the Western educational system many of us have learned in, much of our knowledge of ourselves and the world must be embedded in dissociative consciousness. That means, in varying degrees depending on our social location, we may automatically and unconsciously limit what we can bear to know about ourselves and our environment according to the standards of collective consciousness. In more contemporary language, we are bound by and blind to the social constructions of our home culture while at the same time we both resist and reproduce them. For this to be possible, human consciousness must be profoundly imitative. According to Jung,

Collective psychology cannot dispense with imitation, for without it all mass organizations, the state, and the social order, are impossible. Society is organized, indeed, less by law than by the propensity to imitation, implying equally suggestibility, suggestion, and mental contagion ... We could almost say that as a punishment for this, the uniformity of their minds with those of their neighbors, already real enough, is intensified into an unconscious compulsive bondage to the environment. (Jung, 1966, p. 155)

But if we are all in bondage to our environments, can we ever see the world apart from collective consciousness? How do we know that when we interpret ourselves or others we are not simply trapped in the colonial cultural constructions of our own era? In fact it is very likely that our entire understanding of the world is shaped by the habits of our home-culture, for it is through this formation that we come to know ourselves as gendered, embodied persons with specific identities and norms of behavior. It would not be unusual for most people to be in a state of, at least, partial identification with collective consciousness, which Jung believed would lead to psychological disaster in modern Western culture.

Even if it were a question of some great truth, identification with it would still be a catastrophe, as it arrests all further spiritual development. Instead of knowledge one then has only belief, and sometimes that is more convenient and therefore more attractive. (Jung,1978, p. 219)

If this pressure toward social conformity is so intense, it can be only with the greatest experience of personal conflict or opposition that we can begin to make a break. In other words, from the point of view of Jungian depth psychology, an interior experience of ambivalence, struggle, alienation, and doubt could be the beginning of an important process, enabling an individual to overcome some of the dissociative tendencies constantly reproduced within our culture. Sometimes it is a relationship failure, or our symptoms and wounds that force us to make a break. This is why James Hillman speaks of the "wounded healer." Here, healing is less about shared experience or empathy that can occur within the already constituted social world, and more about a rupture of collective consciousness, a speaking which no longer covers over the absences and silences normalized in modernist uniformity.

This is a dismembered, dissociated consciousness, one that speaks now from the heart, now from the hand, now from the feet that are hurt and can't walk. It is a wounded consciousness that is always sensitively inferior. And this dismemberment and dissociation allows conversation between two persons to go on through the wounds. (Hillman, p. 117)

It is from this sense of wounding and incompleteness that energy arises for differentiation. By questioning the silences inherent in social norms, individuals in conflict can help to deliteralize and transform inherited ways of thinking that have become rigid and deadening. In depth psychology, there is a recognition that what happens in the collective and the individual are intimately related. Though one of the goals of Jungian work is "individuation," this was not theorized by Jung as a splitting of mind and body, psyche and world. Unlike contemporary ego-psychology, the interior life of the individual in Jung's work is not imagined as developing more or less separately from the social context it is embedded in. Jung saw the therapist, the mother, and the family of origin as all located in a collective cultural and historical environment. If this environment is not critiqued in and through analysis, the goal of psychology may become adaptation to the established cultural complex. This type of psychology can produce a sense of a romantic and magical interior where symbols, affiliations, and idealizations are protected from a harsh and uncaring world which cannot be changed. It can lead to conformity with a hierarchical collective life that continues as an unexamined and unconscious ground of thought.

Jung conceptualized the individuation process more as a process of resistance and destabilization to collective norms that would transform both the individual and the social environment.

> It is obvious that a social group consisting of stunted individuals cannot be a healthy and viable institution; only a society that can preserve its internal cohesion and collective values, while at the same time granting the individual the greatest possible freedom, has any prospect of enduring vitality. As the individual is not just a single, separate being, but by his very existence presupposes a collective relationship, it follows that the process of individuation must lead to more intense and broader collective relationships and not to isolation. (Jung, 1971, p. 448)

According to Aniela Jaffé, individuation takes place within the social world and not apart from it.

> Individuation pursues its course in a meaningful way only in our everyday existence. Acceptance of life as it is, of its banality, its extraordinariness, respect for the body and its demands, are just as much a prerequisite for individuation as a relationship to one's fellow men. (Jaffé, p. 82)

This Is What I Know from Blood

As a child, I belonged to an Orthodox Jewish community in a small town in the Adirondacks. Most of the families had arrived in the United States after WWI, and had moved upstate from New York City where they had landed as immigrants, fleeing pogroms in Europe. They carried with them memories of another time and space, another language, and fragments of ritual that they used to recreate an absent environment. At that time, we were the most recent unwanted outsiders to arrive in what had first been Iroquois country, then a French colony, and later contested territory in the "French and Indian War" won by British colonizers. Though I was born in the United States, my childhood space was partway between a Polish *shtetl* and an Adirondack hiking club. My true citizenship originated from an imaginary borderline, a demilitarized zone between several territories at war about meaning and values. This kind of border location can never be precisely mapped anywhere in the visible world, though it can be felt everywhere as affect, symptom, and the presence of absence. Like many other children of recent immigrants, particularly those who hear a second language at home, my identity was constructed in a realm of ambivalence, disorientation, and mixed-messages in a contact zone between cultures. My identification is with disidentification. As a result, I know both peaks and vales quite well, though I usually travel in a crossroads in-between.

Our community was held together through the institution of a thriving synagogue, though we were clearly in transition. Some members had been born in Europe, spoke Yiddish at home, and maintained rituals developed centuries earlier in Eastern Europe. Others, like me, were born in the United States, spoke English as a first language, and were educated partly in "Hebrew School" and partly in the New York State school system. In this complicated geography, our community was in an unacknowledged negotia-tion process over which traditions were old-fashioned and needed to be dropped so we could fit into the larger community and which were crucial to maintain identity. Largely excluded from the economic and social privileges of the dominant culture, the adults around me were creative in developing their own networks of solidarity.

Whether it was acceptable to drive cars on the Sabbath was a major issue. Many people solved the problem privately by driving to the synagogue for Sabbath services but parking a few blocks away so they would not be seen getting out of their cars out front. Nevertheless, each fall on the High Holidays – Yom Kippur and Rosh Hashonah – virtually everyone took days off work and walked to the synagogue. I have a wonderful childhood memory of people streaming out of their houses toward our local "sacred space", walking as if toward a holy mountain. In fact, our sense of place was less connected with the Adirondacks than the "Holy Mount" in Jerusalem, an imaginary peak somewhere in the past to which we could retreat in order to maintain a sense of continuity with 5,000 years of history. This mythological space was recreated as we walked. On these days, time stopped and expanded; extended families gathered and people talked in ways there was no time for on ordinary weekdays. And the ritual pilgrimage worked to create Jewish community and renew spirit, to a degree that from this postmodern vantage point, seems astonishing.

Unlike my parents, however, my earliest memories are rooted equally in the local history of forest preserve with thousands of years of Native-American habitation sites and a contemporary population in active in ethnic and religious conflict. As upstate New York has been an economically depressed area for many years, many of my school friends went away to college and took jobs in other areas as I did. A globalized economy has caused one of the most enormous migrations in human history since World War II. Today, people from many different backgrounds have written about the experience of leaving the close-knit communities of their families, and moving to urban centers where they find themselves in unfamiliar territory. Some people are able to reestablish community ties in the new environment along separate ethnic lines, through religious institutions, country clubs, music groups, community centers, or other social meeting places. Some remain lonely and isolated with a feeling of being in exile from somewhere that no longer exists.

Yet in an urban environment where we are likely to meet others from everywhere in the world in workplaces and public spaces, there can be a destabilization of any simple notion of fixed home and identity. New postco-lonial geographies may be mapped. Where there are many people who are schooled in negotiating between cultures in temporary demilitarized zones, creative languages of solidarity can be invented. As we break away from the older collective consciousness normalized in the era of colonialism, formerly unheard narratives and dialogues can rupture identities and speed up pro-cesses of individuation and differentiation. By participating in this process, we will necessarily discover new, and sometimes disorienting, territories to explore in imagining both ourselves and others. Hybrid rituals and postcolo-nial pilgrimages can then begin to create the cosmopolitan communities of the future.

The First Language Is Not Our Own

The work of Salman Rushdie, who was born in Bombay but educated in England, is a long meditation on postcolonial communication. His novel, *Midnight's Children*, is a fantasy about how a new order of individuated and creative citizens in a hybrid community might develop. He imagines that those children born in India during the first hour of postcolonial independence at midnight on August 15, 1947, "midnight's children," might have a special destiny. Though still influenced by the ethnic, class, and religious hatreds of their parents' collective consciousness, perhaps the rupture of the past which independence and the end of colonialism represent, might create a special moment of openness to the new.

> In fact all over the new India, the dream we all shared, children were being born who were only partially the offspring of their parents – the children of midnight were also the children *of the time*: fathered, you understand, by history. It can happen. (Rushdie, p. 137)

Rushdie imagines that each of the 1001 children born during the first hour of independence have special paranormal powers "although synchronicity on such a scale would stagger even C.G. Jung" (Rushdie, p. 234) An accident on his tenth birthday allows the narrator of *Midnight's Children*, Saleem, to convene telepathic conventions of all the children who can then discuss the future of the India they hope to create. Saleem approaches these conversations with enormous optimism "as though history, arriving at a point of the highest significance and promise, had chosen to sow, in that instant, the seeds of a future which would be genuinely different from anything the world had seen up to that time." (Rushdie, p. 234)

But as the children develop surrounded by the collective consciousness of their parents, they begin to identify with older values.

> I won't deny I was disappointed. I shouldn't have been; there was nothing unusual about the children except for their gifts; their heads were full of all the usual things, fathers mothers money food land possessions fame power God. Nowhere in the thoughts of the Conference could I find anything as new as ourselves ... Children, however magical, are not immune to their parents; and as the prejudices and worldviews of adults began to take over their minds, I found the children from Maharashtra loathing Gujaratis, and fair-skinned northerners reviling Dravidian 'blackies'; there were religious rivalries; and class entered our councils.

The rich children turned up their noses at being in such lowly company; Brahmins began to feel uneasy at permitting even their thoughts to touch the thoughts of untouchables; while, among the low-born, the pressures of poverty and Communism were becoming evident … and on top of all this, there were clashes of personality, and the hundred squalling rows which are unavoidable in a parliament composed entirely of half-grown brats. (Rushdie, p. 273)

Saleem, however, has grown up negotiating opposites in his family. He is already so complicated as a personality that he cannot afford the splitting into binary opposites. He imagines a space in-between, a "third way" or "third principle" whereby what is split apart in the world can be sutured and healed.

Brothers, sisters … Do not let this happen! Do not permit the endless duality of masses-and-classes, capital-and-labor, them-and-us to come between us! We … must be a third principle, we must be the force which drives between the horns of the dilemma; for only by being other, by being new, can we fulfill the promise of our birth! … people are not things; if we come together, if we love each other, this Conference, this children-sticking-together-through-thick-and-thin, can be that third way. (Rushdie, p. 306)

Saleem's rival, Shiva, however, articulates an opposing set of values.

No, little rich boy, there is no third principle; there is only money-and-poverty and have-and-lack, and right-and-left; there is only me-against-the-world! The world is not ideas, rich boy; the world is no place for dreamers and their dreams … (Rushdie, p. 307)

The Midnight's Children Conference fails and eventually Saleem loses the capacity to convene it telepathically. If any reconciliation is to happen in the world, adults will have to want it. Though children are born with a capacity for newness, Saleem decides that "children are the vessels into which adults pour their poison … "

If there is a third principle, its name is childhood. But it dies; or rather it is murdered. (Rushdie, p. 308)

But Rushdie doesn't give up on his dream of reconciliation. He finds a surviving "third principle." The adult Saleem, after many defeats in life, begins to work in a pickle factory and write his life story, which is also a kind of preserving of what has come to him in his life. As chutney is created below by a careful selection of a myriad of different fruits and spices slowly cooked according to old recipes, the writer carries out a "chutnification of history" above the factory, metabolizing the conflicts of the past into meaningful parables and creative images which can help to shape a different future.

> One day, perhaps, the world may taste the pickles of history. They may be too strong for some palates, their smell may be overpowering, tears may rise to the eyes; I hope nevertheless it will be possible to say of them that they possess the authentic taste of truth ... that they are, despite everything, acts of love. (Rushdie, p. 550)

There Are Names Each Thing Has for Itself

Depth psychology has always been a space created by "dreamers and their dreams" outside the literalized vocabulary of official culture. Essentially it is a psychology of the margin, whether the margin is imagined as a breach of collective consciousness, alchemical transformation, dream image, unconscious transference, regression, "wounding", "seeing through," or "pathologizing" cultural fictions. Depth psychology is always about the pull of the future, about what has not yet found expression, experienced at the edge of current consciousness. It is itself a kind of third principle, looking for a path between memory and creativity, conformity and freedom, science and the humanities, theory and practice, religious experience and mental illness. This path has been imagined "in the vale," that is, as located in the local daily life of individuals in struggle with conflicting affiliations, yearnings, and fantasies.

It is not surprising that many well-known depth psychologists have been, like various postcolonial writers, located on the margins of, or in conflict with, the dominant culture of their time. Freud and all the early psychoanalysts, being Jewish, were not allowed to pursue academic careers. Their work was more likely to be presented at Jewish men's clubs like the B'nai B'rith organization, than in any mainstream venue. As they had to leave Austria to avoid being killed in concentration camps, much of their later work was done in second languages in foreign countries. Though Jung was Swiss, and remained in his home country for most of his life, he came from a poor and provincial background and was always considered an eccentric in Zurich. Aniela Jaffé came to Zurich as an immigrant from Nazi Germany. James

Hillman did most of his early writing as an American working in Europe. Each of these writers would have been negotiating conflicting cultural codes on a daily basis.

Jung has described a process he called the "transcendent function" that can arise out of extreme conflicts within an individual, a process that is a third way between extremes. Often in the course of analysis with clients, Jung noticed that opposite possibilities would seem to hang the analysand on a cross of ambivalence. Sometimes the outcome was to jump to one side or the other identifying with a literal solution and demonizing its opposite. However, in some cases, Jung noticed that if the tension of opposite possibilities could be held, if both sides could be heard and symbolized, there was often a third possibility, a new image that united the opposites in some previously unimaginable way, giving the client a rush of new energy and creative possibility. Such a process, according to Jung, is always a "defeat of the ego;" that is, a defeat of old ways of knowing and imaging self and world. The restored self which emerged, would be more aware of its multiplicity, unconscious edges, silenced possibilities, and spontaneous ruptures which puncture previously set ideas. Conflicts would be accepted, perhaps even treasured, as periods of psychological insight and "soul-making." After such experiences, one might live more openly and provisionally in dialogue with what arises synchronistically in both personal and social experience.

Potentially, depth psychology could be in discussion with other disciplines about very complex notions of personal and social identity, always in the process of negotiating internal and external conflicts through dialogue and creativity. If Western official history has been a one-sided and dissociative fiction, there must be a restorative process needed in our social, educational, and community discourse, a "chutnification of history" where the unheard stories and perspectives which have been absent yet preserved, are brought into dialogue with Eurocentric culture. This would result in a decentering of narrative and history parallel with the "defeat of the ego," similar to what Hillman has called a "wounding" process. Depth psychology itself must be implicated in such a process.

It has been particularly those writers who come from postcolonial cultures marginalized by Western official history who have written about a new kind of dialogue in a "third space" which could restore absent narratives in Western academic and social worlds. Homi Bhabha, a British-Asian living in England, has suggested that most discussions about other cultural realities outside of the European and American dominant cultures, simply positions them as "Other."

In fact the sign of the 'cultured' or the 'civilized' attitude is the ability to appreciate cultures in a kind of *musée imaginaire*; as though one should be able to collect and appreciate them. Western connoisseurship is the capacity to understand and locate cultures in a universal time-frame that acknowledges their various historical and social contexts only eventually to transcend them and render them transparent ... A transparent norm is constituted, a norm given by the host society or dominant culture, which says that 'these other cultures are fine, but we must be able to locate them within our own grid.' This is what I mean by a *creation* of cultural diversity and a *containment* of cultural difference ... The whole nature of the public sphere is changing so that we really do need the notion of a politics which is based on unequal, uneven, multiple, and *potentially antagonistic* political identities. (Bhabha, p. 208)

Homi Bhabha asks us to go down in to the vale of intercultural encounter, to see all cultures as "symbol-forming and subject-constituting interpellative practices" which are partly incommensurable and cannot be "accommodated within a universalist framework." This means that people identified with Eurocentric culture will no longer be able to speak through a heroic ego or "sovereign self" that is identified with collective consciousness. Rather, one has to be prepared to have encounters in liminal space, where an always new and hybrid ambivalence tempers an identity-in-process that is both self and other, known and unknown, unified and conflicting, owned and alienated. There is a constant movement in such a third space to reformulate, rethink, and extend what one already knows, in the process of making new alliances.

Gloria Anzaldua, an expert in intercultural conflict as both a Mexican American raised in Texas and a lesbian surrounded by homophobic culture, has named this hybrid third space *mestizaje*. Linking cultural studies and depth psychology, Anzaldua imagines a new consciousness in the making as a result of globalization, a consciousness of the borderlands, or *mestiza* consciousness.

The work takes place underground – subconsciously. It is work that the soul performs. That focal point or fulcrum, that juncture where the *mestiza* stands is where phenomena tend to collide. It is where the possibility of uniting all that is separate occurs. This assembly is not one where severed or separated pieces merely come together. Nor is it a balancing of opposing powers. In attempting to work out a synthesis, the self has added a third element which is greater than the sum of its severed parts. That third element is a new consciousness – a *mestiza* conscious-ness – and though it is a source of intense pain, its energy comes from continual creative motion that keeps breaking down the unitary aspect of each new paradigm. (Anzaldua, p. 79)

Anzaldua imagines that this work will affect both the self and community, in an act of individuation that deepens relationships at every level. It is "the opus," the great alchemical work," a "morphogenesis."

The work of *mestiza* consciousness is to break down the subject-object duality that keeps her a prisoner and to show in the flesh and through the images in her work how duality is transcended. The answer to the problem between the white race and the colored, between males and females, lies in healing the split that originates in the very foundations of our lives, our culture, our languages, our thoughts. A massive uprooting of dualistic thinking in the individual and collective consciousness is the beginning of a long struggle, but one that could, in our best hopes, bring us to the end of rape, of violence, and of war. (Anzaldua, p. 80)

Beneath Us the Other Order Already Moves

At the margin of any cultural complex, whether it is part of individual or community identity, there are always discontinuous and fragmentary images and narratives that may rupture older mythologies. Where there is dialogue at the border, many new forms of expression may arise, leading to a reframing of the issues, a restoration of communication, and a quickening of ideas and images. This dialogue needs to take place in an embodied liminal space where what is unknown can appear with all of its contradictory and uncomfortable presence. Concretely, this can mean the struggle to understand new ideas and ways of being encountered in the social world, or the difficulty of accepting unknown parts of the self that may appear in symptom, desire, or dream image worked through in creative processes.

The response to rupture and disorientation can be either rigid defenses of previous positions or an opening toward new and liberating possibilities. In the best case scenario, we may then begin to relativize our current local social constructions and develop an appreciation of their mythic quality. We could meet the Other in a liminal and creative third space. Unfortunately, there is always fear where there is disorientation, so there may also be a renewed instinct toward dissociation. The response of medieval Europe to intercontinental cultural contact was Crusades, colonialism, and in some cases, the development of xenophobia, scientific racism, discourses of purity and pollution, and genocide. This pattern was repeated in the Americas. Today after five hundred years of colonial dominance which erased many alternative narratives, a postcolonial story is "burning," "dreaming," and "waking up" at the margins of the "forsaken world." People educated in Eurocentric environments will be challenged to wound cherished myths of progress, development, economic and cultural superiority, and white supremacy.

Depth psychology developed in Europe partly as a critique of an exceptionally narrow social code, reframing the discourse to include encounters, texts, and practices connected with marginalized cultural Others. (From the point of view of dominant culture, as well as the contemporary mainstream academic world, many depth psychologists have been and still are marginalized cultural Others.) Depth psychology has always been a decentering dialogue between dominant cultures and silenced cultures, conscious and unconscious, self and other. Though it has developed a language describing the dynamics of projection, transference, and countertransference, its specific expertise may be connected with the appreciation of what the Japanese call *Ma:* a silence or emptiness in the heart of experience that allows profound human encounter and understanding outside the usual norms of social contact. Depth psychology could be seen as a long process of exploration and listening at the margins of all collective thought that now involves practitioners on every continent.

Yet in its institutionalization and success, depth psychology has inevitably developed its own collective consciousness; and even if it is a very great truth, I believe with Jung that identification with it will produce a disaster. Clearly this collective must also have its unconscious margins and a tendency to defend borders. Closed frontiers can lead to isolation and the development of a private idiolect out of communication with potential allies or the enrichment of interesting theoretical challenges. Our borders need to remain open if we are to continue talking from wounds.

As a life-long practitioner of disidentification, it is perhaps predictable I have not felt inclined to attach my theorizing to a specific school of psychoanalytic or analytic thought. I have often found myself mystified by the enmities and attachments formed in relation to specific formulations of various theoreticians. If they are all provisional interpretations or "healing fictions" which help us to "see through" literalized symptoms and mythologies, surely we don't want to literalize or freeze our own interpretations.

Even if in my biographical journey a certain writer or set of mythologies was immensely important, I share the insight of Islamic mysticism that there are many paths up the mountain and that all mountains are connected at the root. In this view, the norm of contact with others would be dialogue through histories and language which are discontinuous and often incommensurable, and we would have to listen to each other in silence for a long time in order to connect in a third space that is neither you framed by my already-known categories or me framed by your already-known categories. We would each learn something new in this encounter. The special talent contributed by an experience with depth psychology might be the patience to create containers for this type of communication and to tolerate learning again and again within them, about our own cultural dissociations and personal blindness.

My dream for the future of depth psychology in globalized communities and environments often in crisis, is that we will enter into the rough and tumble of postcolonial dialogues going on all around us and listen deeply to the suffering and ecstasy to be found there, where "it is burning." For depth psychology to continue to differentiate itself soulfully, it will also have to hear into local histories and embodied fragmentary spaces of encounter beyond its already-mapped territories. It will have to sink into the vale of origin stories different from the normalized Western academic narrative where only great individual European men climbed new peaks of understanding to create "progress." These acts of rugged individualism, unconnected to social environments, would have to be reframed to include a myriad fragmentary historical and textual conversations that have contributed to our discipline. In the continued development of depth psychology, I believe we will have to arrive at what Hillman calls "polytheism."

In postcolonial studies, it is recognized that multiple possible mythologies might represent the past at different moments of the present. Depth psychology might enter into the current hybrid performance-style of auto-ethnography with many other marginalized subjects, where we could view our own past as a series of interesting serial constructions, none of which is definitive. According to Jose Munoz,

> Autoethnography is not interested in searching for some lost and essential experience, because it understands the relationship that subjects have with their own pasts as complicated yet necessary fictions. (Munoz, p. 118)

A polytheistic and autoethnographic depth psychology might come to see its lines of origin developing from many sites of dialogue: Islamic mysticism in the texts of Ibn Arabi interpreted by Henri Corbin, Jewish Kabbala which reemerged in the ideas of Freud, Jaffé, and Neumann, Chinese alchemy in discussions by Jung, D.T. Suzuki, and Richard Wilhelm, Native-American mythologies in the work of Clarissa Pinkola Estes, Latin American folklore in Lopez-Pedraza's thought, or Malidome Somé's work on African ritual. The European Renaissance that is sometimes the origin story of depth psychology could itself be reinterpreted as a centuries-long cultural encounter between an Arabic-speaking African-Mediterranean literary world (which preserved classical texts in Arabic that were lost for centuries in Europe), a Jewish and African Diaspora, and pre-colonial and colonial Europe in contact with Asia, Africa, and Latin America. Disowned for centuries in official histories of Europe, this historic borderlands produced a vibrant intercultural literature by neo-Platonists, Rosicrucians, Cathars, Sufis, Gnostics, alchemists, Troubadors, Kabbalists, poets, and travel writers reporting from the contact zones.

In this schema, much of Jungian depth psychology could be reimagined as part of a fragmentary and discontinuous cultural history that has developed in border areas for centuries. Often its work has been a narrative about myths, symptoms, and images that challenge and resist the current dominant worldview because they have remained unconscious. From this perspective, I am unable to portray depth psychology as originating primarily from the dominant cultures of Europe and America or from any particular culture within Europe; I see it as an attempt at transcultural or intercultural conversation in a third space, historically and currently in dialogue with mythologies and practices from every continent, even though I am aware that some of this conversation was interrupted, Eurocentric, colonial, or appropriating. To the degree that depth psychology can "pathologize" its own stories by relinquishing the heroic constructions of Eurocentric thought that represent European consciousness as an advance over (or a loss of) a "primitive" Other, and itself as the highest stage of consciousness in a Hegelian narrative of world progress, it can enter into a lively contemporary cross-cultural conversation. If it is able to "see through" its own origin stories and bear the ambivalence of polytheism, depth psychology has much to share in dialogue with others about lost histories and values at the margins of dominant cultures.

As practitioners in the creation of liminal spaces where what is new and not-yet thought can emerge, depth psychologists could be helpful in social and cultural dialogues that require the metabolization of conflicting or antagonistic points of view. The "pickles of history" may bring tears to our eyes, but we should be able to bear the strong and overpowering affect that comes with the emergence of disowned symptom and memories, whether individual or cultural. Like midnight's children, we are also living in a unique moment at the end of an era. I believe that the emergence of depth psychology as a discipline is one part of a great "waking up" that could eventually be "another order" growing out of the ruins of the cultural and environmental disasters caused by five-hundred years of colonialism and empire.

As I see it, a vast local and international effort of organization, repair, and dialogue, a project naming the presence of absence, is underway beneath the radar of the nightly news. The cleaning up of polluted streams and soils, the creation of community discussion groups across lines of racial exclusion, programs for mentoring youth, public investigations of corrupt police forces and state security units, alternative films and theater which challenge all the rules of normalized discourse, the spread of world music and dance across continents, worldwide demonstrations against the World Trade Organization, new lifestyles, as well as theoretical explorations of margins and silences in collective culture, are ongoing evidence of something brewing. Introducing their new book, *Cultural Activisms*, Anne Mamary and Gertrude Gonzalez speak of a process of "spinning meaning out of fragmented history, gaps in dominant texts, and stories passed along from generation to generation and spinning off in new directions, reclaiming desire, meaning, magic, and possibility."

> Cultural activisms rework, revisit, recite, and re-cite our cultures of origin, our cultures of choice, our hoped-for cultures and the overlapping of these cultures. We live and write and think and play and paint and draw and dance and sculpt and desire and cry and scream and hope and pray not only to under-mine oppressive foundations, but also to create and nurture living, exciting, sometimes unforeseen realities. (Gonzalez and Mamary, p. xvi)

A public restoration process, which is still an article of faith in most locations, will require much more mature, self-conscious, and sophisticated individuals for the dialogue of the future among communities. Those who are inexperienced in negotiating multiple cultural codes because they live in monocultural environments, will need to learn the arts of *mestizaje* and conversation in uncomfortable borderlands. Many people will be needed to create together the new decentered environments where all can reclaim "desire, meaning, magic, and possibility." If it enters the vale, depth psychology has an important contribution to make in the remapping of discontinuous and multiple notions of self and other, consciousness and unconscious that must be the basis of restorative encounters and acts of love.

References

Anzaldua, G. (1987). *Borderlands / La frontera*. San Francisco: aunt lute books.

Bhabha, H. (1990). The Third Space: Interview with Homi Bhabha. In J. Rutherford (Ed.), *Identity, Community, Culture, Difference*. London: Lawrence and Wishart.

Gonzalez, G. & Mamary, A. (1999). *Cultural Activisms*. Albany: State University of New York Press.

Hillman, J. (1975). *Revisioning Psychology*. New York: Harper Perrenial.

Hillman, J. (1979). *Puer Papers*. Dallas: Spring Publications.

Hogan, L. (1993). *The Book of Medicines*. Minneapolis: Coffee House Press.

Jaffé, A. (1975). *The Myth of Meaning*. New York: Penguin Books, Inc.

Jung, C.G. (1966). *Two Essays on Analytical Psychology*. Princeton: Princeton University Press.

Jung, C.G. (1971). *Psychological Types*. Princeton: Princeton University Press.

Jung, C.G. (1978). *The Structure and Dynamics of the Psyche*. Princeton: Princeton University Press.

Munoz, J. E. (1999). The Autoethnographic Performance: Reading Richard Fung's Queer Hybridity. In M. Joseph & J.N. Fink (Eds.), *Performing Hybridity*. Minneapolis: University of Minnesota Press.

Rushdie, S. (1980). *Midnight's Children*. New York: Penguin Books. Chapter 17.

CHAPTER 17

Prisoners of our Imagination:
The Boys Inside the American Gulag

Aaron Kipnis

On a recent Sunday afternoon five East Side Boys crossed the main street that divides our neighborhoods. They parked their car near the street corner, a few doors from my townhouse. There they hung out, laughing, talking, working on the car, and drinking beers in the sun. They pumped up the bass on the CD player so high their music vibrated my windows. While reading the Sunday paper, one of my more relaxing weekend rituals, I started feeling irritable.

I went to our balcony window and looked out to see what they were up to. I wondered: Are they checking out my street, planning future burglaries, car thefts, or assaults? My wife, Liz, walks through their territory on her way to the post office. My daughter, a student at SBCC, often parks her car right where they were congregating. I felt concerned about my family's safety and the security of our home. For all its rare beauty and fabled enclaves of wealth, Santa Barbara is not immune from the influence of youth gangs and the angry young men that fill their ranks. There are twenty-six known gangs in our region, many loosely confederated by territory as belonging to the East or West side of our city.

It was hard to relax, half expecting to hear the screeching wheels of a West Side Boy's car driving by. Will a bullet shatter our window, I wondered? After all, there have been several gang-related shootings nearby in the last year. "Why don't they stay in their own neighborhood?" I blurted out to Liz.

She looked out the window and said, "They are in their neighborhood, Aaron. That's Carlos. He lives down at the Greenwood Apartments with his mother Carla. She's the manicurist at Heads Up where I get my hair cut. Looks like Carlos got himself an old car to fix up. He's just showing it off to his friends. There's probably no room to park it at the apartments."

"Those boys are really OK," Liz continued. "They're just a little wild. Whenever I walk by them in the neighborhood I just smile and say, 'Hi!' They always smile back. Come back from the window, Aaron, you're going to make them feel weird if they see you."

I laughed, thinking that despite having been a wild child myself, at age fifty-one, I had somehow transformed into a bastion of middle-class sensibilities. Several Italian stone-cutter families, who have lived here for generations, populate my street. And there are various working professionals on the block – a schoolteacher, a therapist, an attorney, a loan officer – as well as several blue-collar workers, small business owners, and others I don't know yet. Most of us own our homes. I share many of my neighbors' values today.

The brighter a light shines the darker and more detailed shadow it casts. In our sunny, whitewashed, seaside community the demarcations of class are as sharply drawn as a border between nations. Income brackets visibly graduate from working class on the flats, near the freeway below my home, to steadily increasing levels of upper classes on the hillsides and ridge tops above. Between the two is the narrow, middle-class band where we live. The demarcations of race are also quite distinct here. On this border between the Upper and Lower East Side, the residents are predominately white.

One block away is a major thoroughfare. On the other side, a higher density of apartments and rental homes exists, and the neighborhood suddenly changes to predominately Latino and African American. Many who live there serve the affluent in the hills above us. They are their gardeners, carpenters, masons, painters, pool maintainers, nannies, plumbers, housekeepers, and maids. Others run small businesses in the neighborhood. Many members of my wife's African Methodist-Episcopal church also live in the Lower East Side.

I gave a last look out the window and tried to reassure myself, thinking, "Hey, they're just kids enjoying a sunny day with no other place to hang out. They're part of my community, as much as Anna, the delightful, retired Italian lady next door who grows ambrosial tomatoes in her back yard every summer."

I went outdoors to take a walk. On the way back, as I passed by the boys, I casually looked their way. We exchanged nods. "How you doin'? Good day, huh?" I said.

"Yeah," Carlos replied.

"Hey, watzup," said another, smiling.

My tension eased. I didn't see any "tats" (gang tattoos); they were just dressed somewhat gang style like most teenaged boys in the neighborhood today. But there was a "tag" (gang graffiti) on the stop sign at the corner I didn't remember seeing before. Anyone could have put it there in the last few days. But it wasn't until the boys later drove away that I could fully relax and enjoy the remains of the day.

* * *

I like most of the young men I've counseled over the years and generally feel sympathetic to their situations. They are often victims of rough treatment, neglect, racism, and the insults of poverty. When those boys gathered outside my home, however, I felt vulnerable and uneasy. I did not feel as understanding as when wearing a professional hat. I have more to lose today than when I was their age. At midlife, I just don't feel so tough anymore. These sorts of fears cause many adults to turn away from young men who do not fit our ideal molds for appearance or behavior. As I thought about it more, my unease felt all the more ironic.

I went out on the deck and smoked a cigar in the afterglow of a sun-drenched day. An ocean breeze stirred our wind chimes and rustled the bougainvillea on the balcony. I suddenly understood more clearly why, when I was Carlos's age, adults displayed so much anxiety around me. I was wild, too. But many people thought I was just "bad." Over the years I've tried to put aside recollections from those days. But the sudden appearance of East Siders, on an otherwise tranquil afternoon, somehow brought these memories to the surface again, like fetid bubbles rising from the muck below an otherwise pristine lake.

I remembered the day the police first arrested me for running away from home after a beating by my stepfather. Incomprehensibly to me at the time, they jailed me but allowed him to remain free. As I entered the Los Angeles Juvenile Detention Center the outer gate crashed shut with the finality of a head-on car collision. Then came the first deadening click as the lock on my new front door slid in place. Click, chunk – the second lock was secured. Click, click – the sound of the guard's hard leather heels striking the concrete floor steadily diminished as he strode away from my seven-by-eight foot, windowless, steel-doored cell, much like the cells in Santa Barbara Juvenile Hall that today house two boys in that space too small for one. My heart grew cold as I sat alone on the sheet metal cot. As I contemplated my future, the singular thought echoing through my mind was click, click, click, click ... I was eleven years old.

During the next seven years of adolescence, when not in juvenile institutions, I spent most of my time living on the streets of Hollywood or San Francisco's Tenderloin and Haight Ashbury districts. The outcast and the outlawed were my friends and family. I lived with Hell's Angels, drag queens, drug dealers, runaways, dropouts, prostitutes, musicians, artists, and thieves.

I rifled cars and stole from shops. I slept in abandoned buildings and cars. I ate out of dumpsters, "dined and dashed" at restaurants, committed acts of prostitution, sold drugs, and did whatever else I could to survive as a teenager alone on the city streets. Understandably, the police repeatedly arrested me.

During my detentions I witnessed numerous beatings, sexual assaults, bloody suicide attempts, stabbings, desperate escape attempts, and young men driven insane from long solitary confinements that broke their spirits. Because of my rebellious behavior in those institutions, I also spent difficult months in dark, isolation cells.

The other prisoners' enraged screams, threats, pounding on the bars and walls, and cursing filled the air with a frightening maelstrom of discontent. These experiences left indelible impressions on my young psyche that still haunt me on occasions. Even though over three decades have passed since my last arrest, those images remain my most vivid memories of adolescence.

As is still true today, the majority of us in those institutions were there for nonviolent crimes. The horrors I witnessed as a child propelled me into adult life with a drive to find alternatives to the juvenile justice system. Most conditions that I encountered as an angry young man have steadily worsened since my era. And I have become painfully aware of ways in which our collective failures as parents, teachers and counselors pave the road for steadily increasing numbers of young men to become incarcerated.

After my first arrest, a judge made me a ward of the state of California. I remained under the state's jurisdiction, on probation or parole, from age eleven to twenty-three. Most friends from this period died long ago from overdoses, suicides, and the perils of street life. But I survived. Eventually, I even thrived. And so can most boys who are similarly abandoned. They do, however, need some specific help, offered at the right time in the right way. It is my personal and professional belief that the majority of difficult, troubled, angry, criminal, and even violent young men can lead whole and productive lives when given the right opportunities and leadership.

Unlike most so-called "bad boys," I had the good fortune to receive a college education. A compassionate parole officer noted that, as a young felon on parole, I might qualify for a rehabilitation grant to cover some college expenses. Though this support was nominal – a few hundred dollars each semester – it gave an impoverished young man enough of a leg up to make college a possibility. Los Angeles City College's policies allowed me conditional admittance as a nineteen-year-old with only a ninth-grade education. It was the first time I went to the same school two years in a row. From there I worked my way through the California State University system and private institutes, culminating my studies with a Ph.D. in clinical psychology.

While I was a psychology undergraduate I counseled numerous boys and young men in residential treatment centers, juvenile halls, on wilderness "rites of passage," and in county jail as a public defender's assistant. Over the years, I also held support groups, seminars, retreats, and private consultations for men and increasingly started receiving requests to train therapists about how to work more effectively with men and boys. Lately much of my attention has been on educators because our teachers and school counselors today are increasingly the last line of defense for kids jumping between the fire of dysfunctional homes and the frying pan of juvenile institutions.

Teaching is a difficult profession. Teachers make much less than prison guards, whose jobs require much less education. Today, however, the teaching profession is equally stressful and, in some schools, almost as dangerous as law enforcement. Failing schools reflect a failure of our culture. Many schools are crumbling and out of date, often lacking adequate textbooks or even basic teaching supplies. In California, graduation rates have steadily fallen over the last twenty years. This drop is coincidental to changes in our state tax code. In 1978, Proposition 13 gave a huge tax break to existing property owners, largely benefiting elderly voters, and gutted the primary source of school funds. Subsequently, our state slipped from the top 10 percent in education spending to the bottom 10 percent. Now, one third of our boys fail to graduate with their class.

Our schools today also often hold many double standards for boys. One common fallacy in gender equity philosophy is the belief that any identified disadvantage for girls corresponds to an advantage for boys. When gender equity programs emphasize the remediation of girls' math or sports deficits, however, without equally spotlighting boys' reading and writing deficits, it's spurious to claim that schools are only "failing at fairness" for girls. Consider for a moment that:

When both girls and boys are equally misbehaving, boys receive more frequent and severe penalties.

Boys, particularly low achievers, receive eight to ten times the reprimands of their female classmates. These reproaches are more likely to occur in front of classmates, whereas girls are more frequently taken aside in private.

Boys are removed from classrooms and serve more detention than girls. They receive 71 percent of school suspensions and are expelled at even higher rates.

Boys are victims of the majority of school violence.

Boys are referred to special education four to one over girls. They represent over 70 percent of students labeled as learning disabled and 80 percent of those sent to programs for the emotionally disturbed. Minority males are highly overrepresented in these categories.

Boys drop out of school four to one over girls.

Boys receive more F's, have lower grade point averages, and fail to graduate more often than girls.

Girls continue to outperform boys in reading and writing by much greater degrees than boys ever outperformed girls in math and science.

Boys are in fewer clubs, student governments, and school newspapers than girls.

Boys are the minority of valedictorians, academic scholarship winners, new college students, and those going on to graduate school.

Nationwide, males now number only 44 percent of college admissions and 41 percent of graduate students. In graduate programs for educators and helping professionals they rarely exceed 25 percent of the students. Subsequently, men, and minority men in particular, are highly underrepresented as primary and secondary teachers, counselors, and therapists to who troubled boys can turn for guidance about their transition to manhood.

Contrary to past studies by gender equity advocates, recent surveys indicate that greater numbers of girls report receiving positive feedback from teachers than boys. The girls reporting the highest levels of teacher attention also have the highest levels of college participation. Minority boys, however, who report the lowest positive attention rates from teachers, have significantly lower college participation. Economically disadvantaged schools have the highest male dropout rates and the lowest male reading scores – as much as four whole grade levels/years below affluent schools.

When boys without good support at home also fall through the widening cracks at school, social services are the next line of defense between at-risk boys and institutions. Today, however, the social net that is supposed to catch youth in free fall has a number of large holes in it. The catcher in the rye is asleep in the field. Tragically, most of the boys who slip through the grasp of parents, teachers, counselors, therapists, social workers, judges, and probation officers do not survive. They go to prison, they go insane, they die. And they create a lot of collateral harm when they go down in flames.

Our national culture today, in many ways, looks a lot like the East Side of Santa Barbara. The divide between opportunity and privilege or exclusion and despair is a double-edged sword that often defends one class and cuts the other. It is harder than any other time in modern history for young men at risk to cross the thickening line that separates them from a good life. This is particularly true for low-income boys and young men of color. In this time of unprecedented prosperity for some segments of our community, child poverty is 50% higher today than it was three decades ago in 1971. One-in-five children in Santa Barbara County live below the poverty line.

American boys today suffer higher rates of homicide, suicide, incarceration, functional illiteracy, school failure, child poverty, gang involvement, gun carrying, drug abuse, violent victimization, male prostitution and sexual assault, AIDS, and homelessness than the youth of any other Western industrialized nation. In many categories we exceed others by far. I believe, however, there are many things we can do to assure that our boys' lives turn toward hope and community instead of nihilism and destruction. Although fundamental changes in our educational, social, and justice institutions' attitudes toward non-conforming boys could help a great deal, the single most important thing we can do is to change our perspective. In essence, the problems with the youth of America reflect a profound failure of our imagination.

From era to era the withered finger of demonization has cast its horrific shadow upon widely diverse segments of human culture. In the 21st century this archetypal fate appears to have selected young men as its most favored creature. Today boys are more pathologized then lauded and it is upon their backs that the sins of the village are heaped before they are driven out of the village and into the barren wilds. How then do we, as a community, meet young men to better help them shoulder the collective burden of their postmillennial scapegoat role?

Once a bad boy arrives at adult prison, our hope for his future dims. Imprisonment signals that we failed to forge crossroads along the prison highway that could have turned him toward community. Some, perhaps, could not have been helped by any intervention. Most young men who pass those gates, however, embody our collective failures in parenting, education, counseling, community support, legislation, economic policy, and juvenile justice.

In 1971, Federal Judge James Doyle wrote, "I am persuaded that the institution of prison probably must end. In many respects it is as intolerable within the United States as was the institution of slavery, equally brutalizing to all involved, equally toxic to the social system, equally subversive of the brotherhood of man, even more costly by some standards, and probably less rational." When Judge Doyle wrote this, the U.S. rate of incarceration was about 100 per 100,000. Today it is 650. Two million Americans are behind bars; four million more are on probation or parole; eight to ten million pass through jails each year. One in thirty-three Americans are in prison, jail, probation, or parole, 95 percent of these prisoners are male. Most were boys or young men when they first entered the "system."

The rate at which we are imprisoning our citizens exceeds that of every other nation but Russia (at 685 per 100,000). But then Russia never has been known as the "land of the free." By comparison, the pre-apartheid rate for South Africa was 368 per 100,000; China's is 342; Romania, 200; and Turkey, 55. The incarceration rates of other Western democracies are all fractions of our own: England and Wales, 120; Spain, 115; Italy, 85; and Scandinavia, 60. Japan's incarceration rate is merely 36 in 100,000.

As our rates skyrocketed, over the last few decades, most European rates remained relatively stable. Sentence length for most nonviolent crime is considerably longer here. For example, Texas's "punitive scale" ranks it between United Arab Emirates and Nigeria. California is not much further down that list.

When Alexander Solzhenitzyn wrote the *Gulag Archipelago*, he inflamed the passions of many and brought the plight of injustice against the Soviet people to the world stage. He said, "If only it were so simple! If only there were evil people somewhere insidiously committing evil deeds, and it were necessary only to separate them from the rest of us and destroy them. But the line dividing good and evil cuts through the heart of every human being." Today, I believe an American Gulag is proliferating, a darkening stain on our national soul, filled with angry young men from our urban wastelands. The world will also judge the true measure of our humanity by how we now deal with this similar crisis. In the winter of 1998, Amnesty International shocked the world by issuing a detailed report documenting the many ways that "people incarcerated in [U.S.] prisons are often the victims of very serious human rights violations." This was the first such action against a Western nation.

In my home state of California, the largest prison system in the nation is filled to about 200% of capacity. Double celling is routine, thus reducing the space allotted a prisoner to twenty-seven square feet. The pressured atmosphere seriously affects prisoners' mental health and undermines the few rehabilitative programs that still exist. In response to prison violence, California created a new, ultrasecure, "super maximum" prison at Pelican Bay, set in the woods, far from human habitations.

Pelican Bay represents a new breed of Orwellian, mechanized, computerized, highly isolative, stark, behavior modification institutions where most of the facility is beneath the ground and direct sunlight never shines. Various investigative reports document "patterns of needless and officially sanctioned brutality" and "cruel, inhuman, and degrading treatment" resulting in serious injury further aggravated by denial of basic medical care. Supermax sensory deprivation, similar to other nations' brainwashing of prisoners of war and political prisoners, has driven some inmates into severe mental illness. Amnesty International finds this factor alone a blatant violation of international guidelines for prisoners' human rights.

Throughout California there are recent and well-documented incidents of torture, beatings, staged "gladiator competitions," medical and mental health neglect, unjustified shootings and deaths. There are also many reports of guards sanctioning the rape of male prisoners as a method to keep them in line. Ex-prisoners report that forced prostitution and sexual slavery are widespread in our prisons with the primary victims of sexual assault being the boys young men transferred to adult prisons. In a nation that prizes openness, prisons remain a largely obscured, shadow world with closed borders. In California, reporters are no longer even allowed to interview prisoners. There is much we do not know. But we continue to send our difficult young men there in record numbers and at increasingly younger ages.

Can we now unabashedly look the new millennium in the face and boldly state that we are still a free society? I believe that failure to respond adequately to this crisis could undermine our status as a civilized culture. How can we better meet the collective fantasy fueling this unprecedented juggernaut of prison expansion in our culture's desperate attempt to quarantine its Shadow? What are the imaginal foundations upon which we have sanctioned the construction of the world's largest penal system?

One reason we imprison more men than the rest of the world is that we can afford to. With six percent of the world's population we have 25% of the world's prisoners. Some analysts aggregate the costs of prison management and construction, county jail administration, judicial systems, law enforcement, and the probation, parole, and social service agencies needed to deal with released prisoners at $100 billion per year. As spending on prisons steadily rose over recent decades, job-training funds plummeted and the rate of higher education spending was stunted.

California built twenty-one prisons and one university from 1984 to 1994, adding over 25,000 corrections employees while eliminating 8,000 from higher education. In 1984 the higher education budget was two and one-half times that of corrections; by 1994 both budgets were equal. Higher education programs for prisoners fell from 350 nationwide in 1990 to only eight in 1997. In 1999 nothing indicates any reversals in this classrooms-to-cellblocks exchange.

The deeper issues are more difficult to name, but they appear to point toward a shift in our collective imagination. From the end of World War II through the 1960s the U.S. rate of imprisonment showed little change. In the early 1970s, however, subsequent to the antiwar movement, civil rights demonstrations, open drug use, and baby-boomer challenges to the established order, new legislation significantly increased the strength of the criminal justice net, and a war against a generation of young men began in earnest. Our prison population then began its relentless ascent to today's previously unimaginable level.

Contrary to conventional wisdom, studies by the Department of Justice indicate little relationship between crime rates and incarceration rates. Incarceration rates are, however, somewhat linked to fluctuations in the total numbers of young men. The larger the ratio young men represent in our population at any given time, the more appear in prison. Various studies also indicate some parallel links between crime and the ebb and flow of young male employment rates. Changing governmental policies that correlate with prison expansion include:

– The criminalization of broader classes of behavior
– Mandatory minimum sentencing and the curtailment of judicial discretion
– The lengthening of sentences and reduction of parole
– Greater scrutiny of parolees, particularly through drug-testing
– Increased allocation of funds for prisons over prevention, treatment, and diversion
– The war on drugs.

A number of psychosocial forces also drive prison expansion:

– A growing public thirst for vengeance, which alternatives to incarceration fail to emotionally satisfy
– A belief that only prisons can appropriately deal with lawbreakers
– Eroding faith in the viability of rehabilitation and treatment
– The voting public's growing fear of violent crime independent of its actual rise and fall
– Racism and poverty
– The widening gap between the rich and the poor
– A growing cultural bias against boys and young men, particularly those of color.

One result of the shift from education to incarceration is that more African-American young men are now in the California criminal justice system than our higher education system.

In an inverse parallel of trends, as crime rates dropped during the mid-to-late 1990s, the rate of crime stories in the media steadily increased, outstripping all other news categories by far. "If it bleeds it leads" is the ratings-competition banner of today's news media. The media are thus highly complicit in generating the disproportional degree of fear that is driving prison expansions. For example, the top ten reasons for Californians entering prison today are: 1) Possession of a controlled substance; 2) Possession of a controlled substance for sale; 3) Robbery; 4) Sale of a controlled substance: 5) Second-degree burglary: 6) Assault with a deadly weapon; 7) Driving under the influence; 8) First-degree burglary; 9) Petty theft with a prior conviction and 10) Vehicle theft.

The crimes heralded by politicians, officials and private investors peddling prisons to a fearful citizenry – murder, rape, child sexual abuse, armed robbery, and kidnapping – are noticeably absent from this list. Those who fear crime the most live in the safest areas, on average, and are the least likely to become victims. Those who complain about crime the least – young, low-income males – live in the most dangerous neighborhoods and represent the majority of crime victims. Politicians know that it is safer to court the first group. They vote. The voter registration of young ethnic minority males, however, is so low that some jury pools lack any young minority men, even where their "peers" represent the majority being judged. In the 1998 elections, one out of seven adult African-American males (1.4 million) were denied the right to vote or sit on juries, due to prior felony convictions. In some communities and several states, 25 to 33 percent of African-American men are now disenfranchised from the electorate by this invisible gerrymandering and covert repeal of the Thirteenth Amendment.

This fundamental right and unique herald of democracy is only denied by other industrial democracies in cases of treason or other direct threats against the democratic process. In South Africa, for example, all prisoners have the right to vote. All together, four million Americans – one out of forty-eight eligible voters, or one in thirty registered voters – have lost their right to vote. Some elections are lost or won by these margins. This is not the vision of American democracy I learned in school. Nor does this practice encourage the marginalized to ever embrace or work within the system. So what can we do?

Some of the influences that helped me transform my own life were:

– Access to affordable education and working hard thereafter.

– Job and financial skills acquisition that led to employment above the minimum wage.

– Introduction to meditation and other healthy practices that helped mitigate the traumatic impact of drugs and abuse on my nervous system.

– Association with "normal" people at work and school. This changed my core identity from a survival-driven affiliation with the criminal class to one defined by learning, caring, creativity, and productivity.

– The attention of older men – teachers, mentors, healers, and social servants – who believed in me and treated me with respect.

– Spiritual experiences, alone and in community, which raised hope and buoyed me against the downward pull of the past.

– Psychological work that lent insight into reasons behind my behavior, helped me become accountable for my actions, and directed me toward alternative ways of being.

– Alcohol and drug recovery through Twelve-Step programs.

– The sealing of my juvenile records, thus giving me a fresh start and allowing me to mainstream.

– The compassion and support of friends, lovers, spouses, teachers, and the miraculous kindness of strangers.

My research into other successful programs around the nation indicates that these are also integral elements needed for most programs to achieve lasting results in drawing forth good men out of bad boys. This work is simple and it is complex. Many young men who lose their way need sustained services from multiple arenas before they can get on the good-man track. They also need room to fail without the specter of unredeemability looming as a consequence.

One-shot programs rarely work. Brash get-tough laws with sound-bite slogans do not breed justice. Half-hearted interventions foster more disappointment and cynicism than they cure. Real change takes time and a dedicated community of responsive adults. We can do better.

* * *

During the course of writing a book on these issues, *Angry Young Men*, a lot of maintenance got deferred around my home. As it mounted up I started feeling overwhelmed. One day, I called one of the program administrators in our Fatherhood Coalition and asked whether any of their young men could use a few days of work. He called that afternoon and said one of his guys was trying to earn some Christmas money and could start the following day. At 8:00 A.M. a sixteen-year-old boy showed up at my door ready to work. He introduced himself as Carlos. He looked familiar. As we talked a bit, I realized that he was the boy with the old car and the loud CD player. I immediately felt a little apprehensive, knowing that he and his friends lived only a few blocks away and now he was going to get a good look at everything in my home. But I was already committed. So we went to work.

He was a great help. He worked hard and thoughtfully. We accomplished a great deal in a few days – more than I could have done alone in a week or more. And we talked a lot along the way about his school, the neighborhood, and other elements of his life.

I referred him to some other friends for more steady part-time work. One thing I learned from my own history of poverty is that offering good employment is often the most sincere demonstration of respect. I paid Carlos and he left, apparently pleased by our brief collaboration. He was grateful for the work; I was extremely grateful for the help. Afterwards, I never felt safer in my neighborhood. I knew that next time he was on the corner that we could talk, easily. Although I could not count on it, I felt I had a better chance of being protected by Carlos than exploited.

During the course of our exchange we came to know one another a little. Now my experience of him as part of my neighborhood is not merely some cerebral exercise, but a genuine experience of being in community with him. It was a small event in both our lives, but within it was the core of what I have attempted to voice here. The building of bridges begins with a single, slender cable stretched between two distant poles. One need not have a Ph.D. in psychology to help most of these boys. A compassionate heart and courage to risk a little goes a very long way. I pray the reader will try, in whatever way he or she can, to look out for the life of at least one young man in their community. If we all did this one thing then, perhaps, America could legitimately rejoin the ranks of civilized nations and put an end to the sacrifice of our children and democracy itself on the procrustean altar of social control.

Note: Documentation for all of the above research and statistics are referenced in: *Angry Young Men: How Parents, Teachers, and Counselors can Help "Bad Boys" become Good Men.* (Jossey-Bass Publishers, Oct. 1999)

Contributors

Stephen Aizenstat, Ph.D., founding president and core faculty member of Pacifica Graduate Institute, is a clinical psychologist whose research centers on a psychodynamic process of "tending the living image," particularly in the context of dreamwork. His approach to the dream is called DreamTending. Dr. Aizenstat brought the insights of depth psychology and dreamwork to the Earth Charter International Workshop, where he was a participant-observer in this United Nations project. Still actively involved in the Earth Charter Project, Dr. Aizenstat has conducted dreamwork seminars for more than 25 years throughout the United States, Europe, and Asia.

Charles Asher, D.Min. is Provost of Pacifica Graduate Institute, a core faculty member, Jungian Analyst, and an Oblate of the Order of St. Benedict, Camaldolese, New Camaldoli Hermitage in Big Sur, California. He is the author of *The Contemplative Self* and *Soundings* as well as other articles on psychology and religion.

Lionel Corbett, M.D., is a British-trained psychiatrist and Jungian analyst and core faculty member at Pacifica Graduate Institute. He is the author of *The Religious Function of the Psyche*. He is also director of the continuing education program, *Psyche and the Sacred*.

Hendrika de Vries M.T.S., M.F.T., teaches in the Mythological Studies program of Pacifica Graduate Institute. Her background is in theology, mythology, and Jungian depth-psychology. She has led workshops and seminars nationally using mythic imagination, dreams, and archetypal mind-body awareness to facilitate psychospiritual development. Hendrika is a licensed Marriage and Family Therapist in private practice in Santa Barbara.

Christine Downing, Ph.D., for 20 years chair of the Religious Studies Department at San Diego State University, has been associated with Pacifica since before it WAS Pacifica and before its move to our beautiful Carpinteria campus, but it is only since the establishment of the Mythological Studies program that it has become the center of her academic life. Indeed, her teaching at Pacifica is so fulfilling and so challenging that although she had earlier published nine books (including *The Goddess*, *Myths and Mysteries of*

Same-Sex Love, and *Gods in Our Midst*), she hasn't managed to complete the Holocaust memoir she began five years ago.

James Hillman, Ph.D., renowned author and psychoanalyst, is a leading scholar of Jungian and Archetypal Psychology. An innovative clinician and an inspiring teacher, Dr. Hillman has led the movement in psychology which aims to broaden the focus of therapy to include in its care disorders of the world soul. Having retired from analytical practice after 40 years, Dr. Hillman now devotes his critical attention to concerns of contemporary culture. Author of Bestsellers, *The Soul's Code: In Search of Character & Calling* and recently *The Force of Character and the Lasting Life.*

Aaron Kipnis, Ph.D., is president of the Fatherhood Coalition, a non-profit organization that supports positive male involvement in family planning, parenting, relationships, and community. He is author of *Angry Young Men; Knights Without Armor*; co-author of *What Women and Men Really Want*; and contributor to many anthologies and journals. Dr. Kipnis is on the core faculty of Pacifica Graduate Institute. He is also a regular speaker and consultant on male psychology and gender issues to professional organizations, governmental agencies, universities, national media, treatment facilities, and training institutes. Please visit www.malepsych.com for more information and an e-mail link to the author.

Patrick Mahaffey, Ph.D., is the Chair of the Mythological Studies Program at Pacifica Graduate Institute. He is a religious studies scholar who teaches courses on Asian religious traditions and hermeneutical research methods. He has published essays on religious pluralism, myth in the context of postmodernity, and on religion in American culture.

Helene Shulman Lorenz, Ph.D., is currently the Academic Dean and a Core Faculty Member at Pacifica Graduate Institute. She has a Ph.D. in Philosophy from Tulane University in New Orleans, LA and a Diploma in Analytical Psychology from the C.G. Jung Institute in Zurich. She is the author of *Living at the Edge of Chaos: Complex Systems in Psyche and Culture.* Active for many years in cultural movements for social justice and development in Latin America and the United States, she has written a number of articles, and is at work on a book, about individuation, decolonization, and community.

David L. Miller, Ph.D., is the Watson-Ledden Professor of Religion at Syracuse University and a core faculty member at Pacifica Graduate Institute. He also teaches at the Jung Institute in Zurich and was a member of the Eranos Circle in Switzerland from 1975 until 1988. Miller is the author of five books and over sixty articles and book chapters.

Maureen Murdock, M.A., M.F.T., is a core faculty member of Pacifica Graduate Institute and the author of *The Heroine's Journey; Fathers' Daughters: Transforming the Father-Daughter Relationship*; and *Spinning Inward: Using Guided Imagery with Children*. Her books have been translated into French, Dutch, German, Italian, Korean, Chinese, Hebrew, Portuguese and Spanish. Murdock is writing a book on the mythic dimension of memoir and teaches creative writing in the UCLA Extension Writers' Program.

Avedis Panajian, Ph.D., is a faculty member at Pacifica Graduate Institute, and training analyst at the Psychoanalytic Center of California, California Graduate Institute, and Newport Psychiatric Institute. He is a Diplomate in Clinical Psychology of the American Board of Professional Psychology. Dr. Panajian is a recipient of the Distinguished Educator Award from the California Psychological Association and is currently in private practice in Beverly Hills.

Ginette Paris, Ph.D., is a psychologist and the author of books on Greek and Roman mythology, among which are *Pagan Meditations*, *Pagan Grace*, and *Mythology: A CD-ROM Encyclopedia of Greek and Roman Mythology*. She is a core faculty member at Pacifica Graduate Institute and the Research Coordinator for Mythological Studies Program.

Robert D. Romanyshyn, Ph.D., is an author, teacher, and international lecturer. In addition to three books, he has published more than fifty articles in journals and edited volumes. He has been described as a master storyteller with a gift for expressing the insights of the soul with the voice of a poet. His primary interest lies in being a spokesperson for the marginalized and neglected values of the soul, including its longing for beauty, its desire for a sense of the sacred, and its hunger to remember its instinctual, vegetative, and mineral roots in nature. Robert lives with his wife, Veronica, and two of their four children in Summerland, California.

Dianne Skafte, Ph.D., lectures widely on oracular traditions in ancient and modern cultures. A past Academic Vice President of Pacifica Graduate Institute, she has taught in the field of depth psychology for over a decade. Her book, *When Oracles Speak*, has been translated into three languages.

Dennis Patrick Slattery, Ph.D., has been teaching for 31 years, including grade school, high school, junior college and university levels. He has written over 160 articles, poems and reviews. He is the author of *The Idiot: Dostoevsky's Fantastic Prince* and *The Wounded Body: Remembering the Markings of Flesh*. His interests are in the area of psyche, mythopoetics, the mimetic impulse of the psyche and body woundedness. He also enjoys writing for newspapers and magazines on current topics seen through a mythological lens. He is married and has two sons.

Mary Watkins, Ph.D., is coordinator of community & ecological fieldwork and research for Pacifica's Depth Psychology Doctoral Program. She has chaired both Master's Program in Counseling Psychology and the Depth Psychology Doctoral Program. She is the author of *Waking Dreams, Invisible Guests: The Development of Imaginal Dialogues*, co-author of *Talking With Young Children About Adoption*, and co-editor of *Psychology and the Promotion of Peace*.

Looking Ahead Academically

Pacifica Graduate Institute's unique educational format is particularly suited to individuals who wish to pursue graduate education while continuing their existing professional and personal commitments. Pacifica's monthly, three-day learning sessions take into account the professional commitments and psychological needs of the adult learner.

Department of Psychology in the Tradition of Depth Psychology

– Ph.D. in Clinical Psychology

– Ph.D. in Depth Psychology

– M.A. in Counseling Psychology

Pacifica provides one of the few accredited academic programs in Depth Psychology, which integrates literature, religion, art, mythology and an awareness of ecological issues into the understanding of the human experience. The Clinical and Counseling Psychology programs include a degree specialization in Depth Psychology and are enhanced by the study of literature, art, and mythology.

Department of Mythological Studies in the Tradition of Depth Psychology

– M.A./Ph.D. in Mythological Studies

The Mythological Studies program offers a strong grounding in theoretical approaches to myth. This innovative program explores world-sacred traditions, symbolism, ritual, and literary classics in light of the concepts of depth and archetypal psychology.

Accredited by the Western Association of Schools and Colleges

Pacifica Graduate Institute
249 Lambert Road – Carpinteria, CA 93013
Phone: 805·969·3626 – Fax: 805·565·1932
E-mail: admissions@pacifica.edu
http://www.pacifica.edu

Index

ENGLISH PUBLICATIONS BY **DAIMON**

Helene Shulman

Living at the Edge of Chaos

Complex Systems in Culture and Psyche

Helene Shulman integrates experiences of synchronicity, altered states of consciousness, trance, ritual, Buddhist meditation practice and creativity into a broad perspective on cross-cultural psychology. What emerges is a comprehensive way to understand psychological illness and healing as a perpetual work-in-progress near "the edge of chaos," where the seeds for new models of reality lie.

With mental illness as the focus, she leads us on a fascinating interdisciplinary exploration, linking such areas as cultural studies, anthropology, evolutionary science and new work in mathematics and computer science – known as complexity theory – to Jungian psychology.

A new paradigm for postmodern psychology emerges as the author presents a dynamic theoretical model containing rational and irrational aspects of individual and collective life. (252 pages, ISBN 3-85630-561-0)

The relevance of this work extends well beyond the field of psychology, for the author is describing the life experience of each of us in our personal and cultural milieu. The current states of our environmental, political and economic realities are presented as an urgent challenge to enter consciously into individual and community restoration work. Living at the edge of chaos, for all its apparent destruction, is nonetheless a source of spontaneity, creativity and hope.

– Tuula Haukioja, Jungian analyst, Toronto

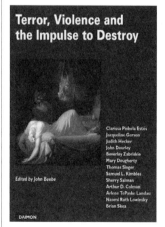

Terror, Violence and the Impulse to Destroy

John Beebe (Ed.)

Papers from the North American Conference of Jungian Analysts

These papers address the process of terror as it confronts us in international situations and in outbreaks of violence in homes and schools. The thirteen contributors, seasoned Jungian analysts and psychotherapists, have often faced the reality of undermining destructiveness in their work with clients. Here they offer their theoretical and therapeutic insights, drawing from their experience of the psyche's healing resources to identify the consciousness we need if we are to survive and reverse the contagion of hostility.

(410 pages, illustrated, ISBN 3-85630-628-5)

ENGLISH PUBLICATIONS BY **DAIMON**

Recent Jungian Conference Proceedings:

Barcelona 2004

Edges of Experience: Memory and Emergence
Proceedings of the 16th International IAAP Congress
for Analytical Psychology.
Edited by Lyn Cowan

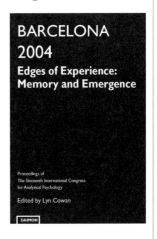

From the Contents:

Cultural Complexes in the Group and the Individual Psyche
Thomas Singer, Sam Kimbles
*Descent and Emergence Symbolized in Four Alchemical
Paintings* Dyane Sherwood
*An Archetypal Approach to Drugs & AIDS: A Brazilian
Perspective* Dartiu Xavier da Silveira
Frida Kahlo Mathy Hemsari Cassab
*Images from ARAS: Healing our Sense of Exile from
Nature* Ami Ronnberg
Trauma and Individuation Ursula Wirtz
Human Being Human: Subjectivity & the Individuation of Culture Christopher Hauke
Studies of Analytical Long-Term Therapy Wolfram Keller, Rainer Dilg, Seth Isaiah Rubin
Analysis in the Shadow of Terror Henry Abramovitch
Ethics in the IAAP – A New Resource Luigi Zoja, Liliana Wahba, Hester Solomon
Hope Abandoned and Recovered in the Psychoanalytic Situation Donald Kalsched
In the Footsteps of Eranos P. Kugler, H. Kawai, D. Miller, G. Quispel, R. Hinshaw
The Self, the Symbolic and Synchronicity George Hogenson
Memory and Emergence John Dourley
Bild, Metapher & Symbol: An der Grenze der kommunizierbaren Erfahrung M. Krapp
*Broken Vessels – Living in two Worlds: Some Aspects of Working with Clients with a
Physical Disability* Kathrin Asper, Elizabeth Martigny

(ca. 900 pages, illustrated, ISBN 3-85630-700-1)

Cambridge 2001

The Fifteenth Triannual Congress of the International
Association for Analytical Psychology (IAAP) took place
on the grounds of St. John's College in Cambridge,
England from August 19-24, 2001. It was a memorable
occasion both in its preparation and its incarnation and
the present volume is meant to preserve at least a
portion of what transpired: the papers comprising the
program. The presentations and events were more far-
reaching and all-inclusive than ever before, incorporating numerous political and intercultural issues and
including representatives from psychoanalysis and other
fields of endeavor for the first time.
(768 pages, illustrated, ISBN 3-85630-609-9)

English Titles from Daimon

English Titles from Daimon

Laurens van der Post - *The Rock Rabbit and the Rainbow*
Jane Reid - *Jung, My Mother and I: The Analytic Diaries*
of Catharine Rush Cabot
R.M. Rilke - *Duino Elegies*
Miguel Serrano - *C.G. Jung and Hermann Hesse*
Helene Shulman - *Living at the Edge of Chaos*
D. Slattery / L. Corbet (Eds.) - *Depth Psychology: Meditations on the Field*
Susan Tiberghien - *Looking for Gold*
Ann Ulanov - *Spirit in Jung*
- *Spiritual Aspects of Clinical Work*
- *Picturing God*
- *Receiving Woman*
- *The Female Ancestors of Christ*
- *The Wisdom of the Psyche*
- *The Wizards' Gate, Picturing Consciousness*
Ann & Barry Ulanov - *Cinderella and her Sisters: The Envied*
and the Envying
- *Healing Imagination: Psyche and Soul*
Erlo van Waveren - *Pilgrimage to the Rebirth*
Harry Wilmer - *How Dreams Help*
- *Quest for Silence*
Luigi Zoja - *Drugs, Addiction and Initiation*
Luigi Zoja & Donald Williams - *Jungian Reflections on September 11*
Jungian Congress Papers - *Jerusalem 1983: Symbolic & Clinical Approaches*
- *Berlin 1986: Archetype of Shadow in a Split World*
- *Paris 1989: Dynamics in Relationship*
- *Chicago 1992: The Transcendent Function*
- *Zürich 1995: Open Questions*
- *Florence 1998: Destruction and Creation*
- *Cambridge 2001*
- *Barcelona 2004*

Available from your bookstore or from our distributors:

In the United States:

Bookworld Trade Inc.
1941 Whitfield Park Loop
Sarasota FL 34243
Order on the web: www.bookworld.com
Fax: 800-777-2525 Phone: 800-444-2524

In Great Britain:

Airlift Book Company
8 The Arena
Enfield, Middlesex EN3 7NJ
Phone: (0181) 804 0400
Fax: (0181) 804 0044

Worldwide:

Daimon Verlag   Hauptstrasse 85   CH-8840 Einsiedeln   Switzerland
Phone: (41)(55) 412 2266   Fax: (41)(55) 412 2231
email: info@daimon.ch
*Visit our website: **www.daimon.ch***
or write for our complete catalog